Also from Catalyst

When Can You Start? The Complete Job Search Guide for Women of All Ages

Making the Most of Your First Job

Marketing Yourself: The Catalyst Women's Guide to Successful Résumés and Interviews

What to Do with the Rest of Your Life: The Catalyst Career Guide for Women in the '80s

Career Options Series for Undergraduate Women

Education Opportunity Series

Career Opportunity Series

Self Guidance Series

Résumé Preparation Manual: A Step-by-Step Guide for Women

How to Go to Work When Your Husband Is Against It, Your Children Aren't Old Enough, and There's Nothing You Can Do Anyhow, by Felice N. Schwartz, Margaret H. Schifter, and Susan S. Gillotti

All books can be ordered directly from Catalyst. For a publications price list and order form, please call 212-759-9700 or write to Catalyst, 14 East 60th Street, New York, N.Y. 10022.

IT'S YOUR FUTURE!

Catalyst's Career Guide for High School Girls

by the Catalyst Staff

Peterson's Guides
Princeton, New Jersey

Excerpt from *The Book of Maggie Owen*, copyright ©1941, by Maggie Owen Wadelton, R. 1969, used by the courtesy of the publisher, The Bobbs-Merrill Company, Inc. • Excerpt from *Kathie's Diary: Leaves from an Old, Old Diary* by Kathie Gray, edited by Margaret Eggleston. Copyright 1926 by George H. Doran Company. Reprinted by permission of Doubleday & Company, Inc. • Excerpt from "Mercedes-Benz" ©1970 Strong Arm Music. All rights reserved. • Excerpt from *The Living of Charlotte Perkins Gilman* reprinted by permission of the Schlesinger Library, Radcliffe College. • Excerpt from *The Three Boxes of Life* by Richard Nelson Bolles. Copyright 1982. Used with permission of Ten Speed Press, P.O. Box 7123, Berkeley, CA 94707. • Excerpt from *An Autobiography* by Agatha Christie reprinted by permission of Dodd, Mead & Company, Inc. • Excerpt from *The Diary of Selma Lagerlof* by Selma Lagerlof. Copyright 1936 by Doubleday & Company, Inc. Reprinted by permission of the publisher. • Excerpt from *Journey Around My Room: The Autobiography of Louise Bogan, A Mosaic* by Ruth Limmer. Copyright ©1980 by Ruth Limmer. Portions of this work were originally published in *The New Yorker*. Reprinted by permission of Viking Penguin Inc. • Excerpt from *Helen and Teacher* by Joseph P. Lash. Copyright ©1980 by Joseph P. Lash. All rights reserved. Reprinted by permission of Delacorte Press/Seymour Lawrence. • Excerpt from *Blackberry Winter* by Margaret Mead. Copyright ©1972 by Margaret Mead. All rights reserved. Reprinted by permission of William Morrow & Company, Inc. • Excerpt from *Enterprising Women* by Caroline Bird reprinted by permission of W. W. Norton & Company, Inc. • Excerpt reprinted by permission of Schocken Books Inc. from *Hannah Senesh—Her Life and Diary* by Hannah Senesh, trans. Marta Cohn. Copyright ©1966 by Hakibbutz Hameuchard Publishing House Ltd. English edition copyright ©1971 Nigel Marsh. • Excerpt reprinted by permission of G. P. Putnam's Sons from *My Life* by Golda Meir. Copyright ©1975 by Golda Meir. • "Disabled? Know Your Rights" ©1981 *Career World*. Reprinted by permission of Curriculum Innovations, Inc., Highland Park, IL 60035. • Excerpt from *Long Road* by Bessie Smith. Used by permission of Frank Music Corp. • Excerpt from *The Diary of Nellie Ptaschkina* edited by M. Jacques Povolotsky reprinted by permission of Jonathan Cape Ltd.

Library of Congress Cataloging in Publication Data
Main entry under title:
It's your future! Catalyst's career guide for high school girls.

   1. Vocational guidance for women—United States.
I. Catalyst, inc. II. Title: Catalyst's career guide for high school girls.
HF5382.5.U5I58   1984   331.7'02'024042   84-4298
ISBN 0-87866-280-4

Printed in the United States of America

10 9 8 7 6 5 4 3 2 1

For information about other Peterson's publications, please see the listing at the back of this volume.

*To women of all ages who move beyond
established boundaries and explore new
vistas as they create full lives*

Contents

Foreword

Do you feel as if you are teetering on the brink of a black hole—the scary, exciting unknown that is the rest of your life? I remember the feeling exactly. I was certain I had no future, and, what was worse, I had no past. Take heart! I found that my future was not a black hole in space but rather in television, which is another black hole of sorts but a future nevertheless. I promise—you have a future too.

The single most important thing I did after I got out of college was to pick up the phone and call the local anchorman at WISH-TV in Indianapolis. I called him out of the blue. Frankly, this was uncharacteristic; I'm not a terrific self-promoter. I chose a time of day when, even as an outsider, I figured things would be slow. He was generous with his time and really talked to me about what the job was like.

Eight months after that phone call, the station was looking for a reporter. Their priorities were, in order, female and inexpensive. I was both. More important, they knew about me because I had introduced myself through my phone call. If I hadn't initiated that first contact—a call I made just to get some information—I wouldn't be co-anchor of the "Today" program now.

My first break may seem more or less like a fluke. The phone call to the station was lucky; I reached the right person, at the right time of day, when he was in the right frame of mind to talk to me and remember me. It wasn't all a matter of luck, however. I had to have the initiative to make the call in the first place. Then, I had to make a sufficiently positive impression on him so that he recalled my name when an opening was available.

It's Your *Future!* will help you discover your own path through the uncharted reaches ahead. The 21-year-old Jane Pauley made a phone call and got a job. I was fortunate to hit upon a strategy that is detailed in this book: do your homework, make contacts, and follow up. The staff of Catalyst designed *It's* Your *Future!* to guide you through the maze of defining and launching a career, hoping at the same time to infuse you with confidence and the willingness to take control of your own life. To a large extent, you will make your own luck. And, if an incredibly wonderful "fluke" does come along, you'll be ready for it.

You are not alone. Women have been breaking the path ahead of you, expanding your career horizons in ways that would have seemed impossible a couple of decades ago. But remember, progress rarely comes in a straight line, and women's progress is no exception.

To have been a woman in her twenties during the 1970s was a unique growth experience. All the doors opened for the first time, and we had the political and emotional readiness to walk through them. We also had the naïveté to think that we could have it all, that our successful career wouldn't change or cut out anything else. I still believe you *can* have it all, if you're prepared for it.

As the second generation of the modern women's movement, you have inherited the best and the worst of it. Your mixed blessing is summed up in that phrase you read at the head of every paragraph written about women these days: "Despite ten years of progress. . . . " Feminist history, as you know, is full of advance and retreat. Let's not let that history repeat itself.

Set a reasonable goal for yourself, work to meet it, then set another. I didn't want to grow up and be Barbara Walters. I couldn't have accomplished anything thinking that. I wanted to be in broadcasting and to see how far I could go, to find out what I could do. I hope you will use this book as a tool in gauging your own interests and potential and then in staking out a career that interests you and fulfills that potential. It's up to you—one person's black hole is someone else's gold mine.

JANE PAULEY

Preface

Catalyst: What It Is, Why We Wrote This Book

Catalyst: something that brings about a change, that initiates a reaction and enables it to take place. Catalyst, the national organization that works to maximize productivity in the workplace by resolving career and family issues, has been making new inroads for the working woman since it was founded in 1962 by its president, Felice N. Schwartz, and 5 college presidents. Today, with a staff of 30 full-time professionals and long-standing contacts in the corporate, professional, and academic communities, Catalyst has a comprehensive national program that

- Informs women, employers, counselors, educators, legislators, and the media about issues of common interest through its multimedia information center, which is open to the public
- Offers career information and guidance to women at all stages of their careers through its filmstrips, videotapes, books, and other publications
- Provides counseling to thousands of women through its network of more than 200 affiliated resource centers nationwide
- Helps corporate women advance in their careers and employers respond to their needs through special programs and research studies
- Offers corporations outstanding women candidates for corporate directorships and assists them with their search through its Corporate Board Resource

- Addresses the specific needs and problems of two-career families and their employers through the Career and Family Center
- Responds to the corporate community's need for comprehensive information on the range of child-care options
- Helps young women and men to consider both their career and family aspirations at an early age through a course developed for the undergraduate, "The Two-Career Couple"

Catalyst's current priorities include addressing the needs of the high school and undergraduate woman, the upwardly mobile woman, and the two-career family. Our role is to facilitate the growing partnership of employers and women by helping women plan and develop their careers and by helping business and industry identify and develop the talent and leadership they need.

Fact: If a woman is married, she can expect to work an average of twenty-five years; if she is single, forty-five years. We at Catalyst realize that you, a teenage woman, need to begin thinking now about your future career and family plans if you are to make the most of this major portion of your lifetime. Very few good materials exist to help you begin this necessary process. Catalyst is filling this gap with a book for high school girls, *It's* Your *Future!*

Without a pool of talented, able women at entry, lower, and middle-management levels, employers cannot select the high-quality women they seek to develop for leadership positions. The increasing numbers of educated women in the work force are a vital new resource for all employers, but the full value of this resource will not be realized unless girls like you are encouraged to consider many career options and to work in traditionally male fields. By exposing yourself to a broad range of possibilities at this time in your life, you will be less likely to eliminate any crucial training you'll need to make the most of the opportunities to come.

Nine out of ten girls will work during their lifetimes. Since it's likely that you'll be among the nine, why not learn the process of career planning now, in order to bring about a successful and satisfying work life in the future? *It's* Your *Future!* provides you with reliable information and the analytical tools you'll need to develop a greater awareness of career options, of yourself, and of what the working world has to offer.

The first half of the book focuses on you: your self-image, the influences that made you what you are, and your needs, talents, values, and interests. The second portion introduces you to the world of work and shows you how to research occupations, evaluate information, set criteria for judging further education, and launch your own job search.

Your whole future lies ahead of you, waiting for you to shape and enjoy it. No one else can do this for you but you—it's *your* future!

Acknowledgments

Catalyst gives warm thanks to the funders who enabled us to undertake the research and writing of this book: International Paper Company Foundation, International Business Machines Corporation, and Helena Rubenstein Foundation, Inc. Their generous support clearly demonstrates their commitment to exposing high school girls to a broad range of career options at an early age and offering these girls reliable information for developing an awareness of the work world and themselves. In this way, our funders are helping to secure women's integral position in tomorrow's work force.

The staff of Catalyst conceived and executed the research, writing, and editing of this book. The publications staff included Elizabeth A. Niles, director of publications; Larayne Gordon, senior editor; Melinda Walsh, editor; Kitty Harmon, editor; and Maureen Zent, editorial assistant.

Our thanks go to free-lance writers Joelle Sander and Priscilla Claman and to contributing editors Dr. Leah Gold Fein, who evaluated and reworked the first half of the book; Dorothy Korber, who edited and consolidated the entire manuscript; Carol Durst; Judy Stone; and Maria Muniz and Lyn Motai of Catalyst's staff.

Interns who helped with research and data collection included Charlotte Milholland, Adrienne Positan, Lois Perelson, Mary Beth Giuffra, Diane Salino, and Gale Fleckner.

To test the self-evaluation exercises and to read and comment on various sections of the book, we formed an advisory board of high school students. These were Darlene Greaux, Karen Andrade, Melissa Degenhardt, Sylvia Rosada, Deedra Everett, Regina Chen, and Linda Chow.

Special thanks go to all those who participated in the Catalyst/ *Seventeen* magazine poetry and cartoon contest, to all the guidance counselors and high school students who helped with the research for the book by distributing and completing our questionnaires, and to the Catalyst Library staff, who helped to acquire the research materials we needed to write the book.

Finally, our sincere thanks to all who devoted their time, advice, experience, and encouragement toward the completion of this much-needed guide.

Introduction

"It was the best of times, it was the worst of times . . . ," wrote Charles Dickens in describing the French Revolution. Today we're in the midst of two revolutions—social and technological—and Dickens' statement again rings true. A young woman entering the American work force today has more opportunities to choose from than at any other time in modern history. The old notions of "man's work" and "woman's work" are going the way of the dinosaur—and they'll be missed about as much as *Tyrannosaurus rex*. At the same time, however, combining a career with the traditional roles of wife and mother, which a growing number of women are doing today, raises a host of new questions for young women. There is also intense competition in the job market and an increasing demand for sophisticated skills.

Making up your mind about what to do after high school isn't simple in these challenging times. There are lots of choices beyond the old equation of marriage + children + housework = happyeverafter. The U.S. Department of Labor's *Dictionary of Occupational Titles* defines more than 20,000 occupations. How do you narrow them down, and then how do you land the job you want? These are the questions that this book will help you answer.

The first portion of the book guides you in sorting out who you are, so you can begin to figure out what you want to become. One thing is already certain: you are a unique individual, with a complicated and fascinating assortment of values, needs, interests, and skills. You have also been influenced by your parents, friends, teachers, television and reading habits, and social and economic background. The book's exercises, which you'll probably find as fun as they are enlightening, will guide you in learning more about who you are. Then, with fresh insights about yourself, you'll be ready to use the practical information that follows.

The second part of the book starts by tackling some myths about the work world, such as the one that says women are "fit" to do only certain kinds of work. Those falsehoods put to rest, you'll learn how to investigate occupations, how to get the training you need for the job you want, and how to be a successful job hunter.

You'll also discover that there's no reason to limit yourself to *one* occupation for the next fifty years. Your decision is not irrevocable. In fact, your career will probably take some interesting twists as you grow and change. The skills and information you'll master preparing for your first job will also help you with your second, and your third, and your fourth. . . .

Maybe this is the best of times; maybe it's not. But it's definitely an *exciting* time to be plunging into the future. The opportunities are there. All you have to do is learn where to look for them and how to take advantage of them.

I

Focusing on You

1
Who Are You?

I want, by understanding myself, to understand others. I want to be all that I am capable of becoming.

—Katherine Mansfield, *writer*

The harried receptionist consulted a list of job applicants, then peered up at the nervous young woman.

"And who are you?" he asked distractedly.

"Lisa Harris," the young woman answered with a weak grin. "Hurray," she thought grimly, "I'm off to a good start. Only one right answer to that one." The receptionist handed her an application and indicated a chair in the waiting room.

Lisa dreaded the interview. She wanted so much to be a summer recreation leader, but friends hired last year had tipped her off about questions she'd be asked—and the interview sounded like torture. What are your strengths? ("That'll kill about 30 seconds," she thought.) What are your weaknesses? ("But we only have half an hour!") What are two adjectives that describe you? ("Crisp and crunchy? Soggy and stale?") How would you handle kids who smoke on the playground? ("With asbestos gloves. Look, all I want to do is play games with the kids and teach them how to make pencil holders out of juice cans.")

3

She finished the application. "It will be about 10 minutes," the receptionist said when she turned it in. The interview questions whirled through her brain. "I'll concentrate on the easy one," she said to herself. "Who are you? I am Lisa Harris. I am 16. I am a job hunter. I am a junior at Hoover High." She began to relax. "I am Marge and Leo's daughter. I am Teddy and Jenny's sister. I am a superb interviewee." She looked at the clock. Nine and a half minutes to kill. "I am a person who can't stand being cooped up in a small room. I am Tom's girlfriend." She paused. "Why didn't I think of that one before? Must be because I'm still mad about his using my biology notes all the time." An unpleasant inspiration struck. "I am a sucker." Lisa hurriedly switched channels.

"I wonder who my mother would say I am?" She could hear her mother's voice: "Who are you? You are your father's daughter. You'd try the patience of a saint. You're a person who always has a smart answer." Lisa had one ready. "I am a person who always speaks her mind," she said to herself with dignity. She thought a minute. "That's not really true. I'd like it to be true, but it's not. If I really spoke my mind, I'd tell Tom to take his own notes." She sighed. Back to pleasant stuff. "Who are you? I am a pretty good gymnast. I am a part-time baby-sitter. I am a faithful friend." Lisa became so absorbed in answering this simple but fascinating question that she was startled when the receptionist called her for the interview. Somehow, butterflies lulled, she felt she'd have plenty of answers when she needed them.

Lisa's accidental dose of self-awareness did more than calm her down and boost her confidence. It helped her sort through her self-image.

Your self-image is the way you see yourself—not the way others think you are or the way you think you ought to be. Your self-image starts to develop at birth and with your earliest experiences with other people. It grows with you. Long before you can remember, you had feelings of pleasure and discomfort. If crying brought a diaper change and smiling earned a hug, you were off to a good start. As you went along, if the responses you got from others made you feel accepted, loved, and appreciated, your self-image is probably good. Except on those occasional days when you'd like to mail yourself to a desert island, you basically like yourself. You have what psychologists call "positive self-regard."

Do you like yourself? Being aware of your self-image is important because, as psychology professor Richard Warga points out, "Our versions of ourselves dictate how we act. If you see yourself as a C student, you will act as a C student. If you see yourself as an A student, you will act as an A student."[1]

Everybody's self-image sags sometimes. The high school years are the time when it's most likely to fluctuate. Luckily, your view of yourself changes and grows as you do. And you can control it. What others have said about you and the way they've treated you may have helped shape your ideas about who you are and what you can do, but they needn't dictate those ideas for all time.

Maybe everyone in your family has always said that you're "just like Grandma." Perhaps you are. Perhaps they only think so because you happen to have Grandma's chin. It's up to you to accept or reject other people's statements about you. That's the one subject about which you are the world's leading expert.

Right now, however, if you designed a T-shirt to proclaim your inner state to the world, it would probably be covered with question marks. You may be asking yourself, "Why do I feel as if I'm 16 going on 3? What do they want from me? What do *I* want from me? How should I act? What's the real me?" People used to ask you what you wanted to be when you grew up. Now you may be asking yourself a more pressing question: "What am I going to do after graduation?" All these queries boil down to one: "Who am I?"

Drawing submitted by Marie Rogoz, 17;
Clark, New Jersey

Discovering who you are is the first step in the not-so-simple task of discovering what you want to be. An important part of what you will be is a worker—such an important part that we often define people by their occupations. "Meet Jane Birnbaum," we say, "she's a lawyer, and she's just back from arguing a case before the Supreme Court."

The U.S. Department of Labor's *Dictionary of Occupational Titles* lists 20,000 possible jobs, from abalone divers to zyglo inspectors (they check for flaws in metal). Self-awareness can help you figure out what you need, what you enjoy, what your goals are. You use your self-awareness constantly. When you say "Yuck!" to liver, when you leave a room rather than blow up at a friend, when you accept a party invitation because you know you'll have fun—in each case you've done a quick self-inventory. You've asked yourself (so quickly you hardly caught yourself doing it), "What do I need, enjoy, value, think, feel, and believe in this situation?"

Like your ideas about yourself, your ideas about work have also been shaped by the people around you. What does it mean to them? Income, certainly. But work can provide more than money in the bank and food on the table. Along with their paychecks, many people take home new ideas, new skills, and good feelings about themselves. Some of the people you know may feel about work the way psychologist Dorothy Jongeward did when she wrote, "Work—whether it's serving food, building bridges, managing a zoo, caring for a child, or running a corporation—gives us one avenue for expressing our outstanding uniqueness. Through work, we can express our intellect, our physical talents, our skills."[2]

How do you feel about work? Is it just a four-letter word, or is it a source of pleasure? How do your parents feel about work? What about your friends? Here is what some famous women have said about their work:

As for me, prizes mean nothing. My prize is my work.

—Katharine Hepburn, *actress*

Work means freedom!

—Eleonora Duse, *actress*

I am independent! I can live alone and I love to work.

—Mary Cassatt, *painter*

I am because I do.

—Lina Wertmuller, *film director*

Work has always been the center of my existence; not work as something one must do in order to earn money, but as an expression of creativity.

—Leonor Fini, *artist*

I still think discovery is the most exciting thing in the world. . . . People come to see me and they say, "Don't you have hobbies?" I say, "What hobbies?" What am I going to do? Ride a horse? Play tennis? This is where the excitement is. Everyday you hope there's something new. This is it!

—Rosalyn Yalow, *nuclear physicist*

This world is the only world I know. To me it's represented a constant challenge. I've seen things I've wanted to do and I've done them.

—Muriel Siebert, *securities analyst*

I had a deep set of convictions about the need to use law not only as a tool for civil rights and justice but also as an instrument of social accommodation and change. The law was the glue that held society together under pressure.

—Shirley Hufstedler, *lawyer, judge,*
and former U.S. Secretary of Education

When I think about what I've contributed to the organized labor movement and what I have received in return, I can only conclude that it has been a profitable venture.

—Addie Wyatt, *labor leader*

To me, winning is doing what I want, what makes me happy, doing the best I can at this given moment in my life. That's all I can ask of myself.

—Billie Jean King, *tennis player*

Have you thought of work not just as a job but as a career? Perhaps more than you know. If you've ever daydreamed about being a movie star, or asked someone what it's like to be a doctor, or taken a class you thought might be useful later in life, or just thought to yourself that you really wouldn't like working with the public—then you're already on the road to making career choices. If you haven't, you can start right now with the question, "Who am I?"

A career can mean a chance to express yourself. But you do have to know who that self is. As you read on, you'll find inventories, questionnaires, fantasy scenarios—all exercises to help you take a good look at yourself. Some of what you learn will make you want to cheer. Some won't. But everything you learn about yourself can be put to good use. If you discover you have a bad habit, you can change it. If you learn that some of the things you always thought were true about yourself aren't true anymore, you can re-create your self-image into a portrait you like better every day.

What you learn about the you-that-was and the you-that-is will help build the you-that-will-be. The future needn't be something that happens to you. It can be something you make happen.

Take a short ride on your time machine. It's next week. A banquet is being given in your honor. Your friends and family surround you. You are being honored for something you do very well. What is it? What is that something—however big or small—at which you excel? Thought of it? You've completed the first exercise in this book, and you've filled in part of the "Who am I?" puzzle.

Seeing that inner you helps you make decisions about your life, just as looking in the mirror helps you decide whether a hairstyle is right for you. Sure, you could ignore that unique person you are inside. Yes, learning your own inner secrets might seem a little risky, even dangerous. But this kind of ignorance isn't bliss. And the risk is necessary if you are to create a future that fits *you.*

WHAT'S IT LIKE BEING A YOUNG WOMAN TODAY?

We asked girls across the country that question as we were writing this book. What do *you* think? What *is* it like being a young woman today? Is it the best of times, the worst of times, or something in between? You may be interested in comparing your answer with some others we received:

"Today, young women have so many more decisions to make about their lives. Twenty years ago, women's lives and how they would be lived were dictated by society."

—Suzanne Hanny, 16; Avon, Connecticut

"Back then, everything, the basic pattern of one's life, was already spelled out. One knew what was expected in terms of career, family, religion, and morals. Nowadays, the responsibility lies solely on the individual."

—Laura Anne Barzune, 18; Dallas, Texas

"In this day and age, young women have much more freedom and do not have to restrain themselves from doing what they really want to."

—Lourdes Noda, 16; Miami, Florida

"I feel it is harder to be a woman today because there are so many opportunities and so many pressures that a young woman is forced to make extremely hard decisions at a very young age."

—Mary Ellen Foy, 17; Plainfield, New Jersey

"The most important thing is that we are given choices."

—Elizabeth C. Chen, 17; Boston, Massachusetts

"It is a more accepted thing that girls can go to college and have a career. Girls who do this are not looked down on nearly as much as in years past. Also, guys do not get as uptight about having girls as competitors."

—Lisa Davis, 16; Camden, Arkansas

"The entire world appears to be opening so many doors for us."

—Almeida J. Toribio, 17; Hicksville, L.I., New York

"I think young women of today are starting to feel more of the same pressures that young men feel concerning success. Schoolwork and career plans are becoming more important to women than they used to be. Young women today think first of a career, then a family. Getting married right after high school has become a thing of the past."

—Beth Lappen, 18; Kaukauna, Wisconsin

"Someone once said, 'Choice is the power in our lives.' Women now have the power to choose their destiny. That is the main difference between today's woman and yesterday's."

—Angele Buefort, 17; Boston, Massachusetts

"I think that being a young woman today is a lot scarier, but more challenging and exciting than it used to be. . . . Just thinking of the possibilities makes me feel a little exhilarated and ready to go out and conquer the world."

—Sue Van Zeeland, 17; Kaukauna, Wisconsin

"Now, there are so many avenues that it is difficult to choose the right direction. But, in a sense, that is good. Today's woman can be whoever she wants to be . . . she can go wherever she wants to go. If she doesn't like the direction she chose the first time, she can back up and take another one."

—Deedra Everett, 16; Camden, Arkansas

"Personally, I prefer being a woman today. I feel that I am respected for what I can do as a person and not just as a female."

—Elizabeth J. Smith, 18; Carmel, Indiana

"Women today are asserting themselves in all phases of life . . . they are exploring who they are and what they are capable of. . . . In my opinion, there is no time when being a woman was better or worse; to me, being a woman ... is great; it's something to always be proud of."

—Kerry Ann Carr, 18; Hicksville, L.I., New York

ON SNAGS, OBSTACLES, AND OTHER HINDRANCES

Nobody said it would be easy to plan or develop a career. Sooner or later, everyone confronts an obstacle, falls into a trap, or gets caught in a snag. But obstacles can be removed, circumvented, or overcome. And some traps and snags can be avoided.

Here's what three women—very successful in their fields—have to say about how they've coped with such things in developing their own careers.

"As simplistic as the statement seems, it is a basic truth that if you know where you want to go, somehow you will get there. The path may take a few unexpected turns, but one learns to adapt a situation into a learning experience and a broadening of one's professional outlook. Eventually, you get back on the right track and you can use your past experience to get you further ahead.

"I owe my success to determination and hard work. I believe that talent will always come through for you; whatever that talent is, it will resurface repeatedly until it is recognized and accepted for its worth."

—Cathy Hardwick, *fashion designer*

"While I was shaping my business career, I thought that being female and poor and wanting to be a chemist were the problems of the first twenty-five years. Those were the years in which I was starting out in a 'nontraditional field' for women.

"Then it seemed that being a female chemist in an industry that did not want women in its senior professional or managerial ranks was the problem for the next twenty-five years of my working life.

"In retrospect, however, these personal circumstances as well as the wars, depressions, and other public disasters of the times were not the obstacles to success. The really crucial problems that had to be overcome were quite different. They came from my own internal failures, which kept me from being sufficiently firm, daring, and imaginative to seize, or make, opportunities.

"It took many wasted years and lost opportunities before I really *believed* that almost any business project can be conquered by simply tackling it—using determination and a modicum of sense. It took even longer to learn that along with successes, some failures are inevitable and must be accepted.

"Developing the courage and skills needed to cope with each tiny individual event as it occurred in the workday turned out to be the key, since I never overcame all the big problems. For example, I was never able to do anything about being female and never had the slightest effect on the economic and political circumstances of the times. Yet I did learn to walk into a routine meeting with indifferent, even hostile people and make myself participate so that I had to be treated as a respected equal. Eventually a lifetime of such modest victories turned out to have built a career."

—Juliette M. Moran, *Executive Vice President, GAF Corporation*

"While I did have a few direct personal experiences of discrimination —being paid less than men in identical positions when I was a high school teacher and being told in a job interview that I could not be a candidate because the school system in question believed that women with children under 2 should stay home—it was through making choices much more than responding to denials that my career was shaped.

"Most careers for both women and men evolve, rather than occur as the result of plans made early in life. Especially today, when opportunities for women are expanding so rapidly, it is probably impossible for young women to set their sights high enough and to have the breadth of vision to know what can be possible in their lives. Making choices is probably both the most precious opportunity and the most difficult responsibility facing young women today. What proportion of our lives do we want to devote to our careers? What kind of family life do we want? How can we create the right mix of career, family, and community activities? The ways in which young women and men can respond to these questions is undergoing constant change.

"In my own case, the single most difficult obstacle to my career development was arranging for good child care. It took an enormous amount of time and energy to arrange for the appropriate kind of help as my children grew from infants needing constant care to teenagers needing transportation, orthodontia, and a way to be with friends. Thanks to my mother, who was a very important source of support for me; a friend and neighbor with whom I made a business arrangement for backup child care; and several very fine women who cared about my children and my home, I was able to work steadily throughout the time my children were growing up, and we all enjoyed rich and rewarding lives separately and as a family.

"Throughout my adult life, a series of people, both women and men, have been important advisers and consultants at various decision points. Some have served as career mentors at various times; others have provided important perspective about life in broader ways. Women especially have a lot to offer one another, and I look forward very much to what I will learn from the next generation as well."

—Alice F. Emerson, *President of Wheaton College, Massachusetts*

Miss Piggy on Overcoming Obstacles

Fortunately, being the singer/actress/dancer/model and Superstar which *moi* am and having the all-consuming love of my frog, I have surmounted all of life's problems. But in the beginning this was not so. Oh no, no, no. Yes, there were obstacles along the way:

1. Being single in a couples' world

2. Being a woman in a man's world

3. Being a pig . . . period

But, I found that the strongest obstacles were in *moi*: my self-doubts, fears, needs, desires, self-image, and, yes, even my disliking of myself. (Can you imagine? *Moi* disliking *moi*?!)

But, I also had dreams and, after following my dreams, here *moi* am! It was difficult, but looking back at those obstacles that seemed so big at the time, they now seem like little powder puffs or mascara wands or those cotton balls that you soak in milk and put on your eyelids. And now, although there are still many obstacles ahead of *moi* (I believe a pig *can* play Shakespeare), I revel in where *moi* am now and, with my frog by my side, I am excited about what is ahead. Of course, I do still get a teensy weensy bit depressed at times and lock my door and eat walnut fudge whips by the carton, but I always bounce back. (Anyway, being depressed is often a good way of getting an expensive gift from someone who feels sorry for you.)

One last word: "obstacle" is just another way of saying, "Go for it!"

Love,

Miss Piggy
xx

WORKING WOMAN

Barbara DeMeo

Real Estate Agent

Matching up a home buyer with a home seller takes a salesperson with the virtues of Wonder Woman—sensitivity, knowledge, charm, and energy. Barbara DeMeo has shown the stuff of a wonder woman, first as a salesperson, then as a sales manager, while trekking the North Shore of Long Island, New York, in search of the perfect condominium or the ideal house for her clients.

"There is no greater feeling than knowing how happy you've made buyers and their families when they've found their new home," she says. "Or when you've enabled homeowners to make a profit from selling their house and they realize what a good investment it was."

Barbara went into real estate after a career in nursing.

"I have found that many people in this field have backgrounds that are completely unrelated to real estate," she comments. "Nursing was very 'people-oriented,' and I think that helped me a great deal in real estate."

In New York State, according to Barbara, it was necessary to find a sponsoring firm before you could work in real estate. Barbara's sponsor spent six weeks training her and preparing her for the real estate licensing examination. She says the New York requirements have changed since then, however, and now novices must be trained at an accredited school of real estate. Training requirements vary from state to state, but all require that anyone wishing to sell real estate pass a state licensing exam first.

"That's a good thing," Barbara feels. "Previously, I'm sure, a lot of companies sent people out to sink or swim with little training. We 'career people' are very happy to see the industry becoming more professional."

After earning her license, Barbara specialized in selling residential real estate. Two years later she was promoted to the post of vice-president and sales manager at a new branch opened by her agency.

"This involves an incredible variety of things," she says. "My responsibilities include public relations in the new community; interviewing, hiring, and firing; training sales associates; conducting weekly sales meetings; and continuing my own education."

Initially, one of her main reasons for going into real estate was her belief that it would be a good part-time career, leaving her plenty of time for her family. She soon found, however, that she wanted to spend more than two or three days a week at her new job.

"Now I find myself working six or seven days a week sometimes," she says. "For example, with out-of-town customers who must buy a house, you might work several days and nights in a row, nonstop, until they find a house. But then, when the house is 'in contract,' you can take a couple of days to recuperate.

"One of the most important things to do in real estate is *work hard.* You have a lot of stiff competition in sales—always. You have to be sure that your customer would rather buy from you than from the next person. Therefore, you can never overextend yourself. Working hard is not just chauffeuring people to and from houses. It also involves area tours—locating and inspecting schools, churches, shopping centers, and so forth for the prospective buyer. Then there are the various obligations the realtor has to the seller of properties as well. You must hold open houses, write ads for the listings, etc."

Obviously, energy is a prerequisite for success in the real estate business. But there are other requirements too.

"All the customers appreciate a friendly, sincere person," Barbara stresses. "If you enjoy people it shows; you'll go to extra lengths to help them. I have known sales associates to go to the grocery store and buy Pampers and orange juice for an out-of-town couple with a new baby."

Women face no sex discrimination in residential sales work, Barbara says. In fact, it may be the sales*men* who have to fight bias.

"Residential real estate is primarily women," she says. "Clients often *expect* to work with women. Often a man doesn't live in a home the same way a woman does. He doesn't spend as much time there.

"If you have ever owned a home, raised children, or decorated a few houses, you are more confident about what kind of house works well for certain kinds of families.

"Perhaps it is more difficult for women in commercial real estate [selling or leasing business properties like stores or office buildings]. I didn't choose commercial because I knew I would be more effective selling a product I was familiar with. I like to know, however, that I have options like commercial real estate open to me in the future, although I still find what I am doing now very challenging."

A good, broad education is important for real estate sales personnel, Barbara believes.

"Education—any and all—will be helpful to you," she says. "You have to work with a lot of different people in order to make something work in real estate. You should know how a lawyer thinks, how a banker thinks, how to talk to an engineer about the construction of a house. I would suggest business or economics as a major in college. One of the exciting things about real estate is that no matter what background you have, it is almost always applicable. Any knowledge of American history, for instance, or architecture would be a valuable sales tool."

Doing an apprenticeship while in high school or college is a good way to find out if real estate is for you, according to Barbara.

"If you do something like this and like it, the ideal way to go into real estate is right after college. When you're starting out, you might want to have six months' or a year's income in the bank for security, because you'll be paid on a commission basis. This means that you would not receive a regular salary," she explains. "Instead, you'd receive a percentage of the selling price of any property your customer buys. If you listed and sold a $300,000 property, you could conceivably end up with a commission of $10,500.

"That's not bad—but keep in mind when you're starting out that it could be months before you get something together. Real estate is definitely not an easy business, especially in the market today, with its very high interest rates. But it can be a very rewarding one, both emotionally and financially."

WHEN SHE WAS YOUNG

Maggie Owen Wadelton

Maggie Owen Wadelton was born in 1897 in Ireland. Her parents died when she was quite young, and she grew up in the homes of various friends and relatives. Given a diary when she was 12, Maggie set out to describe herself for her future grandchildren and dreamt about what she would be like when she was a "woman growen" of 14.

> I am a virgin twelve years of age. Spinster and demoselle and maiden mean the same thing, but not quite. I call meself a virgin and it sounds higher minded and more spiritual. I resolve to be a noble woman but tis hard to be noble in a house along with people not noble. They dont want to be noble and hinder me spiritual effords with teasing. All the well known people you read of have trouble with their families. Look at Joan of Arc and Queen Elizabeth and St. Terese. Their families dident understand them when they started to be noble so they went away from their families. No one understands me either. Some day I will leave Castel Rea and go out in the world and me name will ring down the corridors of time no doubt....
>
> I think it well may be this book will fall to the hands of me grandchildren or me great-grandchildren and they'll wonder what I was like. I will set down what I am like for them. I have red hair with curls to it and wish Ann would let me thrust it up. Twelve years is almost a woman growen, standing with reluctant feet where the brook and river meet (by Alfred Lord Tenneyson I think). It means the time when a girl begins to be a woman and not a girl any more. I have great grey eyes and a nose that turns up but looks all right. Ann says I have a good skin, did I take care of it and not run wild and get burned the like of a red Indian. Me ears are not excellent but you cant see them with all the hair I have. No one will ever see them, not even when I'm married to me husband, if I get one. Bess says husbands are getting scarcer every day. I am four feet in heighth and weigh six stone. I am not beautiful now as when a child, me photografs show me very beautiful then though simpering. I am good at me lessons when I put me mind to them....

2
Threads in the Tapestry

The joy of life is variety.
—Samuel Johnson, *lexicographer, critic, and poet*

Like a master weaver, you have taken the threads of your life and woven them into a unique pattern. Those threads include all the things that influence the kind of person you are. Some of those influences are obvious: your family, friends, schooling. Others are subtle. Did you ever consider, for example, how the fairy tales you heard as a very young child might have shaped your ideas about your-self and the world? Or what effect watching thousands of commercials may have had on your personality? It can be fascinating—and helpful—to unravel some of those strands and examine the influences that af-fect you. Many are positive and help you structure your life in good ways. But some of the strands can tangle you up, limiting your choices for the future. The sections that follow aim to help you sort the positive influences from the limiting ones.

It can be hard work to become aware of these influences and their possible effects, to raise your "Awareness Quotient"; but after some determined soul-searching your A.Q. will be improved and you will have learned something about that extremely interesting creature: you.

ONCE UPON A TIME

> In the thinking out of most stories, the thing the story is about, as apart from merely what happens in it, is of the utmost importance. For a story is not the sum of its happenings.
>
> —Edith Ronald Mirrielees, *writer and educator*

A good place to start is with one of the earliest—and most subtle —influences. You can probably remember listening to or reading fairy tales like "Cinderella," "Sleeping Beauty," and "Hansel and Gretel." Bedtime stories like these did more than make you sleepy. They influenced your view of the world.

As psychologist Bruno Bettelheim points out in *The Uses of Enchantment*, folktales and fairy tales teach children how to deal with the complex and confusing world around them.[1] The stories address fears and problems of young children and offer solutions. But how does a story like "Hansel and Gretel" teach a child to deal with a world noticeably lacking in kid-gobbling witches? Fairy tales use characters and situations that adults might label as unreal but that present children with solutions to very basic human problems: fear of separation from parents or friends, fear of dying, rivalry between brothers and sisters, anger. Think of the plot of your favorite fairy tale. You'll find that on a deeper level, it deals with feelings and problems that all humans share.

Moreover, as Dr. Bettelheim explains, the tales present these problems in very simple terms that are easy for children to understand. Good and evil are obvious and distinct. Good people are good-looking, helpful, kind, and virtuous. These characteristics are attractive to a young child, so the child identifies with the good characters and learns about behavior through their actions.

The bad characters are just as clear-cut. They are ugly, hateful, and hurtful. Their appearance and actions discourage children from identifying with them. What child wants to be like Cinderella's wicked stepmother or stepsisters?

Like the children listening to the tales, the good characters often feel lost, afraid, and confused. They are surrounded by temptations and bad people trying to lead them astray. But, with fortitude and guidance (remember Glinda, the Good Witch, in *The Wizard of Oz*?) the heroes and heroines meet the challenges and emerge victorious. Then they live happily ever after.

So we can see that fairy tales are more than entertainment. They influence children by helping them deal with feelings and learn right from wrong. But the very simplicity that allows a child to understand the meaning of a fairy tale can work negatively. Take "Cinderella," "Sleeping Beauty," "Snow White," and similar stories. They feature a beautiful and docile young woman (often a princess) who becomes the victim of a mean witch or wicked stepmother, but is rescued in the nick of time by a charming and handsome man (usually a prince).

Mature adults know that real women cannot be categorized simply as wicked witches or helpless princesses. Adults also realize that beauty alone never ensures happiness. Young children, however, haven't learned these lessons yet. They are exposed to these tales at a particularly impressionable age—just when they're beginning to form their self-image and to decide how they fit into the world.

You'll recall that most of the heroes in those tales were strong, courageous, handsome, intelligent—and *male.* In contrast, the main female characters were beautiful and dependent upon the kindness and greater intelligence of men. Or worse, they were ugly and wicked. In the stories, beautiful women get happy endings and ugly women get what they "deserve." To many little girls, it must seem that sweetness and good looks are all you need to attain happiness, riches, and a prince. Well, Prince Charles has been married off, and the fairy godmothers have all gone to law school. Sitting around waiting for someone to fit the glass slipper on your perfect little foot can get pretty boring. Even so, some women make a career of waiting, hampering their growth and limiting their potential.

Don't panic. Reading "Cinderella" as a child doesn't automatically make you a passive, helpless adult. One fairy tale won't set your course for life. Anyway, not all fairy-tale heroines are passive. It was Gretel who shoved the witch into the oven, not her mealy-mouthed brother. And, as Bettelheim points out, children tend to identify with the basic goodness of the major characters, regardless of their sex.

AQ: INCREASE YOUR AWARENESS QUOTIENT

Pick a fairy tale and examine the portrayal of female characters. Sniff out the stereotypes. Then create your own version of the tale. Why not have Cinderella march into the castle the day after the ball, demanding to know who has her glass slipper? Or let Snow White sing "I Gotta Be Me" instead of "Some Day My Prince Will Come." Be as creative—and outrageous—as you want. Then test your modern fairy tale on a young child you know.

If you'd like to read some fairy tales with brave, intelligent heroines, find *Tatterhood and Other Tales* (Old Westbury, N.Y.: Feminist Press, 1978) and *The Maid of the North* (New York: Holt, Rinehart & Winston, 1981). Both are by Ethel Johnston Phelps, who spent three years looking for tales with brainy and energetic female characters who rescue men, outsmart demons, and face a fight with courage.

OF WORDS AND IMAGES

It's unfortunate that Hollywood could not visualize a woman of mental acumen unless she was fixing up a mess her man/boss had made, covering a scoop to prove herself to a man, or deftly forging a life of dishonesty.

—Marjorie Rosen, *writer*

The mass media—television, movies, radio, newspapers, magazines, and books—play a central role in influencing and even creating our popular culture. The media tell us who has been elected president and they interpret why that candidate won. They tell us who the beautiful people are (or aren't). They define our heroes and our villains. The average person can't attend an opening of a new play on Broadway, witness the sentencing of a criminal in an important trial, sit in on a Cabinet meeting, or watch the Kentucky Derby from a finish-line seat. We need reporters, critics, commentators, and the magic of technology to bring it to us. Because of this, we see much of our world through a filter, whether that filter is a book, a newspaper, a magazine, a movie, or a television program. The media supply us with all kinds of information we wouldn't have otherwise, but that doesn't mean we have forfeited our ability to question a journalist's perception or an analyst's interpretation.

Sometimes, in trying to attract and entertain a larger audience, the media emphasize the sensational, the dramatic, the glamorous, and the violent—things that will grab attention. You're not likely to read a front-page headline screaming "Responsible Teen Holds Job!"

Of all the media, television is probably the strongest force in shaping today's society. If you don't believe it, listen to this:

By the time you're 18, if you're a typical American, you'll have watched 22,000 hours of television and spent only 11,000 hours in school, according to Action for Children's Television, a consumer group. American Medical Association research shows that the average eighth grader has seen about 18,000 murders committed on TV. More than nine out of ten U.S. households have at least one television set; four out of ten have two or more. The American family has its set on an average of 7 hours a day.

Those are the statistics, but what do they mean? Some experts think that all those hours in front of the tube have lowered the reading and writing skills of TV-generation kids. Studies have shown that children who watch a lot of television are slower learners, are less sociable, and exhibit more sexist and racist tendencies.

Are you starting to feel a little uneasy about those cartoons and sitcom reruns you watched as a child? Good. You need to be aware of the influence that an all-pervasive medium like television can exert over you. You need to approach TV with a critical mind. Television-land is no more realistic than Disneyland; it's a fun place to visit, but nobody could live there.

In real life, problems aren't neatly solved before the next commercial. Real crises are painful and perplexing. Real people are complex and unpredictable. Real jobs, frequently, are routine rather than glamorous. The realistic rewards for a job well done are satisfaction and maybe a promotion; on television, the characters win glory, fame, and untold riches, but only after they discover a cure for cancer or win the Boston Marathon.

Television commercials are often more simple-minded than the programs. They assure us that using the right toothpaste/deodorant/oven cleaner/laundry softener will bring us True Love—if we don't perish first from terminal cases of waxy yellow buildup or horrid age spots.

TV's portrayals of certain segments of our society are frequently one-sided and predictable. Television teenagers, for instance, are generally either totally wholesome kids or totally depraved young hoodlums, crazed with sex and drugs. *TV Guide* magazine, in analyzing one season, pointed out that half the prime-time films dealing with teenagers focused on sexual themes. Among the season's underwhelming offerings: movies about a young hitchhiker who gets raped, a high school boy who has an affair with his teacher, a young female runaway who ends up as a prostitute, and a girl who becomes a victim of child pornography. And you thought *you* had problems!

Women don't come off any better than teenagers. In commercials, particularly, women are depicted as perfectly groomed housewives who agonize over why their husbands don't want a second cup of coffee. A study by the National Organization for Women in the early seventies found that 37.5 percent of all women in commercials were housewives, while less than 1 percent were fulfilling traditional male roles (like doctors or fire fighters). Meanwhile, 90 percent of all voice-over announcers were male, suggesting that those dizzy housewives needed a man's guidance in their quest for the ringless bathtub.

It's easy to make fun of TV's more mindless stereotypes, but the other media are also guilty of portraying women as submissive, frivolous creatures unworthy of little more than a page of society gossip in the "women's" section.

Well, the times they are a-changing—slowly. The news media can hardly ignore the fact that a woman was appointed a Supreme Court justice and another was nominated to the country's vice-presidency. There are more women working as reporters than ever before, and their presence on the staffs of newspapers and television networks makes those media more sensitive to sexism. Even situation comedies are making some headway, following the lead of such pioneers as "The Mary Tyler Moore Show." Mary was a sensible, likable, bright, *single* woman, even if she did "turn the world on with her smile," as the theme song suggested.

So there are some positive role models on television, in films, and in newspapers and magazines. These media images can provide inspiration, but don't feel bad if you don't match the image you see. You don't have to be as perky as Mary Tyler Moore, as intense as Jane Fonda, or as whimsical as Diane Keaton. You have to be yourself.

AQ: INCREASE YOUR AWARENESS QUOTIENT

Pick two or three television shows and watch them regularly for a month. Instead of being a passive viewer, try to see them with a critical eye. Then rate the shows on a scale of 1 to 10 (from least to most realistic). Do they portray men and women in realistic roles, or are the characters stereotypes? What changes, if any, would improve these shows? Watch for:

- Macho Man, a hairy-chested cross between Prince Charming and Mr. Universe who speaks in short sentences and rescues at least one animal, child, or skimpily dressed woman per episode
- Mr. Humanity, who is kind and fair to society's weaklings (animals, children, and women), and is so perfect you want to gag

- Regular Guy, a blundering, likable fellow of the Alan Alda variety, who frequently wears corduroy jackets and is the kind of guy you'd like to fall in love with
- Macho Woman, a brainy, aggressive, unemotional female who doesn't have any life outside her work but who really is looking for an aggressive man to take off her glasses and let down her hair
- Sexy Chick, generally a dumb blonde, who wiggles and jiggles and giggles and is coddled by Macho Men
- Regular Gal, who is bright and funny, like the Regular Guy; thinks Mr. Humanity is a jerk; and gets involved with Regular Guys. She is a rare species in televisionland.

Star Gazing

Looking at the dreary history of sexism, it's easy to cast Hollywood as a villain. The movie industry churned out a long line of sex goddesses, dumb blondes, waspish spinsters, and perfect mothers. Recently, however, things seem to have improved. Jane Fonda played a reporter in *The China Syndrome,* Sally Field was a union organizer in *Norma Rae,* Faye Dunaway portrayed a television executive in *Network,* and Jill Clayburgh was the first female Supreme Court justice in *First Monday in October.* About time, right?

A closer examination of film history, though, reveals that during the 1930s and 1940s many movies celebrated career women. Some legendary actresses created memorable, vital, and interesting characters who weren't always admirable but weren't mere stereotypes either.

Katharine Hepburn—a vibrant, fascinating character in real life—is a prime example of the cinematic career woman. In *Adam's Rib* she was a lawyer, in *Pat and Mike* she played an athlete, and in *Woman of the Year* she was a newspaper political columnist. Her characters are strong women with a streak of stubborn independence that helps them come out ahead in life and in love. (This *is* Hollywood, after all.)

Other notable Hepburn roles are in *Stage Door,* where she's a young actress; *Desk Set,* where she matches wits with Spencer Tracy and a computer; *Christopher Stone,* in which she plays an aviator; and *A Woman Rebels,* where she is publisher of a women's newspaper and a champion of women's rights in Victorian England.

Although Hepburn led the field, other actresses also did their parts. When Gregory Peck needs to be saved from the ravages of mental illness in *Spellbound,* he calls upon the talents of a psychiatrist played by Ingrid Bergman. Other Bergman roles include a spy in *Notorious* and a pianist in *Intermezzo.*

For many people, Joan Crawford came to epitomize the tough, no-nonsense career woman in movies like *Mildred Pierce,* where she's a restaurant owner, and *Daisy Kenyon,* in which she plays a dress designer.

Rosalind Russell was one of the funniest, and best-dressed, career women of the screen. In *His Girl Friday,* Russell is a newspaper reporter; her boss and ex-husband is Cary Grant. And in *Take a Letter Darling,* Russell is a successful advertising executive who hires Fred MacMurray as her secretary!

During World War II, many women poured into the labor market performing what had been, until then, "men's" jobs. And they helped the war effort on the screen as well. In *So Proudly We Hail,* you'll find Claudette Colbert, Veronica Lake, and Paulette Goddard as nurses working behind enemy lines.

Keep an eye open for these "classics" on public television, in movie revival houses, and on late-night and early-afternoon commercial television.

PARENTS

> Parents can only give good advice or put them on the right paths, but the final forming of a person's character lies in their own hands.
>
> —Anne Frank, *diarist*

It's hard to be unbiased about your parents. When you're very young, they are the most perfect, important beings in the world. But as you get older, their pedestals begin to crack. They don't seem to understand you anymore. They're too free with advice, too stingy with permission, and generally wrong about everything. They seldom endorse what you really want to do, but if they support you, you get suspicious. Why, you wonder, do they suddenly approve of your boyfriend? What's wrong with him? You're in a hurry to spread your wings and soar, and they keep hauling you back to earth with reminders to fasten your seat belt and take out flight insurance.

Breaking away from parental influence is a normal part of maturing. It's a process that started when you took that first tentative step in babyhood and will continue long after you consider yourself grown up and on your own. Some conflict is healthy, inevitable, and necessary.

That said, acknowledge that your parents *are* right about many things. The truth is that your parents have had a great deal more experience than you, and there's a fair chance that they can help you avoid some traps that snared them. Maybe you yearn to learn everything on your own, "the hard way," but this can be time-consuming and more than a little painful. It won't hurt to listen.

It's possible that at this stage in your life, your parents know you better than you know yourself. You may be infatuated with the idea of becoming a marine biologist, but your parents remember when you were equally passionate about being a dancer, a doctor, and a forest ranger. It can be irritating to hear it, but their advice at this point can help you keep your options open and give you a perspective you might be lacking.

Your parents were your original role models, and they can continue to be. Try to view them objectively. Pretend for a moment that you are not related to them. As an outsider, how do you view these two adults? How are they handling their lives and their careers? Do they get pleasure from their work? What makes these people tick? What do you admire about each of them? You probably haven't thought of asking these kinds of questions about your own parents before. That's because they're always around—they're like the air you breathe, so you take them for granted.

It's also very important to examine how your parents have influenced your attitudes and your self-image. Both you and your parents may be totally unaware that they could be unintentionally inhibiting your ability to reach your potential. You can assess their influence by taking a close look at the way they've brought you up and by trying to understand them by thinking about the ways *they* were raised.

Ask yourself some questions. If you have sisters and brothers, do your parents treat the boys differently from the girls? Do they encourage your brothers to take on new challenges while protecting you from risks? Do they have higher expectations for your brothers' achievements? Are they willing to spend more on your brothers' educations? Do your achievements scare them? Do they feel you will be less attractive to men if you show your talents or ambitions?

Examine your parents' conceptions of the role of women in society. What part should a woman play in family life? What part has your mother played? If she could do it all again, what would she change? What is her attitude about the changing role of women? How much have her views influenced yours?

When it comes to career planning in particular, parents can provide information. They can talk about their own work histories, and they can put you in contact with people you might not otherwise meet: lawyers, gardeners, accountants, insurance agents, mechanics, real estate brokers, and so on. Sometimes a parent can arrange for part-time work at his or her workplace. It may not be the kind of job you want to spend your life doing, but such an experience can help you pick up some basic work skills (not to mention some cash to finance future schooling or a car).

Parents are neither infallible sages nor incredible dolts. They are people who are familiar with your concerns and interests. They probably remember the feelings of confusion and indecision that accompanied their own early career planning. On the other hand, after being part of your life for so long, parents often develop their own expectations of what you will do or be. And, sometimes, there can be a conflict when a parent's expectations for a daughter are different from her own.

Take Andrea's mother, for instance. She has fond memories of sorority life at good old U. of K. She expects that Andrea will go there also, and have loads of fun in the same sorority. She doesn't understand—or she ignores—the fact that Andrea is a terribly serious scholar and not at all a joiner. There's obviously trouble ahead for these two.

Sometimes a parent who has built up a successful family business may expect a daughter or son to continue the "family tradition" without stopping to think whether that's what the child really wants or would be good at. Part of growing up, of shaping your own life, is learning to separate other people's expectations from your own. This can be especially difficult with parents because they may regard the rejection of their ideas as a rejection of them.

Take Betty's case. Betty's mother never worked outside the home. "When I was growing up," her mother says, "everyone expected me to get married and start a family, and of course that's what I did." She assumed her daughter would do the same, once she finished high school and "settled down." But Betty is not so sure. "When I told my mom that I don't know whether I even want to get married, she really went to pieces," Betty says. "First she yelled, then she cried and told me that I don't love or appreciate her! That's not it at all—I think my mom's great. I wish I could make her understand that it's not *her* I'm questioning, it's myself."

Some parents pass on to their children the limitations that were placed on *them.* For instance, if their own educational aspirations were not encouraged, they might not encourage their children's either. Parents whose aspirations were frustrated might also try to live their dreams through their children. Maria's mother wanted to become a surgeon but couldn't afford medical school. Lately, she's been putting a lot of pressure on her daughter to become a doctor. But Maria, who loves her sociology class, is struggling for a C in basic biology. Her mother is convinced that Maria just isn't "applying" herself. Their arguments are classics.

Parents can also be guilty of "too great expectations." Some, who feel stuck in boring, routine jobs, may develop unrealistically high ambitions for their offspring, demanding that they do everything extremely well.

Then there's the opposite extreme. Melissa's father is a lawyer. He worked hard to get his law degree, and he's become something of a snob about his social standing. He is aghast when Melissa tells him she plans to drop out of college and work full-time as a waitress in the fancy restaurant where she currently has a weekend job. "How can you throw your life away?" he demands. "Whose life is it, anyway?" Melissa retorts.

Well, of course, it's *your* life. You shouldn't have to act out your parents' fantasies or live up to unrealistic expectations. But you shouldn't reject their advice out of hand. And if you do decide to go against their wishes, make it clear you're not rejecting *them.* If you're lucky enough to have parents who love and respect you, you'll have some strong supporters when things go wrong. It beats working the high wire without a net.

AQ: INCREASE YOUR AWARENESS QUOTIENT

Find out what your parents dreamed of doing when they were your age. (It may be a shock.) Ask your folks about the choices they made and the influences that affected them. How did *their* parents feel? Were your parents encouraged or discouraged by your grandparents? By talking to them about their own career and life choices and by trying to understand how they were influenced, you can better understand how (and why) your parents might be influencing you.

I Remember Mama

Mother, may I go out to swim?
Yes, my darling daughter:
Hang your clothes on a hickory limb
And don't go near the water.

—Anonymous

Instructions, orders, advice, wheedling, nagging—whatever you call it, parents usually hold very strong opinions when it comes to their children's concerns. And, whether or not parental advice is sound (or heeded), it's usually offered with the best of intentions. What have your parents and other relatives taught you through their words and examples? Here's what some working women have recalled about their parents.

My father [most influenced me as a child]. . . . He owned his own trucking business. His attitude is always "Shoot for the top. There's *nothing* in between!" He instilled that in me when I was a child, a *little* child. "Shoot for the stars," was his expression. "Shoot for the *stars*." Maybe this was why it never occurred to me that there was any reason that I couldn't do anything I wanted.

—Doris Tarrant, *bank president*

When I look back, my mother very much encouraged my female identity. As far as she was concerned it was a good thing to be a woman. She felt inferior but she experienced it as an injustice imposed from the outside, different from feeling internally inferior.

—Anica Vessel Mander, *writer and founder of Alyssum, a feminist center*

Harlem is a mean place to grow up in; there's always somebody to gall you no matter how much you want to mind your own business. If Daddy hadn't shown me how to look out for myself, I would have got into a lot of fights that I would have lost, and I would have been pretty badly beaten up a lot of times. . . .

—Althea Gibson, *tennis and golf professional and New Jersey State Athletic Commissioner*

My mother's theory was "First finish your housework. Then read."

—Anne Lasoff, *writer*

That one must do some work seriously and must be independent and not merely amuse oneself in life—this our mother [Marie Curie] has told us always, but never that science was the only career worth following.

—Irene Joliot Curie, *scientist*

My grandmother always told me—she worked 22 years in this laundry and she was late maybe once—she said, "I don't work for anybody but *myself*. I don't have *any* bosses! I call *no man* my boss. I'm my own *boss*." And she said, "When you go to work, when you're on top, you're doing that for *you*. I'm only working for myself."

—Sophenia Maxwell, *electrical mechanic*

[My father] had no sexual stereotypes in terms of the way he treated his children. . . . I remember him saying to me, and I guess I was a sophomore in undergraduate school at the time, "Don't you want to do something that will make you independent?"

—Judith Grant McKelvey, *law school dean*

My mother was forever involved with the extended family; she helped relatives and more relatives, mediated, listened to their problems. She was more liberal than my father; never debating him on issues, she quietly voted differently. She was idealistic, concerned about world peace and the role of women in the world. She clipped newspaper and magazine articles—anything with "peace" or "women" in the headline. Eleanor Roosevelt was her heroine. She always encouraged me "to show what women can do."

—Connie Young Yu, *editor/publisher and filmmaker*

My father raised us kids all to be independent, to learn to do for ourselves. He taught us what hard work was, and to always do a job the best we could no matter how big or little it was. He was a very firm, strict man, but a good one.

—Inez Ruth Hill, *lumber mill supervisor*

My mother and father never doubted my ability to take care of myself.

—May Stevens, *painter*

[My mother] has handed down respect for the possibilities— and the will to grasp them.

—Alice Walker, *poet and writer*

FRIENDS

To act the part of a true friend requires more conscientious feeling than to fill with credit and complacency any other station or capacity in life.

—Sarah Ellis, *missionary and writer*

Who is the most important person in your life right now? If your answer is "my best friend" or "my boyfriend" or "my whole gang," it wouldn't be surprising. You probably feel that your friends understand you a lot better than your parents do. Your friends cheer you up when you feel down, don't hassle you, and speak your language. They know what's important to you, and they understand why.

Maybe in school you belong to a group that shares an interest, such as music, theater, or athletics. Maybe your group just likes to hang out together. These friends protect you from loneliness and give you a sense of belonging. That's important. But a tight-knit group can become a little too tight, like a turtleneck sweater that shrinks to strangle-neck proportions. If your friends won't let you grow and develop new interests, if they put you down for taking school seriously, or if they ridicule outsiders you like or laugh at your ambitions for the future, the group becomes a limiting force. It's hard enough to exert your independence, but a critical circle of peers can make it impossible.

How do you reconcile these two forces—the need to be accepted and liked and the need to follow your own interests and instincts? Acting one way in front of your friends when you really believe you should behave another way is likely to make you feel hypocritical and uneasy. And convincing yourself that being part of the crowd is more important than *anything* is likely to make you a dull clone, always following someone else's example. It can also be damaging; if you never make an effort to achieve a goal that will make you stand out from the others, you will probably be considered mediocre in the future when achievements count—by admissions officers and employers.

It's easy to advise you: Be yourself! Ignore the others! Walk to the beat of your own drummer! The advice is easy to give but can be extremely hard to follow. Balancing the need to belong and the need to be an individual is another of the hardest tasks of growing up. How do you tackle it?

Start by taking a look at the elements that make up your social life. Are your good friends supportive and caring, even if you delve into something they don't understand? Are you surrounded by a bunch of conforming, insecure people who ridicule individuality? Do you have some interesting acquaintances you would like to draw into your circle of friends? Are there things you'd really like to do—or really *should* do—but haven't because of peer pressure? Do your friends ever challenge you or push you toward a goal you might not otherwise be motivated to achieve? When you talk about your dreams for the future, do they laugh or do they help you think of ways you can work toward realizing them? Your friends know you well; they should be able to help you with career plans simply by supporting certain ideas your parents might not have found appealing.

What are your friends' goals for themselves? Do female friends aspire to traditionally "female" careers, while male friends plan for "male" careers? How do your friends view women's achievements? How do your male friends feel about women's changing role? How are your opinions influenced by theirs?

Maybe, if your gang is a little too quick to criticize someone different, you could try to show them how their prejudices are self-defeating. They might decide *you're* a weirdo too, but they might also listen.

You've heard this sermon before, but the best kind of friends care about *you*. They may think it's funny that you took a job as a giant rooster to advertise a fried chicken place, but they don't put you down for it. They understand when you'd rather read than go bowling, and they don't get defensive when you excel at something. Friends like these are a rare find. The best way to find friends like them is to *be* that kind of friend.

AQ: Increase Your Awareness Quotient

You're a member of a close circle of girls who have been friends since seventh grade. Now you're in high school, and you're still sharing secrets, sweaters, and jokes. All of you are from the same sort of family background and, though you each plan to go to college, schoolwork is not a high priority. You sit on the same bench at lunch and you laugh about the "bookworms" who study in the library during their breaks.

Then, in your English class, you and a girl named Jane are teamed up to work on a project together. Jane, a loner, dresses a little eccentrically, but she has a biting wit and a wonderful sense of the absurd. You really enjoy working with her, and your oral report—which you deliver as a comedy dialogue—is a hit with the class *and* the teacher.

You want your friendship to continue outside of class, so you invite Jane to come along with your crowd to a basketball game. She has a good time and you have a good time, but you hear later that some of your friends are furious that you included "that smart aleck with the stringy hair."

How do you react? Do you confront your friends and demand that they accept Jane? Do you gently suggest to Jane that she change her hairstyle and try to refrain from laughing too loudly? Do you regretfully forget about developing a friendship with such an outsider? Or do you try to keep your relationship with Jane separate or secret from your other friends?

There are no easy answers. But if you can bring yourself at least to confront the questions, you'll have taken a step toward controlling your own life.

SCHOOL

> ... it has always seemed strange to me that in our endless discussions about education so little stress is ever laid on the pleasure of becoming an educated person, the enormous interest it adds to life. To be able to be caught up into the world of thought— that is to be educated.
>
> —Edith Hamilton, *classics scholar*

When you're sitting at a desk trying to remember if Millard Fillmore came before or after Andrew Jackson, you may well wonder what connection, if any, school has to Real Life. Students sometimes tend to fragment their lives; school is half their existence. Then, beyond the classroom, there is Real Life. When you grow up, you figure, everything is Real Life and you can put biology and social studies behind you forever.

Well, in case you haven't noticed, Real Life *is* biology and social studies. In fact, the elements of our daily lives are merely variations on what you've been doing in school. While few Real Life adults sit around trying to remember how to figure the area of a parallelogram, they are figuring out solutions to other kinds of problems. In school, you get rewarded with a grade; at work, you get a paycheck. But at both places you're presented with problems, you weigh the possible solutions, and you pick the best one.

High school influences you in subtle ways. When you walk through those doors each morning, suddenly you're plunged into a lively broth of personalities. Like them or not, you have to learn to work harmoniously with an assortment of teachers, counselors, coaches, and students. One of the most valuable lessons you master at school is learning to cope with people you don't much like. Just try to remember that the next time Mrs. Feeney looks down her long, sharp nose and demands to know why you're late *again.*

Learning to handle competition and ambition is a useful skill, but sometimes the competitive atmosphere can get out of hand. If getting straight A's or winning the swimming championship blots out everything else, you won't have much time to master other skills.

High school, you may have noticed, isn't perfect. But it sure beats the alternative—dropping out—which can only limit your options and dump you in a rut that will make algebra class look like heaven.

These are the general ways that school influences you, but there are other, more specific influences that affect you every time you open a textbook, listen to a lecture, or seek advice from a counselor. They have molded you in ways you may never have imagined.

Between kindergarten and high school graduation, you will have read about 32,000 textbook pages. That makes for some pretty hefty influencing. Have you ever turned a critical eye on your textbooks? Too frequently, they perpetuate the idea that women played a very insignificant part in history. Some texts might lead you to believe that the last woman who contributed anything useful to America was Betsy Ross. Some history books have treated minorities in the same nonexistent manner. Things have improved somewhat lately. Many schools are making a determined effort to make texts fair and accurate. They know that biased books can have a negative effect on the aspirations of girls and nonwhites.

School is more than the texts you read, and individual teachers can have a profound influence on you. They can inspire you to accomplish things you might have thought you were incapable of doing. A good teacher, enthusiastic and dedicated, can enrich your life and make your mind soar. Poor teachers, dull and regimented, can turn you off so thoroughly that you never want to hear the word "school" mentioned again.

Most teachers have not been trained to give nonsexist education, and most are unaware of the many subtle ways they influence their students every day. The truth is that from your first day of kindergarten on, chances are you were "learning" that teachers perceive students differently according to their sex and that they do not work at providing identical classroom experiences for boys and girls.

Although girls tend to become teachers' pets more often than boys, studies show that because teachers have deep-seated perceptions of male worth in society, it is boys who are actually given more attention. So although you may pay attention, behave, and volunteer often in class, you may find that boys are getting more reinforcement from your teacher—for any type of behavior. Teachers will probably assume that, because you are a hard worker, you are already producing at your maximum potential. Boys, on the other hand, are continually prodded by teachers to push themselves harder. And the more the boys receive the greater amount of attention in class, the more they learn to expect and demand it.

It's not fair to expect perfection from teachers. They have a heavy work load and they're under a lot of pressure. They have papers to grade, lessons to plan, tests to write, and lots of excuses to listen to. They also have personal lives and many of the same problems and concerns as your own family. Have a heart. Your English teacher may not be as funny as Johnny Carson or as dramatic as Sarah Bernhardt, but he or she can teach you *something*. All your teachers can.

The courses you take and the grades you receive become increasingly important as graduation approaches. What made you choose the classes you're in now? Did you listen to suggestions from teachers or counselors? From parents or from friends? Did you choose them solely because they interested you? Did you pick a teacher known for giving easy A's or a teacher known for challenging students? Now that you're in the middle of these classes, are you happy with your choices? What would you change?

In high school you have some power to plan your own curriculum, and it's often tempting to choose easy or fun classes for electives. These are often important for relief from other more demanding classes or for bolstering your grade point average. But it's important to push yourself somewhat too. Your friends might all decide to enroll in the "joke" class to fulfill the history requirement, but maybe you should consider taking the Advanced Placement history class that your last year's history teacher recommended to you. Don't think that college admissions officers don't take a good, hard look at the courses you chose. They know how to compare a B- in AP bio to an A in shop or driver's ed. Employers, too, will often ask about the courses you took and your reasons for choosing them.

Counselors are another significant influence at school. After more than a decade in the educational system, you probably have encountered counselors only occasionally. They were the harried people who helped you figure out a schedule in eighth grade, or passed out the sharpened pencils during diagnostic testing, or told you that if you were late to Mrs. Feeney's class one more time you'd be on probation. After several of these brief encounters, counselors begin to seem like animal cookies. They come in different shapes, but other than that they're all pretty much alike.

Better give counseling one more try. You're going to need it now more than ever before, and it's up to you to press for it. Your counselor can be a one-stop source of information on specific jobs, college requirements, vocational training, scholarships, and test deadlines. He or she can help you interpret your scores on skills and aptitude tests. A good counselor can point you toward the Yellow Brick Road and give you a nudge.

That's a good counselor. By now you've realized that counselors (like parents and teachers) are human, and humans aren't perfect. A counselor can have stereotypes and outdated ideas. And, now and then, bad counseling can steer you in the wrong direction. Here are some examples of bad counseling. Think of them if you sense something is a bit "off" about the counseling you're getting.

- In the bad old days, many counselors routinely handed young women information about such "feminine" occupations as nursing and teaching, but they had to be prodded to talk to girls about such "masculine" jobs as science and engineering.

- Some counselors tend to "track" students; children of wealthy or highly educated parents are encouraged to aim for high-status universities and professions, while minority or poor students are directed to less prestigious schools and lower-level occupations.

- Counselors, who are often oriented toward academics, sometimes hold the notion that jobs involving manual labor are inferior to jobs involving mental labor. They might discourage you from a line of work that you like and could do well.

The point is that *you* will have to evaluate the information you get from a counselor. Be careful of anyone's advice if it pushes you onto a very limited track and prematurely closes up your options. Don't let your future be restricted by the blind spots, prejudices, or ignorance of others.

AQ: INCREASE YOUR AWARENESS QUOTIENT

Analyze the faculty and staff of your school to see if you can detect the results of old-fashioned sex-role stereotyping. Are the science, math, and shop teachers mostly males? Are the art, dance, and homemaking teachers mostly females? Are the cafeteria workers all women and the custodians all men? Is the principal a male, while the one female vice-principal handles mostly girls' disciplinary problems?

35

If your school is arranged on such a "traditional" framework, consider the ways that this might have influenced you. After all, there's really no reason why a woman can't teach woodworking shop or auto repair. And men aren't inherently unable to dish out mashed potatoes in the cafeteria or teach you how to sew on a button.

Drawing submitted by Sandra Lynn Chaney, 16;
Livingston, Montana
Catalyst Cartoon Competition Winner

WORKING WOMAN

Marie Moses

Nursing Consultant

If your conception of a nurse is someone who weighs you at the doctor's office or gives you a shot when you're in the hospital, Marie Moses has news for you.

"It's no longer true that a nurse is a nurse is a nurse," Marie says firmly. "There are lots of subspecialties in nursing, many with requirements beyond the basic R.N. [Registered Nurse] license. Nurses work in schools, prisons, industry, and the military, and some have even hung out a shingle and are treating patients themselves. Wherever there are people there's a need for nurses. It's not a dead-end kind of career; you can grow in the profession."

Not surprisingly, this enthusiastic advocate of nursing is a nurse herself. Currently, she is the nursing consultant for the Indian Health Service in the three-state region of Oregon, Washington, and Idaho. Her work now is administrative and instructional rather than clinical, but Marie began her career in the role of a hospital nurse.

"I guess I always wanted to be a nurse," she says when asked how she chose her profession. "I don't think I made up my mind at one certain point."

Marie had completed one year of nurses' training in her native Japan before she moved to America with her husband. She forfeited that first year, though, when she later resumed her education in the United States.

"I was concerned that my credits from Japan wouldn't transfer to the new program," she recalls, "so I started from scratch."

Marie received her R.N. in 1965 and worked as a hospital nurse until 1972, when she completed her Bachelor of Science degree at Montana State University. She then worked for the Indian Health Service as a public health nurse until 1977, when academia lured her once again.

"I went to graduate school and earned a Master of Nursing degree in 1978, with a major in administration and education," Marie says. "That's when I got my job as nursing consultant for the Portland-area Indian Health Service. The position requires a master's degree.

"I don't do direct patient care as a matter of routine," she explains. "I provide technical and professional consultation to the nurses working on the Indian reservations. I evaluate patient care, nursing procedures, and management. I also assist the tribes in developing a framework for their health programs. And, for the last several months, I've been filling in as director of the public health nurses at a health center. That involves hiring, firing, and counseling. Federal budget cuts are responsible for my dual roles."

Although Marie is employed by the federal government, she is not a member of the civil service. Rather, she is in the commissioned officer corps of the U.S. Public Health Service.

"Not many people are aware of the existence of the corps," she comments. "We don't have open recruitment or posters like the Army or Navy. It's a strictly professional corps, very small, with only about 7,200 Public Health Service officers on active duty. The corps is made up of people in a variety of health-related occupations, including doctors, pharmacists, physical therapists, dietitians, and veterinarians.

"The benefits and responsibilities are pretty much like those in any branch of the uniformed military service, except you don't 'sign up' for a specific stretch of time. The minimum requirement for a nurse in the corps is a bachelor's degree from a college accredited by the National League for Nursing."

One important difference between the corps and the civil service, Marie explains, is the corps' ranking system. In the civil service, each job is designated by a certain grade and pay is determined by that criterion. In the commissioned officer corps, the rank goes with the person who fills the job, not with the job itself.

"Generally, the pay in the corps is lower than in similar civil service jobs when you're starting out," she says. "It gets better the longer you stay, so entering the corps is strictly a long-term career move."

As a nursing consultant providing consultation to seven units, Marie is on the road about half the time, visiting reservations in remote locations.

"One thing I love about my job is the infinite variety. Working with the director of each unit, I get involved in all matters related to nursing," she comments. "The human factor in nursing makes it an unpredictable and interesting way to earn a living.

"Anyone who considers nursing should be aware that it is a very people-oriented profession. If you're more interested in working with things than with people, it probably isn't for you. You must also be able to withstand stress if you plan to become a nurse. It's a high-stress role because you're dealing with human life and there's not much room for error."

But if you like people and can take the strain of life-and-death situations, Marie believes nursing is a fulfilling, satisfying, and useful career choice. Employment prospects are good, too, since there generally seems to be a shortage of nurses.

"The supply of nurses hasn't kept up with the demand," Marie explains. "There are a number of reasons for this. For one thing, women aren't as limited in their career choices as they used to be, so many look for jobs with less stress, better hours, and better pay. Salaries in nursing don't compare with those in electronics or engineering, for example.

"Meanwhile, nursing is an expanding profession. Geriatrics—the care of the aged—is one growing field, and there's a real need for nurses in that area. People are living longer and they tend to need more health care as they grow older.

"There's another very interesting new aspect of nursing—the idea of *keeping* people well rather than just treating them when they are sick. Increasingly, nurses are involved with preventive medicine and health education."

If you ever catch yourself thinking "a nurse is a nurse is a nurse," it's time to revise your stereotype. Remember Marie Moses, out there in the expanses of the Pacific Northwest, as she makes the long drive from one reservation to the next.

WHEN SHE WAS YOUNG

Kathie Gray

Kathie Gray, born in 1864, began her diary when she was 12 years old and living in Ohio. It proved a good companion, perhaps making up for the brothers and sisters she didn't have. Here she talks about braving peer pressure and befriending someone her other friends had shunned.

February 11. This morning most of our class were standing around as usual before the bell rang talking over Lou Hardy's party last night—and laughing and joking—all of course but Harry Rand. He was in his seat drawing and looking as glum as usual. He is never invited to any of the class parties. In the opening exercises Mr. Dean chose "What a Friend We Have in Jesus" and when we came to the words "Do your friends despise—forsake you, Is there trouble any where" Harry stopped singing.... I glanced at him out of the corner of my eye. He was scowling harder than ever but someway he looked so *hurt* too and as though he could hardly hold in—as though he wanted to bolt to the barn and bawl. In a minute as we got our books out I accidentally (?) dropped my silver pencil which rolled nearly to his seat. He stooped to pick it up... and I stooped too, and our heads bumped together quite hard. (*That* part I *didnt* plan.) I laughed (silently) and blushed my becomingest and will you believe it—that misanthrope smiled! Smiled like a sunburst diamond! Why he is very good looking when he doesnt act the part of the heavy villain in the play.

I took it we were introduced after that and at noon as I noticed the far famed drawing book of his on his desk, I stopped and said "Have you finished that last model Harry? I think its dreadfully hard." "Why yes," he answered real eagerly.... Really it was wonderful—rather better than the printed design. I couldnt have helped praising it if I had wanted to—and I asked to see the whole book.... I nearly wore out my adjectives saying so. The poor fellows fingers shook as he turned the pages. My! how ostrachsized he has been feeling....

When I was putting on my wraps I heard Harry Rand actually whistling. Sunny, Mame and Sue were waiting for me in the dressing room—and Sue began to scold "Why Katharine Gray I dont know but that you have spoiled your chance of being chosen for one of our Class Officers!" she stormed. "The idea of your speaking to that stuck up Grumpy—who cheats too!" This made me cross and I told my dear Susan a few things about this being a free country. I told her too that I had been watching out across the isle for a long time and had about made up my mind that we of Class A were a cruel set of Pharasees! Granted that he was seen cheating one day—long ago—no one had ever told me that he did it again. And I said did she think we could reform a sinner by slowly freezing him to death? I reminded her that Bessie Rand was one of our sweetest girls . . . and that she was worried about her brother and that I for one was through treating him so high and mighty unless he should be bad again. We had quite a little spat but kissed and made up afterwards. I am glad I spoke to him. I am glad I stood up for him and I dont care so awfully to be elected to a class office any way.

The Silent One

My friends surround me
at the lunch table
talking about boys
and Friday nights
while I sit nervously
remembering a babysitting job.

My friends surround me
at the lunch table
moaning about weight
and wearing size seven
while I sip Tab
and dream of size nine.

My friends surround me
at the lunch table
wishing for talent
and a direction in life
while I think of
my art scholarship.

My friends surround me
at the lunch table
wanting better grades
and hoping to pass the test
while I am confident
of being on the honor roll.

My friends surround me
at the lunch table
and share their desires
while I sit listening;
I am the silent one.

Poem submitted by Shelly Lynn Sain, 16;
Mound, Minnesota
Catalyst Poetry Competition Winner

3
What Are Your Needs?

Necessity knows no Sunday.

—Agnes Repplier, *writer and social critic*

S urrounded by a dozen stacks of index cards, Amy peers at a book, reading eagerly. Suddenly her eyebrows fly up. She reaches for a blank card and begins scribbling so intently that she doesn't notice her mother entering the room.

"Good grief, Amy, this is the first time in sixteen years that you missed a meal!" her mother says with mock amazement. "Here. I made you a sandwich."

"Thanks, Mom," Amy mumbles, munching. "I'm really wrapped up in this. If we win the debate Friday, we'll be on our way to the state finals." She taps the card in front of her with a finger. "And this is the perfect rebuttal to their strongest point. This'll kill 'em."

"Aren't we bloodthirsty," her mother says. "Give me the plate and I'll let you get back to work."

Amy, without realizing it, is busy fulfilling her needs. She needs food for energy, as well as a warm, safe place to work on her debate. She also needs the work itself. It contributes to her psychological well-being, something she needs as surely as food and shelter.

43

In our society, it's relatively easy to satisfy physiological (body) needs like food and shelter. When you are hungry, thirsty, or sleepy, your body sends out signals and you grab a burger, drink orange juice, or take a nap. Once you've met the need, your body returns to a relaxed state called homeostasis.

But woman does not live by bread—or burgers—alone. Your psychological needs also have to be filled, but it may not be so easy to recognize exactly what you're lacking. Your ego doesn't growl when you need a dose of self-esteem, and your heart doesn't itch when you want to be loved.

Abraham Maslow, a distinguished psychologist, devised a list of basic human needs.[1] Look at the list below and see how your needs fit into his general categories.

- *Physiological needs* (hunger, thirst, and sleep). Without enough food, liquid, and rest, our body mechanisms fail and we cannot survive.

- *Safety needs* (shelter, warmth, and freedom from danger). To be safe—and feel safe—people need protection from danger. We also require physical security, like a dry cave or a cozy condominium, and "social" security, which is provided by family, friends, and various groups. We feel secure if we can rely on these supports when we're threatened, confused, or unable to cope with responsibilities.

- *"Belongingness" and love needs* (companionship and affection). Human beings are social creatures. We require relationships, companionship, and affection in order to thrive, to mature, to achieve. Without this contact, we shrivel and withdraw.

- *Esteem needs* (self-respect and others' respect). We need to respect ourselves, to have confidence in our ability to perform and achieve. We also need the esteem of others. Their recognition gives us prestige and status, while enhancing our self-esteem.

- *Self-actualization needs* (growth, development, and use of potential). To "actualize" means to make actual—to develop the potential each human is born with. Many psychologists believe that most people fail to fulfill their inborn potential; some say we use only 10 or 20 percent of our total potential. Why? Society is one culprit. Its sex-role stereotyping can limit growth. The little girl with great mechanical ability may be told that her talent is inappropriate "for a girl." She may put down her screwdriver forever and concentrate on more "girlish" activities instead. People fail to develop their abilities for other reasons, too. They may lack self-confidence and be afraid to attempt new things. Or time may be a factor. If you practice gymnastics 5 hours a day, you obviously limit the time you have for other activities. The important point about self-actualization is that everyone is born with the potential to grow and develop. Most of us are capable of far more than we give ourselves credit for.

Okay, you may say, so what? Do people really *need* to develop and use their potential abilities? Well, think of something you are good at. Dancing, perhaps. Suppose you break your leg and have to hobble around on crutches for five months. Wouldn't you feel frustrated because you couldn't dance? When the doctor cracked off the cast and you could dance again, you'd click your heels and celebrate. People simply need to develop and grow. We thrive when we are able to use our talents and stretch our abilities.

NEEDS VS. DESIRES

> Oh Lord won't you buy me a Mercedes-Benz?
> My friends all drive Porsches,
> I must make amends.
>
> —Janis Joplin, *singer and songwriter*

It's easy to confuse needs and desires. A need is a basic physiological or psychological lack that threatens our well-being if it isn't gratified. A desire is the wish for something that provides pleasure but is not essential to survival. We live in a society that is comparatively rich both in material things and in pleasant experiences. As a result, it's possible for us to develop limitless desires for pleasures that are entirely unrelated to survival.

In contrast, people who live in poorer parts of the world can be overwhelmed with efforts to gratify basic needs like hunger and thirst. It's easy for them to distinguish between a desire and a need. (They don't long for the newest video game on the market.) There's nothing wrong with having desires, but it's important to realize that fulfilling them is not mandatory.

It's 10 degrees below 0 and you just wore a big hole in the sole of your only pair of boots. You're disappointed because you were planning to take a weekend trip with your friends, but you can't afford both the trip and new boots. You *need* boots, right? By recognizing what's most important, you're able to make the decision to forgo a weekend of fun for a winter of warm feet.

Confusing need and desire can lead to frustration. Suppose you have *four* pairs of boots, but you decide you desperately "need" that high-heeled pair you saw while window-shopping. You depend on your parents for clothing, so you tell your mother, "I can't live without these boots." She looks at you skeptically and points wordlessly to the four pairs in the closet. Obviously, you're going to have to live without the boots. If you're really intent on having that fifth pair of boots, you'll experience intense frustration when you can't have them.

NEEDS RELATED TO WORK

How does working fill your needs? When you're a working adult, you'll assume responsibility for providing for your own physiological and safety necessities. It'll be up to you to see that you have a leak-proof roof over your head, a dead-bolt lock on your door, and three square meals a day. Your work will pay the bills for these needs.

Companionship will continue to be as essential to you as it is now. At school, you form friendships with students you enjoy, respect, and share interests with. Similarly, on the job you will look for companionship and seek friends among coworkers you respect and who share your interests.

Often, the people you work with can make the difference between liking or hating a particular job. People who work alone most of the time, such as artists, scientists, and writers, have to seek companionship outside their immediate workplace.

Self-esteem is an ongoing need too, so you will want to choose work that you enjoy and take pride in your competence. Your self-esteem will be enhanced by recognition in the form of praise, promotions, and pay raises.

For many people, work is the main route to self-actualization. As you master the job at hand or move on to one that involves new challenges, you will tap many potential abilities that otherwise might have remained dormant.

MEETING YOUR OWN NEEDS

Adults are always telling teenagers to "be mature." Generally, they are referring to behavior. They want you to stop giggling at the concert or to start writing your term paper more than 24 hours before it's due. But maturing is more than that. It means learning to recognize your own needs and becoming responsible for attending to them. The transition from a totally dependent infant to an independent adult is a long, and sometimes painful, process.

You've made a lot of progress since you took a first toddling step away from your parents. Remember those frightening first few days at school when you had to face a new situation alone? Or the first time you went to a party by yourself and had to swallow your shyness when you marched through the door? Or the first time you stayed home by yourself or raced through an oral report? Or the time you took your driver's test?

In each case, you were fulfilling needs and discovering that you *could* take care of them. Sometimes you blew it. Sometimes you wished you could return to the snug security of childhood. But there is also something delicious about handling things on your own, about facing up to something that is difficult for you.

One of the hardest things about taking on more responsibility is dealing with other people's reactions and your fears of how they might react. Parents can feel threatened when they see their daughters and sons maturing, viewing them as children even when they are almost adults.

Let's go back to Amy, the debater. She obviously loves this expression of her skills. She's good at it; she enjoys it; it gratifies her needs for friends, accomplishment, self-esteem, and recognition. Her mother (remember Mom, with the sandwich?) doesn't see things Amy's way. A very proper lady, she can't understand why Amy insists on "making a spectacle of herself" in public debates. Amy is an independent sort, so she continues with the debating team despite her mother's objections. But she is also sensitive and respects her mother's feelings. She doesn't want to disappoint her. Balancing needs can be tricky—and the results may occasionally be unpleasant.

At a time when you are clarifying your own needs and setting goals, it may be difficult to tell your parents that what they want for you isn't necessarily what you want for yourself. Even so, it's important to discuss these issues with them. If the gap seems too wide, talk with a teacher, with someone who works in the field you're interested in, or with your school counselor. Sometimes it helps to get a more objective perspective.

FRIENDSHIPS

Friends can pose dilemmas too. You need—and enjoy—their companionship and affection. They feel the same way. But what happens when your need for friendship clashes with another of your needs?

Imagine that summer is approaching, and you've applied for and landed an internship at a nearby natural history museum. You're delighted by the prospect, but there is one nagging problem: your boyfriend. He wants you to be a counselor with him at a summer camp in the mountains 100 miles from home. "It'll be fantastic," he assures you. "We'll have the whole summer together, and we'll be out of reach of our parents for once." You haven't been able to bring yourself to tell him about the internship yet.

Meanwhile, there are your parents. They're pressuring you to take the internship, but you suspect that their real reason is a desire to split up you and your boyfriend. They're pushing so hard you're beginning to balk at the idea of the internship just to assert yourself.

"*I* need to be with you this summer," your boyfriend pleads. "*We* need you here at home this summer," your parents argue. What are *your* needs in this situation? Is it more important to be with your boyfriend, to assert your independence, or to capitalize on a good chance to use your abilities at the museum?

What would your decision be? Now, imagine that your best friend faces this situation. What advice would you give him or her?

Weighing your needs against a friend's can be hard in other ways. Have there been times you felt nervous after doing something better than a friend, like being elected to a class office, or winning a swim meet, or earning the top grade on a test? Were you a little reluctant to acknowledge your accomplishment? If such situations sound familiar and made you feel anxious, ask yourself why. Were you afraid that you would lose friends because of your achievements? Frequently, girls worry about being successful because they think their friends will see them as competitive overachievers.

Working out these problems requires you to think about your needs in a particular situation, to weigh them, and to decide what's most important to you. Sometimes you will have to compromise or forfeit one thing to gain another. Conflicts like this will confront you throughout your life, but being aware of your own needs will help you settle on a course of action that is best for you.

THE GREAT JUGGLING ACT: KIDS AND JOBS

Another conflict that may confront you later is balancing work, babies, a husband, chores, leisure, and rest. That's like juggling a dozen eggs while riding a bicycle—backwards. It's possible, but it's certainly not easy.

Raising a family and maintaining a career require forethought, hard work, and compromise. Most couples find that they must make some sacrifices, like giving up the idea of a clutter-free home or a two-seater convertible. They work out their own solutions by dividing up tasks and responsibilities. Of course, families have always had to make sacrifices, compromise, and work out their own solutions, but in the past, for many families, the husband's role was usually that of breadwinner while the wife managed things at home. Today, that old order has been changed by the need for two paychecks coupled with women's drive for equality in the workplace.

Starting a career is an exciting prospect. At some point, you will probably consider starting a family as well. You'll face questions like these:

- When should I have children, or should I have them at all?
- If my husband and I both have jobs, who will care for the children while we work?
- Will I want to put my career on "hold" for several years while I care for my young children?
- How will I reconcile the many demands on me—my children's needs, my husband's, my employer's, and my own?

Drawing submitted by Marie Rogoz, 17;
Clark, New Jersey

Some couples postpone having children until their careers are firmly established and they can take time off without jeopardizing their jobs. Others wait until they are earning enough money to afford child care comfortably. Many women, in fact, are waiting until they're in their thirties before beginning a family.

Some couples hire housekeepers or baby-sitters to help them cope with the responsibilities of a family. Others negotiate special work schedules so husband and wife can swap baby duties. Sometimes one parent is able to work at home and care for the kids during the day. Other possibilities are home care by other parents who take in a few children in addition to their own, government-sponsored or private child-care centers, or child care provided by the employer.

You may want to take care of your child yourself during the early years, but that doesn't mean you're confined forever to a life of diapers and dirty dishes. You could take an extended leave of absence, if your employer agrees, or you could reenter the job market when you are ready to do so.

Fantasize a bit. If you could arrange your work and family life any way you wanted, what would you do? Bring your children to work with you? Share a job with your husband or someone else? It's not too early to begin thinking about how you will work this out.

WORKING WOMAN

Wende Jones

Computer Programmer

Wende Jones perches on a deck chair in her West Los Angeles back-yard, soaking up the warm California sunshine. Her tan is enviable. So's her job, for Wende—bathing suit and all—is at work.

Wende is a computer programmer. Her employer provides her with a home terminal that's connected to the big computer at her office. This way she can work from her backyard deck—or living room, or bedroom—designing and testing software to be used by Citibank. The home terminal allows her to have an extremely flexible work schedule, something that's important to her as a parent of a toddler. Her current assignment, coincidentally, is to develop programs for bank customers who own personal computers.

"I'm working on a home terminal program—on *my* home terminal," she explains, laughing. "Confused? My assignment is writing the programs so customers can do all their banking from their residences. This means developing and testing the instructions that tell the computer what to do."

She enjoys working at home but emphasizes that she still has deadlines to meet.

"Citibank has been very flexible in letting me schedule my own time," she says. "Working at home is great, but of course I'm expected to put in all the hours necessary to get the job done. And sometimes it's necessary or desirable to go to the office to work."

Wende's actual employer is Citibank's Transaction Technology, Inc., which develops banking systems for Citibank. Her first position with the company was as a clerk in the personnel department. She had no idea at that time that she would eventually become a programmer.

"I was back in Los Angeles after a few years at San Jose State University, and I needed a job," Wende recalls. "So I went to work as a Kelly Girl, doing temporary secretarial jobs. I was sent to Transaction Technology, and I hit it off with the people there. They offered me a permanent job."

They offered a job, but what she got was an education.

"I learned programming on the job," she says. "At the same time, the company sent me to Pepperdine University, where I earned my

Bachelor of Science degree. Now I'm working on my M.B.A. [Master of Business Administration] at Loyola Marymount, also paid for by the company. I never could have afforded this kind of an education on my own. Needless to say, I think Citibank is a wonderful employer!"

Balancing motherhood, a career, and a graduate education takes skill, guts, and a delicate touch. Wende attributes her success to good time management and "tremendous self-motivation." It was this motivation that made Citibank notice her and want to help her as much as it has. But she wasn't always this motivated, Wende concedes.

"I don't recall having any career goals at all in high school," she says. "In fact, I wasn't very serious about college, either. I didn't really know where I was going then. Things didn't start to come together until I went to work for Transaction Technology. There I was, a personnel clerk without a very good education. I realized *only* secretarial work was ahead for me unless I did something positive. That's why I went into programming."

It looks as if Wende's self-motivation will now propel her into management.

"Management is my next goal; it's the next logical step," she believes. "It appeals to me, and it's where my education is leading."

Looking back, Wende believes that her work as a temporary employee was a good first step in exploring her career options.

"It's a fantastic way to get a taste of all kinds of different fields," she says. "You can test yourself in any number of businesses—banks, telephone companies, computer firms. It's a good way to get an inside look at a career you might want to follow."

But working as a temporary isn't the best way to begin a career in computer programming, she cautions.

"The best training for computer programming is a Bachelor of Science degree in computer science or electrical engineering," advises Wende, "followed by a master's in the same. The competition is tough in this field and you have to have a formal education to compete."

Once you have that education, however, computer programming is an excellent career choice for a young woman, Wende says. Her enthusiasm, in fact, seems boundless.

"This is a fabulous field for women," she says. "There are lots of employers trying to hire women to meet their equal opportunity obligations. The pay is good, the work is challenging, and you use your brains. I have found absolutely *no* sex discrimination in programming. It is simply a fabulous field for women," she repeats.

After 5½ years with Citibank, during which she's mastered programming and chalked up several suntans, Wende Jones should know.

WHEN SHE WAS YOUNG

Mathilde von Buddenbroch

Mathilde von Buddenbroch was born in 1520 in German-speaking Switzerland and lived during the time of the Protestant Reformation. Her reaction to her first marriage proposal 450 years ago is not so very different from the mixed feelings many young girls today have about marriage.

Here I am, seventeen years old, being proposed to! My good neighbor Michon, what could you be thinking of? Why in Heaven's name do you wish to marry me? I assure you, it doesn't appeal to me. My sister's example has hardly served as a guide. I don't want to leave my father, my mother, my brothers and my friends to enter into the confined household of Michon. My father asked me, "Don't you want to consider it awhile?" "Consider what?" I retorted, horrified that my father could conceive of letting me go. He realized my distress and burst out laughing, "All right, my child, I guess you are decided." So, the matter is settled. Although I am dead set against this marriage, I want to understand the meaning of marriage.... Marriage, I believe, is an indissoluble bond which obliges the woman to leave everything behind and follow her husband. Really, it's awful. Could I do such a thing for the love of Michon? Certainly not! To live only with him—I shudder at the thought. Marriage is a cage which locks you in, and even if this cage is made of diamonds and gold, it is still a cage.... I don't want any of it. I want to stay with my parents. Of course I would continue to visit them, if I were married, but then everyone would be reminding me of my wifely duties and telling me about what a husband desires and what a husband allows. My mother is an exception to this rule, but only because my father is also an exception. There is not another man like my father, and that is why I choose not to marry. In any case, I could never be happier than I am right now. I have work, diversions, inspired discussions... what more could I want?

Two Worlds

Little house on a hill;
white picket fence;
Six kids in a big yard;
a dog and cat.

A high rise office,
my name on the door;
Park Avenue apartment;
no roommate, just me.

Such a decision—
how does one choose?
Wouldn't you like to have a
little of each world?

Poem submitted by Dusty Suzanne Pierce, 15;
Edmond, Oklahoma
Catalyst Poetry Competition Winner

4
What Are Your Values?

> You have to know exactly what you want out of your career. If you want to be a star, you don't bother with other things.
>
> —Marilyn Horne, *opera singer*

As a noun, value means the worth of something. A new car and a friendship are both valuable. Which is worth more? Only you can say. One has a dollar value; the other doesn't. Values have a way of shifting, too. If you are in the middle of the Sahara and there are no roads, you won't be able to use a car. You probably won't be able to sell one, either. A jug of water would have greater value.

Your values are the standards that guide your life. They dictate your choice of friends, jobs, politics, where to spend the weekend, and whether to order a hamburger "with the works" or "hold the onions." (You may have to decide between pleasing your palate or your classmates.)

In making these choices, big and small, we are guided by our values, even if we're not always conscious of it. Suppose you are buying a suit to wear to a job interview. You'll probably consider cost, color, style, fit, quality, and the need to make a good impression. Your best friend goes shopping with you, and she urges you to buy a flashy style with a split skirt. You know, however, that the job you want is with a rather conservative company. You believe you should buy a businesslike tweed suit, but you don't like to ignore your friend, either. Your choice will depend on which you value most in this particular case: your friend's feelings or your desire to get the job. You decide on the conservative outfit.

Obviously, not everything can have equal value, and our values generally range from most important to least important. This hierarchy of values isn't rigid—you might take your friend's advice on a dress to wear dancing—but it's consistent enough to be called a system. It is this system that helps us to make choices and decisions, to decide what is important to us.

Your value system is at work when you decide how to vote, for example. Candidate Jones, running for the U.S. Senate, argues for reducing federal welfare programs while building a stronger defense. Her opponent, candidate Smith, promises to limit the spread of nuclear weapons and to expand social programs like welfare. If you think government welfare has gotten out of hand while national defense has grown weaker, you will probably choose Jones. If you believe enough weapons are stockpiled and you worry about the plight of the poor, you will probably choose Smith.

In similar ways, your value system helps you make career choices. Imagine that you are talented musically and have been practicing hard since kindergarten. You aim to be a concert pianist. You know you must study with top-flight musicians, so you hope to attend a certain university with a world-famous pianist on its faculty. This school is located several hundred miles from your home town, though, and you know living and studying there will be expensive. You just don't have the money.

What are your choices?

You could take a few years off from studying music, get a good job, and save money to continue your training later. Your playing might get rusty, but you wouldn't starve. Or you might change your career goals and study at a nearby relatively inexpensive college where you could get an education that would make you an excellent music teacher. A third possibility could be to try for a scholarship or borrow money, move near the university, and find a part-time job to provide the bare essentials while you study with the maestro.

If you feel you'd be truly unhappy living the life of the penniless artist for four years, you might decide a music teacher's career is appealing after all. Or you might choose to postpone your studies until you can afford the more comfortable life-style that is important to you. But if a concert career is an all-consuming passion, you will forget comfort—and steak dinners—and head for the university that promises the training you crave. Your decision depends on your value system.

WORK VALUES EXERCISE

Awareness of your own value system is essential in career planning. You have difficult decisions to make. Is a large income extremely important to you, are you content to live modestly, or are you indifferent to money altogether? Is it more important to you to work independently or to be part of a team? We all need some recognition, but is it vital to you to become famous? Knowing your values will guide you in making decisions that are right for you. Here is a list of some work-related values that can help you explore your own value system.

First read the entire list. As you do, look carefully at the definitions. How important are these things to *you*? Then go over the list again. This time, rate each item on the list, using the scale below.

1 = Not important at all

2 = Not very important

3 = Reasonably important

4 = Very important in my choice of career

_____ *Help Society:* Do something to contribute to the betterment of the world I live in.

_____ *Help Others:* Be involved in helping other people in a direct way, either individually or in small groups.

_____ *Public Contact:* Have a lot of day-to-day contact with people.

_____ *Work with Others:* Have close working relationships with a group; work as a team toward common goals.

_____ *Affiliation:* Be recognized as a member of a particular organization.

_____ *Friendships:* Develop close personal relationships with people as a result of my work activities.

_____ *Competition:* Engage in activities which pit my abilities against others where there are clear win-and-lose outcomes.

Reprinted by permission of The Carroll Press, Cranston, R.I., from *PATH: A Career Workbook for Liberal Arts Students,* by Howard E. Figler, ©Copyright 1975, from page 77 to 79.

_____ *Make Decisions:* Have the power to decide courses of action, policies, etc.

_____ *Work under Pressure:* Work in situations where time pressure is prevalent and/or the quality of my work is judged critically by supervisors, customers, or others.

_____ *Power and Authority:* Control the work activities or (partially) the destinies of other people.

_____ *Influence People:* Be in a position to change attitudes or opinions of other people.

_____ *Work Alone:* Do projects by myself, without any significant amount of contact with others.

_____ *Knowledge:* Engage myself in the pursuit of knowledge, truth, and understanding.

_____ *Intellectual Status:* Be regarded as a person of high intellectual prowess or as one who is an acknowledged "expert" in a given field.

_____ *Artistic Creativity:* Engage in creative work in any of several art forms.

_____ *Creativity (general):* Create new ideas, programs, organizational structures, or anything else not following a format previously developed by others.

_____ *Aesthetics:* Be involved in studying or appreciating the beauty of things, ideas, etc.

_____ *Supervision:* Have a job in which I am directly responsible for the work done by others.

_____ *Change and Variety:* Have work responsibilities which frequently change in their content and setting.

_____ *Precision Work:* Work in situations where there is very little tolerance for error.

_____ *Stability:* Have a work routine and job duties that are largely predictable and not likely to change over a long period of time.

_____ *Security:* Be assured of keeping my job and a reasonable financial reward.

_____ *Fast Pace:* Work in circumstances where there is a high pace of activity; work must be done rapidly.

_____ *Recognition:* Be recognized for the quality of my work in some visible or public way.

_____ *Excitement:* Experience a high degree of (or frequent) excitement in the course of my work.

_____ *Adventure:* Have work duties which involve frequent risk-taking.

_____ *Profit, Gain:* Have a strong likelihood of accumulating large amounts of money or other material gain.

_____ *Independence:* Be able to determine the nature of my work without significant direction from others; not have to do what others tell me to.

_____ *Moral Fulfillment:* Feel that my work is contributing significantly to a set of moral standards which I feel are very important.

_____ *Location:* Find a place to live (town, geographical area) which is conducive to my life-style and affords me the opportunity to do the things I enjoy most.

_____ *Community:* Live in a town or city where I can get involved in community affairs.

_____ *Physical Challenge:* Have a job that makes physical demands which I would find rewarding.

_____ *Time Freedom:* Have work responsibilities which I can work at according to my own time schedule; no specific working hours required.

Now that you've rated each of these work values, list on another sheet of paper the ones you ranked most important. Add any of your own important values that weren't in the exercise.

This should give you a clearer sense of what's important to you in a career. Later in this book, you will learn how to research occupations that appeal to you, and you can ask yourself how these jobs complement your own values. If *security* is highly important to you, you probably wouldn't want a job that pays employees a commission rather than a fixed salary. If *physical challenge* is a key value in your hierarchy, you might feel trapped behind a desk but could thrive as a ski instructor or tree surgeon.

Or consider occupations from the perspective of what is *unimportant* to you. If *creativity* ranks low in your value hierarchy, you'll want to avoid jobs like writing or architecture. If being able to *help others* isn't a key value to you, teaching or social work would probably be out.

YOUR VALUES AND THEIR VALUES

Your parents were your first source of values. You learned what their values were by watching their behavior and listening to their judgments. As you've gotten older, you have also observed other value systems—those of teachers, friends, religious leaders, politicians, and celebrities. These people enriched and modified your views.

That doesn't mean you're a robot programmed only to echo other people. Your value system is already a unique reflection of you. If you're skeptical, ask a parent or a friend to do the work-related values exercise and see how different their results are from your own. And your value system will probably continue to change over time, as you do.

Sometimes conflicts arise from differences in values. You may find, for example, that you no longer share many of your parents' values.

Suppose that you are deeply committed to the effort to block the construction of nuclear power plants. You wear "No Nukes" T-shirts, you've donated a little money to the cause, and you stuck a bumper sticker on your parents' car. But now you want to do more. You want to attend a demonstration against nuclear power at a site 50 miles from home. And you want to spend the summer before college volunteering your time to work at the antinuclear headquarters.

Your parents think you're wasting your time. Conservative folks that they are, they modestly favor the increased use of nuclear power. More than that, though, they disapprove of the kind of people they imagine you'll meet working for such a cause. They place a heavy value on social respectability, and they don't want you to embarrass them by being arrested at a rowdy demonstration. Furthermore, they don't want you to spend the summer stuffing envelopes in a run-down office. They want you to work at a clerical job at your father's company.

"Stuffing envelopes in a ritzy office?" you yell. "What's the difference? I want to do something that's important to *me*!"

Instead of yelling, stop and think through your reasons for what you want to do. Then approach your parents and speak to them calmly and openly. This won't guarantee that they will adopt your views, but if you show them that you have given the issue careful thought and aren't just jumping on another bandwagon, they may take your commitment more seriously and allow you to devote your summer to it.

Your values also differ from your friends', and this can trigger some clashes. Maybe you think it's dumb to jog 5 miles a day, as your friend Amanda does. This attitude annoys Amanda, who insists that *you* spend too much time sitting around reading. If you respect each other, you'll recognize that there's room in the world for both of you. You may even learn something from one another while you're at it.

Like individuals, cultures develop their own general value systems. In our society, people who reflect these cultural values are rewarded with money or status or both. For example, our culture generally values beautiful and youthful bodies, so beautiful young models can earn big salaries.

It is vital that you be alert to what society values and rewards, even though your personal values may differ in some respects. You might choose an occupation that you regard highly but that society values less. In fact, many of the jobs that women have traditionally held, such as nursing, are not rewarded with really high pay or with great prestige. People who thoughtlessly accept society's values might treat you as if your work had little importance. It will be up to you to be true to your own values.

All your life you will deal with people whose values differ from yours. The more conscious you are of your own values, and the more confident you are of their validity, the less vulnerable you will be to outside pressures. This will make you better able to evaluate advice and take from it what is useful.

VALUES, THEY ARE A-CHANGIN'

Just as your personal values change over time, society's values change as well. Not all of them, and not completely, of course. A happy family life, for instance, is valued just as much today as it was back in 1920. Sharing close relationships with family and friends has remained one of our most important values—one that seems to have grown *more* important.[1] But other values *have* changed—especially some related to career and life decisions.

Probably the most obvious change is that more women are working outside the home than ever before. More than three fourths of all high school senior girls in a 1980 poll said that they would probably work after marriage, and over half planned to continue working after they have children.[2] Work clearly has a new value for today's young women. In contrast, in the 1950s about 70 percent of all women spent most of their work lives in the home, taking care of house and children.[3]

Did you ever hear someone say that girls go to college just to find a husband? It's no longer true, if it ever was. Today young women view college as a way to prepare for a rewarding career. And rather than getting a general liberal arts education as their mothers might have, most plan to go for specific majors to help them net the jobs they want.[4] In fact, a survey by the University of California at Los Angeles and the American Council on Education reported that at more than 500 colleges, 27.2 percent of the female freshmen were planning careers in law, engineering, medicine, and business. This is more than four times the number of women interested in these traditionally male fields in 1966.[5]

What do women value in a job? Female professionals and managers place "good chance for advancement" highest on the list, and female blue-collar workers and clerical workers rate "good pay" as most important to them.[6] Doubtless this is because many women stay single for a longer time and are responsible for their own support. Also, divorce is more common, and many women end up supporting themselves and their children too. (So much for the traditional notion of women's income being "pin money" for extras!) Next to advancement and money, they value "recognition for good work" and "good fringe benefits."[7] In the 1960s, young people said "work that helps society" was just as important to them as challenging work. Today, though, "social" work is given lower priority.[8]

Is there any broad value change that affects not only our attitudes about work—where we work, who we work with, and how far we can go—but *all* of our social attitudes? Yes—it's tolerance.[9] People are far more tolerant of different life-styles today than they were a generation ago. They're also less rigid about who can (and may) do what. Fifty years ago, only one third of the people in the United States could imagine voting for a qualified woman for president. Today, well over two thirds say they would definitely vote for a qualified woman.[10] So while some women set their sights on the Oval Office, others may decide to forgo careers and stay at home to run a household. There are still those who would question either of these decisions, but society as a whole now accepts women in all roles.

The changes in values that have taken place over the years have brought us all more responsibility—but more freedom as well.

WORKING WOMAN

Arie Taylor

Politician

Arie Taylor's job involves long hours, exhausting work, and low pay. Stress and conflict are fringe benefits. And every two years, her boss has the option of firing her without so much as a warning or a thank you. Still, Arie Taylor is a woman who loves her job.

For ten years, she's been a member of the Colorado House of Representatives, the state legislature's lower house. Arie is 1 of 25 women in the 100-member legislature (called the Colorado General Assembly). She is also 1 of only 3 blacks in that body. And, since she's a Democrat in a heavily Republican state, Arie finds herself battling for three minorities. The challenges are gigantic, but she says the rewards are worth it. And, slowly but steadily, gains have been made.

"When I first went to the General Assembly, there were only 8 women out of 100 members," she recalls. "I was the first black woman in *any* part of state government. Now, a quarter of the Assembly members are women. You can see how our clout is increasing."

Arie's district, located in Denver, is 55 percent black, 80 percent Democratic.

"Because of the nature of my district, I have some problems that are unique in Colorado," she explains. "Urban blacks have different problems than the majority of Colorado residents. That's why my legislation relates mostly to the poor, to minorities, and to women. I've carried all the women's legislation.

"It's very frustrating, and you get tired, no doubt about it. This is a very conservative state. For six years, for example, I fought to remove the sales tax on food. *Six* years. Then, when the Republicans were finally ready to do it, they voted to remove it. Still, I know that without my efforts it wouldn't have happened at all. There's a real satisfaction in knowing you can get *some* things done, even if you're thwarted on others."

Arie, 55, has been active in politics since she was a teenager. At 21, she was the administrative assistant for the first black city councilwoman in Cleveland, Ohio.

Time passed. Arie, married now, was increasingly caught up in Democratic party politics.

"Then I just got burned out on politics, burned out on marriage," she says. "So I got a divorce, left Ohio for Colorado, and vowed never to get involved with either marriage or politics again." Arie chuckles ruefully. "Well, I kept *half* of it."

Arie was drafted by her party to run for office in 1972, after district lines were redrawn following the 1970 census. Before that, she'd been a state Democratic Committee member and a delegate to two national conventions.

"The best way to launch a political career is to start young at the bottom rung," she advises. "At least in the Democratic party, you've got to get active in grass-roots politics. You have to get out there and walk precincts, stuff envelopes, work your way up. I've got 13- and 14-year-olds out walking in my campaigns, passing out literature. That kind of help is always welcome and appreciated. Get to know candidates, issues, party leaders. Work hard. You'll be noticed."

If you do get noticed, *and* you run for office, *and* you are elected, there are more problems ahead—and possibly not much else in the way of pay or security.

"In Colorado, the General Assembly is paid on a part-time basis," Arie says. "That's a joke. Last year we were in session from January through November. In California, where they have a 'full-time' legislature, they're actually in session *less* than we are, but they get paid twice as much. We're only paid $14,000 a year. The result is that many of Colorado's legislators are very wealthy people who can afford to treat politics as a hobby. Meanwhile, we lose some of our best legislators because they simply can't afford it. It's nearly impossible to be gainfully employed when you may be called back to the capitol at any time."

Arie, who is also an accountant, has a tax preparation business but spends the bulk of her 14-hour workdays either campaigning or legislating.

"Young people considering politics have to be individuals who are willing to assume big responsibilities," she believes. "Their rewards will probably not be commensurate with their capabilities. And, if they're women, they will run into some bias. But I will tell young women that this is a new day," Arie stresses. "Because of all the activity generated by the Equal Rights Amendment, women are expected to take positions and speak out. Both political parties are seeking capable women to run for office.

"The ERA fight has been positive in another way. Women are angry in states that failed to ratify the amendment. They're running for office against men—and women—incumbents who are hostile to women's rights."

In her own career, Arie says the next logical step would probably be a bid for a state Senate seat. She doesn't foresee a move to Washington, D.C., and national politics.

"Fortunately, we already have an excellent congresswoman representing our district, so I don't aspire to that seat," she explains. "She's younger than I am, and I'll probably retire before she does."

So Arie will stay in Denver, pounding the pavement seeking votes, fighting tough—and sometimes impossible—battles, living with the fact that every two years the whole cycle will repeat itself. Why not retire to her comfortable tax preparation business?

"It's nice to be respected," Arie says. "I'm not saying loved, but respected. That's important to me. And when you help somebody, it makes you feel good. That's what makes the sacrifice and the commitment worthwhile."

Drawing submitted by Maureen Pepper, 17; Scotia, New York
Catalyst Cartoon Competition Winner

WHEN SHE WAS YOUNG

Charlotte Perkins Gilman

Charlotte Perkins Gilman was born in 1860 in Hartford, Connecticut. Her father left home soon after her birth, returning only occasionally, until her parents were finally divorced thirteen years later. The bitterness of this experience caused her mother, trying to prevent her children from someday suffering the same hurt and disillusionment, to refrain from showing affection toward her two children. Charlotte grew up with little attention from her mother, in a family that was poor and forced to move frequently as her mother looked for work. Her first marriage ended in divorce, and, to support herself and her daughter, she began writing short stories and poetry, as well as giving lectures on themes relating to women, labor, and social organization. Through this activity, she became a major spokesperson for the women's movement, speaking across the country and writing several books. In this excerpt from her autobiography, Charlotte describes how, as a young girl, she came to see herself as an individual, one who has freedom and the ultimate responsibility for that freedom.

Scene, the little bedroom I shared with mother. I was sitting up in bed, my hands clasped around my knees. She stood by the bureau, combing her hair, holding it at the crown of her head in one hand while she combed. The kerosene lamp threw moving shadows on the ceiling.

"You must do it," said mother, "or you must leave me." "It" was to apologize to Mrs. Stevens—for a thing I had not done. The alleged offense was this: there was a grapevine in the back yard. Mrs. S. had eaten a bunch of grapes from it. I, sitting at a window, had observed her. She, being something of a psychic, asserted that I had thought harsh things of her—that as one of a cooperative group she had no right to eat those grapes. I denied having thought anything about it, which was true, but mother, being greatly under this woman's influence, believed her, and insisted that I apologize. This I declined to do. Hence the ultimatum.

"You must leave me" was no threat of being cast off deliberately, it was an expression of her profound belief that the only *modus vivendi* for a child with a parent was absolute obedience. Never before had my own conscience come squarely against hers. To apologize for what I had not done was flatly dishonest, a lie, it was wrong.

So I sat there and made answer, slowly, meaning to say the first part, and the last part saying itself: "I am not going to do it—and I am not going to leave you—and what are you going to do about it?"

Doubtless she was horrified beyond words at this first absolute rebellion from a hitherto docile child. She came over and struck me. I did not care in the least. She might do what she would, it could not alter my decision. I was realizing with an immense illumination that neither she, nor any one, could *make* me do anything. One could suffer, one could die if it came to that, but one could not be coerced. I was born. . . .

The incident passed with no visible consequences at the time, but the great discovery remained, and there followed a period of mental turmoil, with large ultimate results. If I was a free agent what was I going to do with my freedom? If I could develop character as I chose, what kind of character was I going to develop? This at fifteen. . . .

Out of much consideration I finally came to a definite decision as to my duty. The old condition of compelled obedience was gone forever. I was a free agent, but as such I decided that until I was twenty-one I would still obey. I saw that mother was probably wiser than I, that she had nothing to live for but us two children and would probably suffer much if we were rebellious, and that, furthermore, she had a right to her methods of education, while we were minors. So I told her that I would obey her until I was of age, and then stop.

Growing Up

I used to feel my cat's life was the best,
living as if sheltered in a nest.
He hasn't any decisions to make,
no figuring out what road he'll take.
College? . . . you bet,
but where and which one?
A career? . . . of course,
but should I write or teach,
or study the sun?
Should I go for it all—
career, husband, and a child?
Or instead, total devotion to career
and a family after awhile?
Fame, money, or happiness,
should I settle for anything less than the best?
Do I want tuna on rye or nothing but caviar,
winter trips to Hawaii or perhaps a sports car?
What's important, and what do I really want?
. . . inner happiness or possessions to flaunt?
A feeling of achievement? Why yes, that's the ultimate.
Wait, sure there are decisions, but so what?
You, my sweet cat, don't have any of this;
But oh, you poor thing, look what you'll miss.

Poem submitted by Jennifer E. Price, 17;
Roseville, Minnesota
Catalyst Poetry Competition Winner

5
What Are Your Skills?

I do not want to die ... until I have faithfully made the most of my talent and cultivated the seed that was placed in me until the last small twig has grown.

—Kathe Kollwitz, *graphic artist and sculptor*

Have you ever taken stock of your skills? Do you take them for granted or compare them unfavorably with the skills of other people? When it comes to planning your career, it's crucial that you try to have an objective view of your skills and talents. Then you can match those abilities with specific jobs and hone your skills until you are a competent professional.

In this chapter, you'll inventory your skills and probably discover that a rather capable, talented person lurks inside you.

EXERCISE 1: IDENTIFYING YOUR SKILLS

This exercise, a "Skills Inventory Checklist," will help you zero in on your abilities. Skills are listed in the left-hand column; on the right are examples of activities that call for each skill. As you go through the checklist, keep two things in mind: (1) You don't have to be an expert before you can check off a particular skill. Don't feel that you must be able to write like Jane Austen or Toni Morrison to assert that you have some basic writing ability. Can you write a clear and interesting letter or essay? This is evidence of writing skill, so you would put a check mark next to it. Can you change a tire or learn a new dance quickly? That's evidence of good muscular coordination. Do people laugh when you tell jokes? Then you are articulate and probably have some performing ability as well. (2) Don't let the titles of the categories turn you off or scare you. You may think, for example, that you're a klutz and feel inclined to skip entirely the "using my hands" section. Don't do it! Perhaps your "all thumbs" opinion of yourself is all wrong. Read the whole list carefully, and give yourself the benefit of the doubt.

Skills Inventory Checklist

Instructions:

1. Put a check mark next to those skills you think you have.
2. Put two check marks next to your "best" skills.
3. Circle the skills that you really enjoy using.

A. USING MY HANDS

☐	1. assembling	as with kits, etc.
☐	2. constructing	as with carpentry, etc.
☐	3. or building	
☐	4. operating tools	as with drills, mixers, etc.
☐	5. or machinery	as with sewing machines, etc.
☐	6. or equipment	as with trucks, stationwagons, etc.
☐	7. showing manual or finger dexterity	as with throwing, sewing, etc.
☐	8. handling with precision and/or speed	as with assembly line, etc.
☐	9. fixing or repairing	as with autos or mending, etc.
☐	10. other:	

B. USING MY BODY

☐	11. muscular coordination	as in skiing, gymnastics, etc.
☐	12. being physically active	as in exercising, hiking, etc.
☐	13. doing outdoor activities	as in camping, etc.
☐	14. other:	

C. USING WORDS

☐ 15. reading   as with books; with understanding

☐ 16. copying   as with manuscripts; skillfully

☐ 17. writing or communicating   as with letters; interestingly

☐ 18. talking or speaking   as on the telephone; interestingly

☐ 19. teaching, training   as in front of groups; with animation

☐ 20. editing   as in improving a child's sentences in an essay, etc.

☐ 21. memory for words   as in remembering people's names, book titles, etc.

☐ 22. other:

D. USING MY SENSES
(Eyes, Ears, Nose, Taste or Touch)

☐ 23. observing, surveying   as in watching something with the eyes, etc.

☐ 24. examining or inspecting   as in looking at a child's bumps, etc.

☐ 25. diagnosing, determining   as in deciding if food is cooked yet

☐ 26. showing attention to detail   as in shop, in sewing, etc.

☐ 27. other:

E. USING NUMBERS

☐ 28. taking inventory   as in the pantry, shop, etc.

☐ 29. counting   as in a classroom, bureau drawers

☐ 30. calculating, computing   as in a checkbook, arithmetic

☐ 31. keeping financial records, bookkeeping   as with a budget, etc.

☐ 32. managing money   as in a checking account, bank, store, etc.

☐ 33. developing a budget   as for a family, etc.

☐ 34. number memory   as with telephone numbers, etc.

☐ 35. rapid manipulation of numbers   as with doing arithmetic in the head

☐ 36. other:

F. USING INTUITION

☐ 37. showing foresight   as in planning ahead, predicting consequences, etc.

☐ 38. quickly sizing up a person or situation accurately   as in everything, rather than just one or two details about them, etc.

☐ 39. having insight   as to why people act the way they do, etc.

☐ 40. acting on gut reactions   as in making decisions, deciding to trust someone, etc.

☐ 41. ability to visualize third-dimension   as in drawings, models, blueprints, memory for faces, etc.

☐ 42. other:

G. USING ANALYTICAL THINKING OR LOGIC

☐ 43. researching, information gathering   as in finding out where a particular street is in a strange city

☐ 44. analyzing, dissecting   as with the ingredients in a recipe, material, etc.

☐ 45. organizing, classifying   as with laundry, etc.

☐ 46. problem-solving   as with figuring out how to get to a place, etc.

☐ 47. separating important from unimportant   as with complaints, or cleaning the attic, etc.

☐ 48. diagnosing   as in cause and effect relations, tracing problems to their sources

☐ 49. systematizing, putting things in order   as in laying out tools or utensils in the order you will be using them

☐ 50. comparing, perceiving similarities   as with different brands in the supermarket, etc.

☐ 51. testing, screening   as with cooking, deciding what to wear, etc.

☐ 52. reviewing, evaluating   as in looking at something you made, to see how you could have made it better, faster

☐ 53. other:

H. USING ORIGINALITY OR CREATIVITY

☐ 54. imaginative, imagining   as in figuring out new ways to do things, or making up stories, etc.

☐ 55. inventing, creating   as with processes, products, figures, words, etc.

☐ 56. designing, developing   as with new recipes, new gadgets

☐ 57. improvising, experiments   as in camping, when you've left some of the equipment home, etc.

☐ 58. adapting, improving   as with something that doesn't work quite right, etc.

☐ 59. other:

I. USING HELPFULNESS

☐ 60. helping, being of service   as when someone is in need, etc.

☐ 61. showing sensitivity to others' feelings   as in a heated discussion, argument

☐ 62. listening

☐ 63. developing rapport — as with someone who is initially a stranger, etc.

☐ 64. conveying warmth, caring — as with someone who is upset, ill

☐ 65. understanding — as when someone tells how they feel, etc.

☐ 66. drawing out people — as when someone is reluctant to talk, share

☐ 67. offering support — as when someone is facing a difficulty alone, etc.

☐ 68. demonstrating empathy — as in weeping with those who weep

☐ 69. representing others' wishes accurately — as when one parent tells the other what a child of theirs wants, etc.

☐ 70. motivating — as in getting people past hangups, and into action, etc.

☐ 71. sharing credit, appreciation — as when working in teams, etc.

☐ 72. raising others' self-esteem — as when you make someone feel better, less guilty, etc.

☐ 73. healing, curing — as with physical, emotional and spiritual ailments, etc.

☐ 74. counseling, guiding — as when someone doesn't know what to do, etc.

☐ 75. other:

J. USING ARTISTIC ABILITIES

☐ 76. composing music

☐ 77. playing (a) musical instrument(s), singing

☐ 78. fashioning or shaping things, materials — as in handicrafts, sculpturing, etc.

☐ 79. dealing creatively with symbols or images — as in stained glass, jewelry, etc.

☐ 80. dealing creatively with spaces, shapes or faces — as in photography, art, architectural design, etc.

☐ 81. dealing creatively with colors — as in painting, decorating, making clothes, etc.

☐ 82. conveying feelings and thoughts through body, face and/or voice tone — as in acting, public speaking, teaching, dancing, etc.

☐ 83. conveying feelings and thoughts through drawing, paintings — as in art, etc.

☐ 84. using words on a very high level   as in poetry, playwriting, novels

☐ 85. other:

K. USING LEADERSHIP, BEING UP FRONT

☐ 86. beginning new tasks, ideas, projects   as in starting a group, initiating a clothing drive, etc.

☐ 87. taking first move in relationships   as with stranger on bus, plane, train, etc.

☐ 88. organizing   as with a Scout troop, a team, a game at a picnic, etc.

☐ 89. leading, directing others   as with a field trip, cheerleading

☐ 90. promoting change   as in a family, community, organization, etc.

☐ 91. making decisions   as in places where decisions affect others, etc.

☐ 92. taking risks   as in sticking up for someone in a fight, etc.

☐ 93. getting up before a group, performing   as in demonstrating a product, lecturing, making people laugh, entertaining, public speaking

☐ 94. selling, promoting, negotiating, persuading   as with a product, idea, materials, in a garage sale, argument, recruiting, changing someone's mind

☐ 95. other:

L. USING FOLLOW-THROUGH

☐ 96. using what others have developed   as in working with a kit, etc.

☐ 97. following through on plans, instructions   as in picking up children on schedule

☐ 98. attending to details   as with embroidering a design on a shirt, etc.

☐ 99. classifying, recording, filing, retrieving   as with data, materials, letters, ideas, information, etc.

☐ 100. other:

EXERCISE 2: IDENTIFYING YOUR ACCOMPLISHMENTS

Now set aside the checklist (you'll get back to it later), and get seven sheets of blank paper. At the top of each page, write down one accomplishment that has given you a lot of satisfaction. You might include things like these:

- Earning enough money to buy a car
- Making new friends when your family moved, although you were extremely shy
- Getting an A in history, a subject you've always hated
- Overcoming your fear of water and learning to swim
- Writing a short story that was published in the school magazine
- Making the debate team
- Setting a new school record for running the 440
- Heading the publicity committee for the school musical, which sold out every night

If, once you get started, you can think of more than seven accomplishments, keep going! Then use the rest of the sheet to write down all the skills you can think of that helped you achieve each accomplishment.

Suppose you listed "heading the publicity committee for the school musical." Skills that you used probably included planning the publicity campaign, making decisions, organizing people and materials, delegating assignments to other people, overseeing their work, calling the local newspapers, managing a budget, and designing posters and fliers.

Something as general as "making new friends" also requires many specific skills. Among them are memory for names, imagination, conversational ability, and developing rapport with strangers.

Beyond such "bread-and-butter" skills, also recognize "personal" skills like patience, perseverance, confidence, enthusiasm, poise, flexibility, honesty, and stamina. A publicity manager, for example, probably needs a lot of stamina and patience. A newcomer to town has to have courage to overcome shyness and talk to strangers, as well as determination and perseverance.

Once you have noted the skills required for your accomplishments, go back to the skills inventory and add any new ones to the list.

Are you amazed to see how many different abilities you have? Many people never really evaluate their skills. If you've discovered that you're pretty wonderful, give yourself a hand. But remember, skills are like roller skates; if they sit in the closet unused, they aren't doing you much good—and they may get rusty. It's time to think about ways to put your skills to good use.

Suppose you checked "researching, information gathering" as one of your best skills because of excellent papers you wrote on the life of Margaret Sanger, on the habits of dolphins, and on the works of Willa Cather. You knew where to find the facts, how to compile and organize them, and how to present them effectively. Many occupations use research ability, ranging from the saleswoman who studies her potential clients to the travel agent who collects information on hotels, airfares, and tours. In fact, each of the skills in the inventory can be used in many different jobs.

Whodunit? Shedunit!

Use your sleuthing skills to deduce the identity of the twentieth-century mystery writer who assessed herself this way:

> I was never good at games; I am not and never shall be a good conversationalist; I am so easily suggestible that I have to get away by myself before I know what I really think or need to do. I can't draw; I can't paint; I can't model or do any kind of sculpture; I can't hurry without getting rattled; I can't say what I mean easily—I can write it better. I can stand fast on a matter of principle, but not on anything else. Although I know tomorrow is Tuesday, if somebody tells me more than four times that tomorrow is Wednesday, after the fourth time I shall accept that it *is* Wednesday, and act accordingly.
>
> What *can* I do? Well, I can write. I could be a reasonable musician, but not a professional one. I am a good accompanist to singers. I can improvise things when in difficulties—this has been a most useful accomplishment; the things I can do with hairpins and safety pins when in domestic difficulties would surprise you. It was I who fashioned bread into a sticky pill, stuck it on a hairpin, attached the hairpin with sealing wax on the end of a window pole, and managed to pick up my mother's false teeth from where they had fallen on to the conservatory roof! I successfully chloroformed a hedgehog that was entangled in the tennis net and so managed to release it. I can claim to be useful about the house. And so on and so forth.

The person who arrestingly cataloged her pluses and minuses is Agatha Christie, author of sixty-eight novels and writer of one of the longest-running plays in theater history. She arrived at these insights after a lifetime of self-analysis and included them in her autobiography. It's reassuring to know that even a person who can chloroform a hedgehog can't do *everything* supremely well.

DEVELOPING YOUR SKILLS

But, you may protest, does the research involved in writing a school report really compare with the kind of expertise it takes to be a successful saleswoman or travel agent? It's true that knowing how to impress a client or book a camel caravan probably takes skills you haven't acquired yet. But people aren't *born* with those skills, only with the potential to develop them. The skills themselves are developed, refined, and maintained—the "self-actualization" discussed in the chapter on your needs. It's a long process, but you've already begun.

Obviously, you can't fully develop every skill for which you have the potential. You develop some skills because you deliberately choose to and others simply because you must to do the job at hand. Some of your skills will improve over time, others will emerge, and still others will atrophy from lack of use. Consider the story of the Doodler Who Made Good:

Lisa loved to draw, and draw she did, even when she was supposed to be doing something else. When she was a child, most of her doodles ended up in the wastebasket, but when she reached high school she began to take her art more seriously. She submitted some of her drawings to the school newspaper, and the thrill of seeing her work in print was almost as rewarding as the work itself.

The summer after eleventh grade, Lisa designed some greeting cards and convinced a local stationery store to carry them. They sold out in the first week, and customers began clamoring for T-shirts emblazoned with her character, a pudgy penguin named Puddles. The manager begged her to make some shirts, and Lisa agreed—hesitantly. She had no idea how to silk-screen her design onto a T-shirt. She was resourceful, though, and discovered a course at the local Y that taught her the skill she lacked. The Puddles shirts were an even bigger hit than the cards.

Back in school that fall, Lisa enrolled in art classes. For her special senior project, she created a portfolio of new designs for cards, T-shirts, handbags, posters, and wristwatches. With each design she learned something new. By graduation, Lisa was sure she wanted to be a designer. She attended an art institute, took some marketing classes on the side, and within a few years was manufacturing her own line of clothing and accessories.

Lisa took a hobby of hers—sketching—and capitalized on it. She sharpened her skills, found an outlet for them, and, with a combination of hard work and good luck, shaped a career out of them. Lisa also recognized that her innate talent wasn't enough by itself. She actively sought to improve her abilities by enrolling in art classes in high school, in her spare time, and, after graduation, at an institute. If she hadn't taken the classes—or had dropped out of school entirely— her sketches would have ended up in the wastebasket.

In today's highly competitive job market, education can mean the difference between an interesting career and a dull, routine job. Furthermore, the dull jobs are generally the lowest-paying ones. As you attain more sophisticated skills and higher educational degrees, though, your prospects brighten considerably. High school dropouts are obviously at the bottom of the heap. High school graduates have more options, but their range of choices is still comparatively limited. Add a college degree or specialized training, and options multiply like rabbits in springtime.

The day is gone—and good riddance—when the only skills a "lady" needed were pouring tea properly or removing her gloves gracefully. (And that was about *all* she was allowed to do, day after day.) You might wear gloves if you're a welder or a ski instructor, but nobody will care how you take them off. Today you can select from a wide spectrum of jobs, but once you choose you'll have to see that you've got the skills to match.

Drawing submitted by Marie Rogoz, 17;
Clark, New Jersey

WORKING WOMAN

Linda Zink

Union Representative

It's a tense moment. Two groups of people sit glaring at each other across a long table in a newspaper's conference room. Ranged down one side is an assortment of burly truck drivers, pale reporters, and an occasional young circulation clerk in a T-shirt and jeans. They represent the Los Angeles Newspaper Guild.

On the other side sit four men in three-piece suits, all wearing blue dress shirts and subtle neckties. Even their haircuts are similar.

Linda Zink, a small woman sitting in the middle of the Guild side, glances at the four vests across from her.

"Does your mom always dress you boys identically," she asks, "or does she sometimes let you choose your own outfits?" The Guild members chortle appreciatively. Management is annoyed. It's another small point for the union in the continuing battle of wills known as labor negotiations.

As administrative officer for the Los Angeles local of the Newspaper Guild, Linda spends a lot of time facing management across bargaining tables in conference rooms. An odd role for the daughter of a conservative Republican businessman? Linda would be the first to agree. She says, in fact, that the course of her life has been determined to some degree by her early rebellion against the upper-middle-class life-style her parents represented.

"I knew by junior high that I didn't want a big house with a white picket fence," she says. "My mother was a traditional, nonworking housewife, and she was very unhappy in that role. I knew I didn't want that kind of life. Meanwhile, my father, to his credit, always told me I could do anything I wanted to do.

"So, in my girlhood fantasies, I was always living in a New York City penthouse and had married an older man with grown children—not mine. I was still conventional enough to require a husband of some sort. I knew I wanted to be a writer, maybe a foreign correspondent who traveled to Hong Kong. Journalism seemed like a romantic sort of career—a totally unrealistic impression, I learned as soon as I got into the business."

She chose a small private college far enough away from home to be certain that no one would have heard of her family. She knew the school had a religious affiliation, but she had no idea how strict its rules were until she arrived.

"There were special curfews for female students and rules against allowing single women to live off campus," she remembers. "I was a real tester of the status quo, though, and was in the forefront of the battle to get the rules changed."

Although her college had no journalism major, its student newspaper was nationally respected. Linda, who majored in history, signed up to work on the paper "the minute I arrived."

"Traditionally, interested students could apply for a summer internship through the Newspaper Fund," she explains. "The internship provided a few weeks of training and then placement with a pretty good newspaper for the summer. But up until 1968 that internship was closed to women. I began lobbying with the Newspaper Fund's director to include women. And, between my junior and senior years, I was among the first women to win an internship."

Hers was in Grand Island, Nebraska, population 30,000. She found life there to be somewhat different from what she was used to.

"Remember," she says, "I was a girl who'd lived her entire life in southern California. Going to Nebraska was an incredible culture shock."

She was a copy editor in Grand Island, not a reporter, as in her dream, but she benefited from the experience anyway. "It was a useful internship, although it didn't have much application to reporting. It looked good on a résumé, too, and when you're starting out, you've got nothing *but* a résumé.

"The Nebraska experience was a real turning point for me because I discovered that the production employees made more money than the reporters and editors. The back-shop people were treated better, paid better, and worked better hours. That's because they had a union. This was an education in itself."

Four months after she graduated from college, Linda was hired at the *Press-Telegram* in her hometown of Long Beach, California. It was a union newspaper, with editorial and circulation employees represented by the Los Angeles Newspaper Guild. She worked at the *Press-Telegram* for the next eight years, primarily as a feature writer in the Life/Style department. Toward the end of that period, she became increasingly aware that it was time for a career change.

"I felt I was headed for a real dead end in the newspaper business," she explains. "Like a lot of women journalists, I'd been stereotyped as a feature writer and, in the hierarchy of the place, Life/Style was the pits. Things are better for women journalists now, by the way. About the same time I reached this conclusion, I became active in the union as a volunteer. I was on the Guild's bargaining team, so I saw the administrative officer in action. I thought it looked like an interesting job that I could do well."

Linda worked as a Guild volunteer three years before there was an opening for an administrative officer. At 30, she knew she was ready for a change. Now, five years later, she's glad she made the jump.

"I want a career that offers a lot of variety in terms of skills and situations," she explains. My job as administrative officer is like that. One day I'm a writer, the next day I'm a salesman, the next day I'm representing a member at an arbitration hearing. I'll always want a job with variety, but perhaps I could do with a little less stress."

Stress is a constant, Linda admits, because a union representative is so frequently in an adversarial role. She is also responsible for protecting the careers and livelihoods of the 400 members in her local.

"It's very draining to have that kind of responsibility," she says. "During bargaining, the wrong word at the wrong time and you could end up with your members out on the street.

"It's a combative job. Women from my generation were not trained to be combatants. We were told to catch flies with honey, not vinegar. But in labor negotiations, the more strength you show, the more successful you are. I'm not concerned with people viewing me as unfeminine. As a girl, I realized that I was never going to be a candidate for Miss California. But there are other problems with being a woman in a male role. Always in the back of my mind is the question, 'Are they not taking me seriously because I'm a woman?' That doubt has been proven untrue, but still I feel I have to prove myself over and over.

"I must say that my male colleagues in the Newspaper Guild have been terrifically supportive. They push me out there and say, 'Of course you can do it!' "

She sees a good future for women who want to work for labor unions.

"Women in professional positions are becoming more and more important to the whole American labor movement," she says. "This is a good time to get into it, whether you come from the rank and file as I did or you get hired from outside. Just in the Newspaper Guild, a relatively small union, there are 3 women permanently in the field around the country. That's out of a staff of 10. Before, there was only 1 token woman."

Linda says she's given up the penthouse-in-New-York fantasy, but it took a long time to accept the fact that she was an independent person who was responsible for her own life.

"There's a tendency among young women to put off serious financial planning," she comments. "In the backs of their minds they're still waiting for Prince Charming to come along. For too long, I didn't take my *whole* self seriously. I didn't want to take on serious obligations until I was married. Finally, I realized that no one was going to provide me with a penthouse, so I bought a condominium. It was scary but it was a good decision.

"You have to learn to handle your fears. I was afraid of making the change in careers. I was afraid of bargaining my first contract. Then, every time I did something, I'd look back and say 'That wasn't so hard.'

"The first few times I went into bargaining sessions, I had a written script for everything I planned to say. I was afraid I would be tongue-tied." She gives her characteristic grin and says, "Now I find it's much harder to *listen* than it is to talk!"

WHEN SHE WAS YOUNG

Selma Lagerlöf

Selma Lagerlöf was the first woman to win the Nobel Prize for Literature. Born in Sweden in 1858, she kept a diary as a young girl. When she was 13, she went to stay with her aunt and uncle in Stockholm, where she received treatments at a clinic for her lame leg. Writing in her diary while she was there, she wishes she was more like another girl her age whom she's met and thinks everyone else admires. She believes herself to be "dull and unresponsive" in contrast—until she sees herself through someone else's eyes and discovers that she's really fine the way she is.

Friday morning, February 21. In the sitting room. I have thought all day of Fröken W. Now I know what Aunt Georgina meant when she said that I was dull and unresponsive. I understand that she wishes me to be like Fröken W.—friendly and talkative and amusing and open and natural as every young girl ought to be.

But how, how, oh how, am I to become like her!

Much as I admired Fröken W., I felt rather downhearted after she had gone because I was so unlike her. Auntie and Uncle had gone to the theatre... and I sat in the bedchamber writing until I grew sleepy and went to bed.

I had not slept long when I awoke. Auntie had come home from the theatre and stopped in the nursery to talk with Ulla, who had been sitting up for her. I heard them speak of a young girl whom they praised extravagantly. I understood, of course, they were speaking of Fröken W. That made me keep my eyes shut and pretend to be asleep. I admired Fröken W. greatly and wanted so much to be like her, but in any case...

"Ulla, don't you think she is a very nice and well-brought-up girl?" said Auntie.

"Do you know, Fru," answered Ulla, in her clear and positive voice, "I don't believe you could find a nicer or a better-behaved young girl anywhere."

"No airs, nor stories about young men. She comes and goes as she should. And she is gifted, too, Ulla. Baroness H. says she speaks English remarkably well."

I was not a little astonished that the Baroness H. knew all about Fröken W. It was also queer that Auntie should say she had no stories to tell about gentlemen.

"The little girl who was here today was very sweet," Auntie continued. "But, Ulla, don't you think it would be rather trying to have a person like her living in your home?"

"Yes, it would be rather trying at times," Ulla conceded.

I understood now that it was of me they were speaking, and I was so happy that I wanted to jump out of bed and give Auntie a great big hug. But then I thought that perhaps she might be angry if she knew that I had been listening—and I kept still.

In the Middle

The sun set slowly as I sat,
alone, by the lake so still;
I could hear the grownups' chat
and the childrens' shrill
But I sat there all alone
not knowing where I belong.
You see, I am not a child
who likes to run and play,
Nor am I a grownup
who must have her say.
I am in the middle—
no one else around—
I do not fit in either group
and a third one can't be found.

Poem submitted by Lisa Kapela, 14;
Napanoch, New York
Catalyst Poetry Competition Winner

6
What Are Your Interests?

> ... from the first days of dawning individuality, I have longed
> unceasingly to make pictures of people ... to make likenesses that are
> biographies, to bring out in each photograph the essential personality
> that is variously called temperament, soul, humanity.
>
> —Gertrude Kasebier, *photographer*

I f you come from a family that enjoyed playing folk songs and pinochle as they ate popcorn every Saturday evening, you were probably a guitar-strumming, pinochle-playing, popcorn-eating little girl. These early interests of yours were nurtured by your parents and siblings, who needed a fourth at the card table and a strong elbow at the corn popper.

Then you discovered there was a big world out there beyond your pinochle hand. Your folks soon were competing with friends who took you camping and your soccer teammates who took you to the league play-offs.

You grew some more, changed some more, and soccer fell by the wayside as you developed your singing style and joined a bluegrass group. Occasionally you could be cajoled into a hand of pinochle. And you still loved popcorn. But one of the guys in your band was an expert at preparing Japanese cuisine, and slowly sushi and sashimi became staples in your menus.

Your interests—preferences for certain activities, events, and ideas—sometimes change as you grow and gain experience and as your situation changes. And, conversely, your situation often reflects your interests. This is an important thing to consider when you're casting about for career possibilities. Would you be happy as a forest ranger if your ideal vacation is two weeks of sight-seeing in London? Would you enjoy being a research librarian if you get claustrophobic in a space smaller than Yosemite National Park?

It's time to ask yourself what your interests are. You'll be happier and work better at something that you enjoy, something that interests you. Sorting your interests also will help you clarify "who you are."

IDENTIFYING YOUR CAREER INTERESTS

What are your interests? Sometimes the direct approach is best, so grab a pencil and make a list. Pose questions like these:

- If I could spend a weekend doing what I enjoy most, what would I do?
- What topics pop up most frequently in my conversations?
- Which shelves do I head for at the library or bookstore?
- What clubs have I really enjoyed?
- If I could study anything I wanted, what would it be?

Obviously, you don't have an equal interest in everything. It's very unlikely that you will be able to incorporate all of your interests in a single occupation, anyway. Try arranging them in order from strongest to weakest. To do this, either number your interests or group them into three categories: an "A" list of your strongest interests, a "B" list of slightly less strong interests, and a "C" list of moderate interests.

Psychologist John L. Holland has defined six categories of people that are related to career interests: realistic, investigative, artistic, social, enterprising, and conventional.[1] Now look at your strongest interests and try to think of what kind of person you might be and what occupations fit your interests best. If you like working with your hands—taking shop classes, sewing, or fixing electrical things—you might like to be a farmer, laboratory researcher or technician, or toolmaker (realistic). If you enjoy taking science courses, solving math or chess puzzles, or reading scientific magazines and books, you might make a good research scientist, psychologist, or anthropologist (investigative). If your interests include reading popular fiction, drawing or painting, taking photographs, writing poetry, or playing a musical instrument, you might be interested in being an author, painter, musician, actress, or dancer (artistic). If you like to go to parties, make new friends, or help others with personal problems, you could be a good doctor, lawyer, teacher, nurse, social worker, guidance counselor, or athletic coach (social). If you serve as an officer of any group, follow and discuss politics, or can influence people, you might like to be a top-level corporate executive, politician, or entrepreneur (enterprising). Finally, if you take business and typing courses, keep detailed records of expenses, or operate business machines, your calling might be as an office manager, corporation treasurer, or word processor (conventional).

Now where do your interests fall? Are they spread out over several categories or concentrated in just a couple? In which categories fall most of your "A" interests, or your "B" and "C" interests?

HOW YOUR INTERESTS RELATE TO WORK CHOICES

Probably your interests fall under several headings. By organizing them, you may find that you are able to incorporate several interests into your choice of occupation, the way Marta did. She enjoyed working with others, especially children, and she was interested in research and psychology. She combined these things by joining a research team that was studying child development. She might also have considered being a guidance counselor, a social worker, or an elementary school teacher. Rather than feeling that her interests pulled her in different directions, she found a field that incorporated several of them.

Or maybe you are more like Jennifer, who enjoyed persuading others to adopt her point of view. She was articulate and talkative and liked writing and solving other people's problems for them. In fact, while she was growing up, other kids called her a smart aleck— or worse. As an adult, she discovered that her interests and skills teamed up to make her a hotshot criminal lawyer.

The next exercise will help you see how different interests relate to various types of work. Read through the checklist of occupations and check off how much they appeal to you. Then identify the occupations with interest patterns similar to your own. Those jobs are ones you would be likely to enjoy. Of course, this checklist is only a small sampling, to get you started, of the thousands of different jobs that exist, but it does illustrate how different jobs involve a variety of interests.

Some Occupational Titles
and Requirements/Interests

Occupational title	*Requirements/ interests*	*Very appealing*	*Somewhat appealing*	*Not very appealing*
Airline pilot	precision, concentration, communication			
Attorney	writing and speaking, research, persuasion			
Auditor	analysis, precision			
Bank officer	leadership, communication			
Barber	working with people, dexterity			
Broadcast technician	communication, working with people, concentration			
Carpenter	agility, physical strength			
College professor	communication, interacting with people, research			
Construction laborer	agility, physical strength, working outdoors			
Dietitian	working with people, communication			
Editor	thoroughness, creativity, facility with language			
Engineer	creativity, precision			
Fire fighter	physical exertion, working with people			
Geologist	investigation, working outdoors			
Graphic artist	artistic ability, communication			

Occupational title	Requirements/ interests	Very appealing	Somewhat appealing	Not very appealing
Health inspector	investigation, attention to detail			
Hotel manager	interaction with people, communication, responsibility			
Insurance broker	communication, persuasion			
Medical laboratory worker	thoroughness, precision			
Merchant marine sailor	communications, physical strength			
Nurse	interacting with people, communication			
Postal clerk	working with people, organization			
Public relations worker	creativity, communications, persuasion			
School administrator	leadership, communication			
Security sales worker	persuasion, analysis, communication			
Stenographer	memory, concentration			
Surveyor	precision, working outdoors			
Truck driver	precision			
Underwriter	analysis, working with figures, evaluation			
Urban planner	organization, originality, communication			

Recognizing your interests not only helps you select potential occupations, it also should encourage you to find out more about these fields. It's a good idea to seek out people working in jobs that are related to your major interests. Then find out exactly what they do, their educational background, how they got started, what they are paid, and what their career plans are. You'll find details on how to research an occupation later in this book.

Pinpointing your interests also guides you in developing and perfecting skills related to these interests. When you have a strong interest in something, you feel motivated to increase your expertise in that field. This may lead to a career that flourishes for a lifetime.

IF 2 + 2 = ANXIETY

Are you tempted to skip this section because you dislike anything to do with numbers? Do you get sweaty palms when you have to figure a percentage? If you plan to take the Scholastic Aptitude Test, does the mere *thought* of the math portion give you a stomachache? If your answers are "yes," you may have a case of math anxiety. It's not fatal, but it can be serious. It means you can't do math—not because you lack the ability but because you *believe* you lack the ability.

Lorelei R. Brush, author of *Encouraging Girls in Mathematics*, defines math anxiety as "an extreme negative reaction . . . which results in discomfort and may also cause restlessness and irritability. It is a reaction which takes dislike a step further, adding a suggestion of fear."[2] Even if you're not afraid of math, you may try to avoid it as much as possible or freeze when confronted by a math test.

Boys can suffer from this problem, of course, but it seems to hit girls especially hard. Some experts blame this on our culture's sex-role stereotyping, which labels math and science as "unfeminine" and tends to steer girls away from them. By the time they're in high school, even girls who have excelled in math may develop a mental block against it. Bette Korber, who attended a large high school in southern California, is a real-life example of this very situation:

"I had always enjoyed math classes in junior high, so I looked forward to taking a second year of algebra when I was a sophomore in high school," she recalled. "I was doing fairly well—a B+—but I felt I wasn't understanding a lot of it and I was getting in deeper and deeper over my head. When I look back on it, I know that I was a victim of a poor teacher. Then, though, I blamed myself.

"So I went to the teacher for some advice. I told him I wanted to go into math or science as a career, and he stopped me right there. He told me to give up any such notion. He was very friendly and fatherly, but the message was pretty clear: I wasn't cut out for such things. The implication was that no girl is.

"So I just stopped taking math. I didn't take physics or chemistry, either. I thought I wasn't capable of such 'hard' subjects. Even when I was a National Merit Scholar—with a higher score in math than in English—I still doubted myself because of that one teacher's influence.

"I didn't take another math class till my second year in college —I had to for my major. That time, I had a very encouraging teacher. He cured my math anxiety and boosted my self-confidence. The next semester, I took a chemistry course and fell in love with it. I never looked back."

Today, Bette is earning her doctorate in chemistry from a prestigious scientific institute. Even so, the effects of sex-role stereotyping are still apparent: there are only 4 women in Bette Korber's doctoral program of 64 candidates in chemistry.

Even if you don't plan to be a mathematician or chemist, don't kid yourself that you can get by without math. Many jobs require knowledge beyond your twenty toes and fingers. Consider this:[3]

You will need at least *two years* of high school mathematics, beginning with one year of algebra, for a career as a

policewoman	carpenter
fire fighter	bricklayer
bank teller	social worker
hotel desk clerk	dental assistant
postal clerk	medical assistant
electrician	cabinetmaker
machinist	plumber
construction worker	

You will need at least *three years* of high school mathematics, beginning with one year of algebra, for a career as a

computer programmer	pharmacist
mental health worker	forestry aide
drafter	sociologist
accountant	dietitian
home economist	physical therapist
teacher	nurse
dental hygienist	photographer
medical secretary	

You will need at least *four years* of high school mathematics—two of algebra, one of geometry, and one of precalculus mathematics—for a career as a

veterinarian	physician
airline pilot	medical researcher
political scientist	chemist
biochemist	astronomer
engineer	mathematics teacher
geologist	economist
statistician	computer scientist
meteorologist	

If you feel panicked at the inadequacy of your math background, it's not too late to do something about it. Speak to your math teacher or guidance counselor. The support and encouragement you receive might be enough to convince you that you *can* learn math and give you the courage to go back and tackle it on your own. If you need more help, ask about special "catch-up" or intensive math courses you can take, either at your high school or at another school in your area.

People of all ages suffer from math anxiety and some communities offer math anxiety clinics or workshops, often sponsored by universities or community colleges. In these special programs, you will receive support from others who have been scared off by math just as you have, as well as the assistance of teachers who understand your problem and who will try to make math comprehensible and demonstrate its relevance.

Fear of math is learned, and that means it can be unlearned. Don't be discouraged. Once you realize that you have a case of math anxiety rather than an inborn inability to work with numbers, you've taken the first step toward solving the problem.

WORKING WOMAN

Eva Mauer

Pediatrician

When Eva Mauer was a sophomore in high school, her father asked her if she had any idea what she wanted to do with her life. Nearly twenty years later, she can recall his words verbatim. No wonder. That question triggered a discussion that set the course for her future.

Watching her own children playing in the backyard, Eva sits in a sunny room of her big old house in Pasadena, California, and remembers how her father helped her map out a career.

"I told him I had no idea what I wanted to do," she says, smiling at the memory. "So he said, 'Let's look at what you're good at, and what your interests are. Now, all you talk about at home is your human physiology class. And your spare time is spent doing volunteer work at the hospital. It looks like you're interested in medicine. Have you considered becoming a nurse?'

"I told him I didn't want to be a nurse because in my experience they mostly changed beds and bedpans. Since becoming a doctor, incidentally, my view of nurses has changed radically. When I saw what intensive care nurses do, for example, I realized that they certainly knew more about caring for critically ill people than I did.

"So then my father said, 'Be a doctor.' My first reaction was that boys are doctors, not girls. He told me that wasn't always true."

But Eva, who loved art almost as much as she loved science, still had some doubts. And her father had more advice.

"He told me it made more sense to have medicine as a career and art as a hobby than it did to have art as a career and medicine as a hobby," she recalls. "I had to agree that seemed like a reasonable analysis. But I was still worried. What if I couldn't make it, if I failed at medical school? He said it was important to aim for the *most* you can accomplish, even if you eventually have to settle for less. I thought it over and decided he was right."

Once she resolved to aim for medical school, Eva enrolled in high school courses that would help her achieve her goal: physics, chemistry, more biology, calculus. Competition for admission to medical school is fierce, and applicants are expected to have not only top grades, but top grades in difficult classes.

She applied to Boston University's six-year program, which combines an undergraduate education with medical training. It's a rigorous, year-round course of study, and graduates receive both Bachelor of Arts and Medical Doctor's degrees. (Most future doctors attend a regular four-year college where they take a prescribed series of "pre-med" courses that generally tie in with a science major.) Eva was accepted into the elite program and started at Boston U. after her high school graduation.

The modern medical profession is male-dominated (although for generations women have been midwives and healers). Though Eva downplays the role of sex bias in medicine, still things weren't exactly equal between male medical students and female medical students.

"During an interview before I was accepted into medical school, I was asked what my marriage and family plans were," she says. "I lied and said I didn't even have a boyfriend. And I found out later that only women applicants were asked that question; none of the men were. There's an attitude that a woman medical student is taking a place that could have gone to a man, so the woman shouldn't 'waste' the training if she's going to raise a family. That kind of pressure is never applied to male doctors."

The pressures and stresses felt by all medical students were intensified in the speeded-up Boston program, and Eva seriously considered dropping out during her first year.

"At the beginning there were a couple of courses in physics and physical chemistry—I just don't have any aptitude for those subjects. I *hated* them," she remembers. "I was really depressed and I think the only thing that kept me going was the admiration that people had for me for getting into the program in the first place.

"I didn't enjoy the program until my fifth year, when we began working with patients. I *loved* it from that point on. Oh, I had periods of insecurity, but I was sure I was in the right profession."

Eva graduated with both degrees at age 23, even though she took a year off between the fifth and sixth years to spend time with her then new husband, Patrick, who is also a doctor.

Doctors are not made by degrees alone, and Eva still had an internship and two years of residency before her. During this training period new doctors get to sample a range of specialities, and Eva's own choice evolved from dermatology to psychiatry to pediatrics.

"My pediatrics unit was the first time I loved every day of work," she says. "There was never any doubt."

As a practicing pediatrician, her day begins around 8 A.M. when she makes her rounds at the hospital, visiting newborns and sick patients.

"Hopefully, I finish with that by 9," she explains. "Then I have office hours from 9 to 12:30 and from 2 to 6. During that time I see children for routine checkups or for illnesses."

It's a long day for a working mother with two children (ages 4 and 2) of her own. Now that Eva's been a doctor for ten years, she's finding herself at another crossroads.

"Now I'm trying to decide how to spend the *next* ten years," she says. "The logistics of caring for two children—and keeping up my own medical practice—are more than I can handle, I'm afraid. One child is much more manageable—working women considering starting a family should keep that in mind.

"I'm also beginning to suspect that private practice is not for me. The demanding mothers are really getting to me, the ones who demand treatments or medicines I don't feel are right for the child. It's a constant battle with them, but the real problem may be my own inability to stand up to people."

That calm, reassuring self-confidence exuded by most doctors isn't as easy as it looks. But what does a physician do if she doesn't have a private practice?

"I'm planning to look for a job in a clinic, where my hours will be regular and my relationships with patients will be less personal and demanding," Eva says. "Then, when my own children are older, I may be able to handle the mothers better—I'll be a more experienced mother myself—and I may return to a private practice. What I need now is to find a way to keep my skills up until that time comes."

If she's found that being a doctor isn't exactly what she'd expected, Eva says philosophically that few things in life are exactly what you expect them to be. She still believes that her father's counsel is relevant and applicable for anyone trying to choose an occupation.

"I like the way my father looked at it," she says. "Even as a sophomore in high school, you're already showing where your aptitudes and interests lie. Examine them and make your decision based on them."

WHEN SHE WAS YOUNG

Louise Bogan

Louise Bogan was born in Maine in 1897. She began writing verse when she was 14 to escape from frequent family quarrels, a temperamental mother, and the separations and reconciliations of her parents that caused her to lead a somewhat nomadic existence. By age 24, her work had been published in several literary magazines. Her first book of poetry appeared in 1923, and she continued writing and publishing until her death in 1970. In this selection from her autobiography, she recalls the disillusionment she felt at 15 when she realized that Miss Cooper, a teacher she had idolized, was really human after all.

The enchantment worked for two years. In the autumn of the third, something had changed. In a pupil, the abstracted look in Miss Cooper's eye could have been put down to a loss of interest; in a teacher, I could not account for it. Miss Cooper lived in my mind at a continual point of perfection; she was like a picture: she existed, but not in any degree did she live or change. She existed beyond simple human needs, beyond hunger and thirst, beyond loneliness, weariness, below the heights of joy and despair. She could not quarrel and she could not sigh. I had assigned to her the words and the smile by which I first knew her, and I refused to believe her capable of any others. But now, behind my shoulder, those October afternoons, I often heard her sigh, and she spent more time in the closet-like kitchen, rattling china and spoons, than she spent in the studio itself. I knew that she was having a cup of tea alone, while I worked in the fading light. She was still gentle, still kind. But she was not wholly there. I had lost her.

It was always ourselves that we blame for such losses, when we are young. For weeks I went about inventing reasons for Miss Cooper's defection.... My ears became sharpened to every tired tone in her voice, to every clink of china and spoon, to every long period of her silence. One afternoon she came out of the kitchen and stood behind me. She had something in her hand that crackled like paper, and when she spoke she mumbled as though her mouth were full. I turned and looked at her: she was standing with a greasy paper bag in one hand and a half-eaten doughnut in the other. Her hair was still beautifully arranged; she still wore the silver and fire-opal ring on the little finger of her right hand. But in that moment she died for me. She died and the room died and the still life died a second death. She had betrayed me. She had betrayed the Hotel Oxford and the replica of the Leaning Tower of Pisa and the whole world of romantic notions built up around her. She had let me down; she had appeared as she was: a tired old woman who fed herself for comfort. With perfect ruthlessness I rejected her utterly. And for weeks, at night, in the bedroom of the frame house in Harold Street, I shed tears that rose from anger as much as disappointment, from disillusion and from dismay. I can't remember that for one moment I entertained pity for her. It was for myself that I kept that tender and cleansing emotion. Yes, it was for myself and for dignity and gentility soiled and broken that I shed those tears. At fifteen and for a long time thereafter, it is a monstrous thing, the heart.

Drawing submitted by Peggy Ann Ritchey, 16; St. Louis, Missouri
Catalyst Cartoon Competition Winner

All Grown Up

when i was small
i didn't like to wash up;
i played in the mud
and didn't wear no shoes,
and got all dirty.
when i was small
i didn't like to dress up
or go to church,
or go shopping.
when i was small
i loved running through fields
newly planted,
following the rows
sinking my toes in
soft, warm dirt.
and when i was small
i liked to climb trees
jumping out to play Tarzan.
when i was small
i liked to yell real loud
whistle, dance and chew Bazooka bubble gum.
                    But now
that I am all grown up
I don't do those antics anymore
                    'cept of course
when no one is lookin'.

Poem submitted by Monica Lynn Valentine, 17;
Grayslake, Illinois
Catalyst Poetry Competition Winner

7
The Greatest Puzzle

> Who in the world am I?
> Oh, that's the greatest puzzle.
>
> —Lewis Carroll, *mathematician and writer*

A keen-witted sleuth, you've been racing up and down the halls of your personality trying to deduce who in the world you are. You've picked up clues here and there, like dropped handkerchiefs in a mystery story, as you've explored your needs, values, skills, and interests. And you've turned a magnifying glass on the influences in your life: your parents, friends, teachers, and television set. The aim of all this self-analysis is to help you get a handle on what is important to you—and why. Then you can begin to approach career planning with a bit more precision than "well-I-always-kinda-sorta-wanted-ta-be-a-stewardess." You also can weed out self-defeating stereotypes, outdated values, and less-than-necessary "needs." Then, your mental housekeeping done, turn on the little projector in your head and see which of your daydreams can be nudged into reality.

If anyone has ever told you that only fools and loafers daydream, they were wrong. Fools *live* in their daydreams. But visionaries *use* their daydreams to spark creativity and creation. You can use day-

99

dreams constructively too. Fantasizing is an entertaining, liberating way of thinking about yourself and your future. In fact, some career counselors use guided fantasy exercises to help their clients explore job goals.

Here's your invitation to a daydream—four of them, really. If you're feeling industrious, get out some paper and write down the fantasy inspired by each of the following scenarios. If that doesn't appeal to you, just relax and put your imagination on automatic pilot as you read them.

- *Fantasy #1: Twenty-five Million Dollars*
  Pretend that it is your high school graduation day. When you are handed your diploma, you are also—much to your amazement—handed a check for 25 million dollars! What would you do with all that money? Invest it? In what? Would you give away some or all of it? To whom, and why? How would you live? How might having all that money affect your plans for the future? Would you continue to go to school? Travel? Retreat to a tropical island and paint? Be specific. What, if anything, would you do differently, and why? Would having so much money affect your feelings about yourself? About others?

- *Fantasy #2: TV*
  You have been hired by a national television network to produce a one-hour show. The network executives gave you a free hand, the show can be whatever you want, and the budget is virtually unlimited. What will your show be about? Will it be a documentary, a situation comedy, a talk show, a drama, a variety program? What audience is it for? What time of day will it be on? Will it be taped or live? Who will sponsor the show? Who will star? Will you? What will you do?

- *Fantasy #3: At 25 Years*
  You are 25 years old. Picture yourself getting up in the morning. What kind of home do you have? Is it a small apartment in a city, a house in the suburbs, a cottage by a lake? Imagine that you are getting ready for work. What kind of clothes do you put on—a tailored suit? Jeans, a flannel shirt, and sturdy shoes? A white coat with a stethoscope? A hard hat? Next, think about the place you work in. Is it a large corporation? An office at home? A department store? A hospital? Do you work out-of-doors? Is it quiet or bustling with activity? Do you sit behind a desk, stand in front of a class, bend over an operating table? Who are your colleagues? Do you work alone much of the time? What's your salary? How many hours a

week do you work? What do you do after work? Who shares this life with you?

- *Fantasy #4: This Is Your Life*
  Imagine that you are now 40. You're seated in a movie theater, the lights darken, and suddenly you realize that you are about to watch a movie of *your* life! What's the title of the movie? What actress portrays you as an adult? What important experiences and relationships are highlighted? Is it funny, sad, poignant, artistic, adventurous? What's the background music like? How does the audience respond? How do you feel when the film ends?

To make this exercise profitable, you need to get more out of it than a craving for popcorn. Try examining each fantasy in light of your needs, values, skills, and interests. In the 25-million-dollar fantasy, for example, what you did with your money may tell you something about your values. Did you spend it on luxuries for yourself? Did you buy your mother that sailboat she's always wanted? Did you donate some money to cancer research or to the Metropolitan Museum of Art? Did you use it to buy a home in Paris, or Muncie, or Fairbanks?

Now consider your television show. Was it an off-the-wall comedy designed to make people laugh hysterically? A showcase for unknown singers and dancers? A drama about child abuse?

The goal here is to use these fantasies as a tool for increasing your self-knowledge, but the exercise is not supposed to be a test of you or your values. And don't worry if you can't apply all four things —needs, values, skills, and interests—to each fantasy.

It might be fun and interesting to discuss these scenarios with your friends, maybe at lunch or on the way home from school. What would *they* do with 25 million dollars? Their answers can give you some insights into their values and interests.

A FRIENDLY EAR

All the exercises and activities in this book are designed to help you assemble and examine the pieces in the puzzle that constitute your personality. This information will help you make informed decisions about what to do with your life. Looking back on the exercises you've done, you may feel that some of the pieces are still missing or don't fit together quite right. That's when it can be very helpful to talk to someone who will lend you a friendly ear. Sometimes they can see something you've never been aware of.

If you're feeling confused, ask other people who know you well to envision what *they* think you'll be doing after you finish school. Some of their ideas may surprise you, some may make you laugh, and some may even make you mad, but they can give you a perspective different from your own. Perhaps your Aunt Carol will recognize a special skill of yours that you take for granted. Or your history teacher might suggest an occupation that combines several of your interests. Anyway, it's always interesting to catch a glimpse of yourself through someone else's eyes.

If you're lucky enough to get all the support you need from family and friends, that's great. But if you don't, or you think an outsider's help would be useful, consider talking with a counselor. Counselors are not just for people with "serious" problems, but rather they are for anyone who has a problem they want to talk out or who's confused about something. They serve as sounding boards and can often help people work out solutions. You've probably been a counselor yourself, listening to the problems of your friends or family.

A good counselor will listen carefully to you and help you clarify your own thoughts and feelings. You can find counselors at school, of course, or among members of the clergy. If these don't seem right, some other potential sources are your doctor, your teachers, a local community mental health association, graduate schools with programs in psychology, the "Y," or the Girl Scouts.

TRY A LITTLE JOURNAL-ISM

A really excellent way to assess yourself and your life is to keep a journal. A diary forces you to think about yourself and to take yourself seriously. Furthermore, just the process of writing things down helps to organize thoughts and feelings. Once you start keeping a journal, you may well become like the drama critic who doesn't know what he thinks of a play till he gets back to the office and writes the review.

Tristine Rainer has this advice in her book on journal keeping:

> To make full use of the diary, you need to forget all the requirements and restrictions you have probably been taught about writing.... Diary writing is free of such conventions and rules. Everything and anything goes. You cannot do it wrong. There are no mistakes. At any time you can change your point of view, your style, your books, the pen you write with, the direction you write on the pages, the language in which you write, the subjects you include, or the audience you write to.

You can misspell, write ungrammatically, enter incorrect dates, exaggerate, curse, pray, brag, write poetically, eloquently, angrily, lovingly. You can paste in photographs, newspaper clippings, cancelled checks, letters, quotes, drawings, doodles, dried flowers, business cards, or labels. You can write on lined paper or blank paper, violet paper or yellow, expensive bond or newsprint.... It's your book, yours alone. It can be neat or sloppy, big or little, carefully organized or as gravity-free as a Chagall skyscape.

Your journal is for you alone, to share with others only if you choose. If you keep this in mind, you will feel freer to honestly express yourself.

Many people approach a diary as if it were merely a matter of record keeping: "Today I spent $33.99 for a pair of running shoes. It rained." Journals like this serve a purpose, but they aren't very revealing or even very interesting to read a few years later. That's because the person behind the endless lists is missing. *Why* did you buy running shoes? Planning to run in your first marathon? Pressured by the shoe clerk? How did the rain affect your mood? How did the shoes feel the first time you laced them up? Diaries that limit themselves to listing activities could belong to almost anyone, but a diary that includes thoughts and feelings becomes a very personal document.

One way to start a journal that avoids the "bought-shoes-it-rained" syndrome is to gather five or six pictures that say something important about you. They might be photos, drawings, or clippings. Then paste the pictures in your diary and write a caption for each one.

It can also be fascinating to read the diaries of other people. (No, not your sister's that you discovered in her underwear drawer.) Virginia Woolf, Katherine Mansfield, Frances Burney, and Anaïs Nin —all well-known women writers—each have published journals. Other diaries and diary collections include

Boulton, Jane, and Opal Whitely. *Opal.* New York: Macmillan Publishing Co., 1976.

Evans, Elizabeth. *Weathering the Storm: Women of the American Revolution.* New York: Charles Scribner's Sons, 1975.

Frank, Anne. *Diary of a Young Girl.* Garden City, N.Y.: Doubleday Publishing Co., 1952.

Holiday, Laurel. *Heart Songs: The Intimate Diaries of Young Girls.* New York: Methuen, 1980.

Moffat, Mary Jane, and Charlotte Painter, eds. *Revelations: Diaries of Women.* New York: Random House, 1975.

GO FLY A KITE

What did you do last week that was really different or totally new? How about in the last two or three weeks? Did you do anything novel and exciting? Come on. Be honest. If you can't think of anything, you just might be in a rut.

Ruts are nasty things. Sure, they may feel safe and secure and comfortable, like that old pair of slippers you've been wearing since you were 12. But who wants to wear the same slippers night in and night out forever? And who wants to do the same old things for a lifetime? Ruts can put you off from new experiences, from developing new interests and skills. In this way they can limit your career planning, because you may be afraid to grow and change and try new things.

How can you boost yourself out of that rut? Well, you got into it a step at a time, and you can climb out the same way. Next time you turn on the same old television program, or pour the same old cornflakes, or read the same old kind of novel, stop and reconsider. Isn't there something you'd rather do instead? Here are some possibilities:

- Write a letter to the editor of the local newspaper on a topic that concerns you.
- Learn to change a tire.
- Sit in on a Board of Education meeting and speak up during the "public comment" portion.
- Go see a foreign film. By yourself.
- Listen to your parents' old records.
- Learn to cook something exotic (ever try dim sum?).
- Walk through a new neighborhood, or take a new route home.
- Read a science fiction book if you've never read one before. If you have, read something entirely different.
- Write your autobiography, for your children if you plan to have them, but mostly for yourself.
- Learn how to read the financial pages of the paper, and then buy yourself a share or two of stock, if you can afford it. Or pretend you have and follow its progress.
- Tape oral interviews with old folks in your community about life in the past.
- Build something—a model plane, a bookshelf, a sand castle.
- Help a child learn something you're good at.
- If you're not a musician, learn to play the recorder.

- Join a club you've always wanted to be in but never had the time for.
- Learn a self-defense skill like karate or judo.
- Wear a hat if you don't, or don't if you do.
- Take a friend out to dinner.
- Take an enemy out to dinner.
- Read some books by an author you liked or studied only fleetingly in school.
- Tutor in an English as a Second Language program.
- Ban television from your life for a week.
- Eat pizza for breakfast.
- Strive to be open-minded about something you've always detested.

If none of these suits your fancy, dream up some new activities of your own. Start with something fairly easy, progress steadily, and the next thing you know you'll have mastered Italian or something else and the rut will be behind you. Then on to something else!

Drawing submitted by Marie Rogoz, 17; Clark, New Jersey

Working Woman

Kathleen Riley

Cable Splicing Technician

Bundled up in a parka against the winter chill, Kathleen Riley was perched atop a telephone pole in Yakima, Washington, fixing a cable. A little old man stood on the pavement, gazing up at the padded, indistinct figure straddling the pole above.

"Hey," he yelled. "How do you like all these women taking the jobs away from you guys?"

Kathleen peered down at him and laughed. "I think it's wonderful!" she yelled back.

Kathleen Riley has been working on poles and under streets for the past ten years, repairing cables for Pacific Northwest Bell. She describes herself as the first woman "this side of the mountains" to go to work for the phone company in an outside job. She didn't take the job to make a point, however. She took it to make a living.

"I became a cable splicer because there were openings for them," she explains. "It made sense because I've always loved the outdoors; that's where I seemed to be in my element and where I excelled." She pauses and chuckles. "And anyway, I couldn't find a teaching job."

After graduating from high school, Kathleen worked three years to finance a college education. Then she earned her bachelor's degree in history and planned to teach. Things turned out differently, however, and now she's glad.

"The pay and benefits I get as a cable splicer are much better than they would have been if I'd become a teacher," she notes. "And my job gives me a lot of freedom and mobility. Those are things I value highly now, although that's not to say that someday I won't want to 'settle down' in another job."

As a cable splicing technician, Kathleen maintains the cables required to operate a telephone system.

"I work from a central office where the switches are located," she explains. "The larger cables are kept under air pressure, and my job is to find and repair leaks in both aerial and underground cables."

She concedes that it's somewhat risky to spend your days dangling from telephone poles.

"There's an element of danger, that's true," Kathleen says. "Every morning we get a little safety message. I've never been injured, though, and I don't really worry about it."

Learning how to climb was part of the curriculum in the five-week session Kathleen attended at the phone company's central training center in Seattle.

"We had a week of pole climbing, a week of driving and first aid, then several weeks working on splicing and learning how to operate the equipment," she says.

Although Kathleen enjoys the freedom and pay, she says there are some definite drawbacks to her kind of job. The winters can be cold and blustery in Washington, but splicers have to work in bad weather as well as good. It also tends to be a physically dirty job, "especially if you're working in a manhole!"

Another problem was reflected in the Yakima man's comment— the feeling among coworkers and customers that she is a woman taking a job that "rightfully" belongs to a muscle-bound "guy."

"The one constant thing is having to prove myself over and over again," Kathleen comments thoughtfully. "And every day having to answer the same questions. Many of the men I worked with just couldn't accept the fact that I simply needed a job, that I wasn't out to prove something."

Kathleen ran into sexual bias almost immediately. Her supervisor was convinced that she just wasn't strong enough to do the job properly and told her she wasn't going to make it to the end of the six-month probationary period.

"One day he saw me having trouble lifting a manhole cover," she recalls. "I hadn't learned the trick of removing them yet. But, based on that one observation, he decided I wasn't *strong* enough to do it. After that, I made it a point to be the one to take the covers off. Still, my boss said I was too weak. I'm pretty husky, and I *knew* I was strong enough to do anything the guys could do. I got mad. I told him, 'It wouldn't matter to you if I could lift a *truck*!'

"That same day, just by coincidence, the company's equal employment opportunity officer came by. He asked me how things were going, and I told him the truth. He set up a conference between me and my bosses, and my supervisor agreed they would give me two weeks to build up my strength; then they'd test me." Kathleen chuckles. "It was incredible how strong I got in those two weeks! I passed all the tests, got a permanent position, and the supervisor saved face—which was really the point of the whole thing."

Although, her college education isn't directly applicable to her current work, Kathleen says she's glad she got her degree.

"My college experience was very valuable to me as a person," she explains. "I grew up a lot there. And, in the future, it will help me advance into management, if that's where I decide to go next. I don't really think I'll want to be climbing poles and going into manholes when I'm 60."

Kathleen's got a quarter-century before she reaches 60, and she figures she'll keep working in the out-of-doors she loves for a while yet. She's learned more than how to climb poles on this job. She's learned something about herself.

"Basically, try and get to know yourself," she advises. "Learn your capabilities, your strengths and weaknesses. Have faith in yourself and trust your instincts.

"I used to look to the guys I worked with for validation of what I was doing. I never got it, and I never understood why until a friend taught me that I should look to myself instead of to my coworkers. They saw me as a kind of threat, and they didn't like to admit I was doing a good job. Now, *I* know I'm doing a good job, and that's what's important."

When She Was Young

Anne Sullivan Macy

The woman who later became the famous "Teacher" of Helen Keller was born in 1866 in Massachusetts to very poor parents. She was raised in a state almshouse, where she was known as a spitfire. Here she writes about the influence one of her own teachers had on her when she was about 14.

Miss Moore exerted a salutary influence over me. I respected her mind, and I fancied she did not think I was quite such a dyed-in-the-wool black sheep as the others did. When I was deliberately rude, or expressed opinions which betrayed the meagerness of my information, she often pretended not to notice it. She changed the subject so adroitly that I was not sure she had really noticed it. Sometimes I had the uncomfortable feeling that she was getting me under her thumb, which made me uneasy and suspicious. The mind was willing and docile, but the spirit carried a chip on its shoulder. I now wonder at her good-will towards me. It might easily have collapsed before a student so intractable as I was. Little by little she disciplined my unorderly mind.

Piece by Piece

I sat down at my desk
to write about my growing independence.
I had thought of certain phrases
and words that would be just perfect
to express the ideas in my head.
But as I sat
staring at the blankness
of the page before me,
I threw out my old ideas,
realising they were merely illusions
to make myself believe that I
was truly becoming more independent.
Sure,
I've taken some chances
that I might not have taken a few years ago,
and it feels good . . .
but it's also scary.
And I've made a few decisions on my own
that I've benefitted from.
Maybe this is what independence
is really like.
Grabbing on to it,
piece by piece,
but still being uncertain
about how hard you should hold on.

Poem submitted by Natalia Taylor, 15;
Atlanta, Georgia
Catalyst Poetry Competition Winner

II

Focusing on the World of Work

Like a double feature, this book is divided into two parts. In the first half, you've been concentrating on you—identifying influences and needs, examining values, pinpointing skills and interests, even diagraming daydreams. Now it's time to change focus.

In the next part, you'll be taking a look at the world of work and learning how to apply what you've discovered about yourself to the nitty-gritty of selecting a job, landing a job, and actually *doing* a job. The next chapters explore (and explode) some myths, describe the work world, teach how to investigate jobs that interest you, discuss education and training options, prepare you for job hunting, and enumerate the skills required for success.

And now back to the show....

8
The Great Beyond: Of Myths, and Women

The future is made of the same stuff as the present.

—Simone Weil, *theologian, philosopher, and writer*

At this point in your life, you might think of yourself as poised on the brink of the Great Beyond—a vast, unknown territory waiting to be explored, if not conquered. In a way, that's an accurate representation. You won't *really* know what it's like out there until you *are* out there. In the meantime, you fantasize and wonder what's in store for you. That sense of anticipation can have both good and bad results. Good, because it can lead you to explore your career and life-style choices in order to make the future seem a little less uncertain. And bad because, not having any actual experience yet, you might develop misconceptions and form opinions about the work world based on hearsay rather than facts.

Primitive people have always invented myths and tales to explain things they didn't understand—their own Great Beyond. In the beginning, these stories had some basis in reality. But as time went on and the stories were passed from generation to generation, they were gradually altered until it was impossible to separate fantasy from fact.

People in modern cultures are also prone to believe in myths, even about something as down-to-earth as work. They develop beliefs about the work world that aren't based on fact, but rather on "things I've always heard," or on what a friend's older sister said to a friend's friend at a party two months ago, or what some teacher told them six years ago. It's sometimes hard to tell just where these beliefs did originate, let alone distinguish between fact and fiction.

This chapter discusses some common misconceptions about work and about women—and shows how they can affect your career planning.

MYTH NO. 1: *There Is One Right Job for Every Person*

False. Career planning isn't like an algebraic problem. At the end of the process, you won't come up with one "right" answer, one "right" job. In fact, you won't come to the end at all. Career planning is a lifelong process, and you'll arrive at many different "right" answers to your questions throughout your work life.

The old pattern of one occupation per lifetime is gradually giving way. According to the U.S. Department of Labor, the average person changes fields or occupations three to five times during his or her lifetime. Just take a look at these well-known "career changers":

- Congresswoman Barbara Jordan gave up public office at the age of 43 to become a professor of political science.
- Grandma Moses was an avid and skillful embroiderer, but, as she got older, her fingers became too stiff to do delicate needlework. So at age 78, she turned to another art form, oil painting, and became one of America's best-known painters.
- Phyllis Diller was a homemaker until age 37, when she made her debut as a professional comedienne in San Francisco.
- Beatrix Potter gained fame as the creator and writer of the Peter Rabbit stories, but at 47 she became a farmer.

A person's goals, interests, and skills often change over time, and a career change reflects that. Longer life spans and early retirement are making it possible for many people to make career changes in midlife. A new commitment to lifelong learning encourages people to return to school for more or different training—at any age. Some people even combine two entirely different occupations simultaneously in their careers.

The poet Wallace Stevens was also a lawyer and a vice-president of the Hartford Accident and Indemnity Company. He worked on his poems on weekends and while going to and from the office. His formal study was in law. His genius was in poetry.

Rachel Carson worked as a marine biologist for the U.S. government for sixteen years, doing field research and writing pamphlets to educate the public. In her spare time, she produced newspaper and magazine articles as well as her first widely acclaimed book, *The Sea Around Us.* With the earnings of this book, she quit her job and devoted herself to researching and writing *Silent Spring,* a prize-winning book about the dangers of DDT and other pesticides. Its publication caused an uproar and marked the beginning of the age of ecology.

Charles Ives's formal study was in music, and he was one of America's great composers. But after he discovered that he couldn't make much of a living playing piano in New York City saloons or writing the adventurous music he felt compelled to create, he too joined the ranks of the "career combiners," becoming a partner in an insurance agency—and a multimillionaire.

The author of over forty books for children and adults, Lois Wyse is also the president of Wyse Advertising, a company she and her husband started in 1951. (As a copywriter, she came up with the slogan, "With a name like Smucker's, it has to be good.") Also the mother of two children, Ms. Wyse manages to do most of her writing on weekends.

Academy Award–winning actress Jane Fonda has been in over thirty films; she is also a partner in her own film company, IPC Films. Perhaps equally well known for her strong political convictions, Ms. Fonda started three successful fitness centers to raise money for a grassroots political organization she and her husband support. She designed and manages the fitness centers and occasionally teaches classes.

It is possible that once you enter an occupation, you will decide to work in it all your life. That's fine. It is also possible that you will be among those who will take a very different direction at some point in their lives. That's okay too. You don't marry a job "till death do you part." If you take a job you end up hating, you can still learn from it. Finding out what you don't like—and why—is almost as important as finding out what you do like. Even the wrong job can teach you skills that can be used elsewhere, such as good work habits, the discipline of doing tasks you don't particularly enjoy, and the ability to communicate clearly with coworkers and superiors.

Oh! There's another prominent career changer you might have heard of. He's been rather successful at it, too. After working as an actor for much of his adult life, he turned to politics. At age 56, he became governor of California. Just before he turned 70, he was elected president of the United States. Not a bad career change for Ronald Reagan.

MYTH NO. 2: *What You Study in High School Has Little to Do with Your Future Career*

False. At this stage in your life, you might believe that your high school studies have no connection with the real world of work. Think again. What you do—or don't—study in high school not only can but *will* affect your career options. For one thing, the skills learned and refined in high school will be the basis for all your future educational and vocational training. And in today's complex society, you need to know how to read, write, compute, and think logically just to survive, unless you plan to move to Tahiti and take up grass-skirt weaving.

Another point: High school gives you the opportunity to learn the discipline of good study and work habits. You might hate physical education class, but you work at it anyway because you know you won't get that diploma if you don't. That's called disciplining yourself, and the same discipline that gets you through gym class (or English or math) can get you through a lot of other things later on. In the work world, everyone is faced with doing tasks they find boring or distasteful. But no work, no pay; and workers find they have to use discipline every so often to keep from "flunking out."

High school can help you test out career interests as well. If there's a subject you love and do well in, it's probably worthwhile to explore occupations that involve that subject. Class assignments can be used for occupational research. Suppose you're required to prepare a paper for your civics class, a course you find interesting. Why not do a paper on the work of a city planner? In that way, you can explore an occupation and fulfill class requirements at the same time.

What you *don't* take in high school can also affect your future career options. Suppose you absolutely hate math, have trouble with it, and are thinking of dropping it next semester. Don't be too hasty. If you're planning to go to college (or into a trade or apprenticeship program), math is necessary just to gain admission. Also, some of the most promising career opportunities are in high-technology fields, such as computer science and engineering, which require strong math and science backgrounds. While you might not now see yourself as a systems analyst or an engineer, it's best to keep your options open in case you change your mind. And this means taking those math and science courses.

MYTH NO. 3: *If You Don't Go to College You Will Never Get a Good Job*

False. A college education is not your only option. A college diploma was once considered a sure-fire guarantee of a high-paying, high-status job. Not anymore. In fact, if there's one thing certain about the current world of work, it's that there are *no* guarantees—for college graduates or anyone else.

Some college graduates have to take jobs that traditionally have been held by people with less schooling. College graduates are sometimes unemployed. But there are workers of every educational level who are unemployed. The better and more versatile your skills, however, the better your chances will be of working.

Being highly skilled doesn't necessarily mean having a college degree, although such a degree *is* a minimum requirement for entry into some occupations. Remember, too, that training requirements vary *within* an occupational field. Suppose you want to work in dentistry. The training you would need to become a dentist, including college, is longer and costlier than the training needed to become a dental technician or a dental hygienist.

There are many different ways you can satisfy your needs. Just because one occupation demands more education than another doesn't mean that it is more interesting, better paid, or more important. It takes more time and training to become a doctor than a plumber, but both of these jobs are important. Just ask the doctor whose house is flooding because the pipes have burst or the plumber who is sick in bed and can't work.

The Bureau of Labor Statistics (BLS) predicts that many of the most favorable job opportunities in the coming decades will be for highly skilled workers such as plumbers, electricians, and mechanics. Salaries in these occupations are expected to be quite good. Even now, it's not all that unusual to find a carpenter who makes more money than a college graduate who works in an office. Well, prestige may be in the mind of the college graduate, but the money is in the pocket of the carpenter!

To sum up: If you want to go to college and think that a college degree will best meet your career goals, by all means do so. If you think that your career goals are best met otherwise, that's also a valid choice.

MYTH NO. 4: *Everyone Works a 9-to-5, 40-Hour Week*

False. The phrases "9 to 5" and "40 hours" are often used to denote the typical workday and workweek. But in the work world, there are lots of variations. Many employers do use 40 hours as the standard in determining overtime pay. For other employers or fields of work, the 40-hour week doesn't apply.

In some fields, like advertising, corporate management, law, and publishing, 40 hours might often be a *minimum* workweek. People in these fields frequently work late at the office, take work home, and sometimes work on weekends. Self-employed people, owners of small shops, for instance, might put in far more than 40 hours during their workweeks.

There are also part-time workers who do not work a full workweek. Generally, they work under 35 hours per week. According to the Association of Part-Time Professionals, 1 out of 6 Americans works part-time. Another statistic: According to the International Labor Organization, the United States *actually* has an average workweek of 35.1 hours (not counting agricultural workers), the shortest in the world. (Egypt has the world's longest workweek—56 hours.)

The workday doesn't necessarily begin at 9 A.M. or end at 5 P.M., either. One variation of the 9-to-5 day that some employers are experimenting with is called "flexitime." This system permits employees to choose (within certain limits) the time they will begin and end their workday, as long as they work the total required number of hours. According to the BLS, 12 percent of America's nonagricultural workers were on flexitime in 1980. Among them were clerical and sales workers, managers, and real estate workers.

Still another variation is the compressed workweek. Under this system, a worker is given the option of dividing 40 hours (or whatever the employer considers a standard workweek) into 3, 4, or 4½ days. The BLS reports that 2.7 percent of full-time workers participate in this system, among them some factory workers, police officers, and fire fighters. Other variations include job sharing (two workers share the responsibilities of one job but work different schedules in coordination with each other), temporary work (a worker agrees to work for an employer for a specified number of hours/weeks/months and is not required to stay with any one job or employer), and free-lancing.

Many free-lance workers, because they are not considered "regular" employees but "hire themselves out" to employers to do shorter-term projects, are often able to schedule their workweeks at their own discretion. A free-lance writer working on a magazine article assignment, for example, might choose to do her writing from 10 P.M. to 5 A.M., if she's most productive during those hours. Of course, if she must interview people for the article, she may have to juggle her schedule to avoid 2 A.M. interviews with very sleepy, irate people.

Keep these variations of work schedules in mind as you research career possibilities. Is there any system that you would strongly prefer?

How do you feel about overtime work, night work, or working on weekends? You may have other considerations, such as family commitments, schooling, and avocational pursuits, that will affect your decision. It's important to think these things over before you decide on a job that forces you to stick to a schedule you might hate.

MYTH NO. 5: *Women Don't Have to Worry About Working Because They End Up Getting Married*

Oh yeah? First of all, more women are remaining single for longer periods than in the past. The proportion of American women between the ages of 20 and 24 who had never married rose to 50 percent in 1980, up from 36 percent in 1970. When women *do* marry, the majority continue working. In 1981, 51 percent of all married women were either working or looking for work. And they don't necessarily stop working when they have children. In fact, in 1981 there were a record 18.4 million women in the labor force who had children under 18 years old—an increase of 44 percent since 1970.[1]

By 1990, the BLS predicts, 80 percent of American women aged 25 to 34 will be in the labor force. And, according to a study done in 1979, these women (married or single) can expect to spend at least twenty-five years working for pay outside their homes.[2]

Regardless of whether women are married, single, divorced, widowed, or with or without children, most work because of economic need. Increasing educational and career opportunities have also contributed to the growing numbers of working women. Unfortunately, the fantasy of Prince Charming bringing home the bacon—and everything else—is still alive in the minds of some students. The National Institute of Education recently reported that 46 percent of the eleventh graders in a sample of 32,000 believed that women *never* work after marriage. Students who swallow this myth will underestimate the importance of career planning and are in danger of being unprepared for dealing with the realities of the work world.

MYTH NO. 6: *Sexism Is a Thing of the Past*

> Equality of rights under the law shall not be denied or abridged by the United States or by any State on account of sex.
>
> —The Equal Rights Amendment

This basic constitutional guarantee of women's equality was rejected in 1982. Although the amendment passed in thirty-five states, fifteen refused to ratify it. However, the struggle continues today to gain the same rights for women as for men.

That's not to say that women haven't continued to make great strides. Sex discrimination in employment was made illegal by Title VII of the 1964 Civil Rights Act; the Equal Pay Act of 1963 requires that men and women receive equal pay for equal work performed under similar working conditions. Women are working in greater numbers than ever before in all kinds of occupations.

In spite of the legislative and social gains made during the past twenty years, however, sexism hasn't been eradicated. Following are a few statistics that will put things into perspective.

Women may have the right to vote now, but as of November 1, 1981, only 12 percent of all elected officials in this country were women. And, although Sandra Day O'Connor became the first woman to sit on the United States Supreme Court in 1981, women still account for only 6.6 percent of the total federal judiciary.[3]

Women are entering the work force in ever greater numbers, but what jobs are they getting? In the beginning of the 1980s, according to BLS, 36.9 percent of all working women were concentrated in just 10 occupations (out of a possible 400-plus categories): secretary, bookkeeper, retail sales worker, cashier, waitress, registered nurse, elementary school teacher, private-household worker, typist, and nurses' aide/orderly/attendant. Given the high concentration of women in undervalued and underpaid jobs, it's not surprising that women take home less money than men do. The average full-time working woman earns only 62¢ for every dollar earned by men today.

Part of the problem is slowly changing attitudes, which prevent women from advancing to positions that are more powerful and better paid. Half of the 8,000 male managers who responded to a recent survey agreed with the statement, "Generally, women are not as career-oriented as men."[4] In addition, although affirmative action has helped to increase the number of women and minorities getting hired and promoted, when a company's business falls off, a common practice is "last hired, first fired"—which can mean most of the women employees who have been newly hired or promoted.

The struggle for equality is as important today as it was in the days of our foremothers. We should rejoice in the advances made by women and take advantage of the many new opportunities available to us, but we should never forget that full equality is still a goal.

MYTH NO. 7: *Until Very Recently, the Only Contributions Women Have Made Have Been as Wives and Mothers*

False. Judging from all the fanfare and attention given the "new working woman," you'd think she was some sort of recent invention. But the truth is that women have always worked, both in and outside the home. From the early Colonial women who ran the first "industries" in their homes, to the black slave women who labored in the cotton empire of the South, to the women who toiled in northern factories for 10 or more hours a day, the labor of American women has played a great part in building and developing our country. As Barbara Mayer Wertheimer, a leading women's historian, explains, "Women were part of the work force all along; they have always been part of building society."[5] It's just that, until recently, women's contributions to our country's past—and present—have been virtually ignored.

Working women are not a new phenomenon. What *is* new is that women are finally beginning to get credit for their achievements.

FAMOUS FOREMOTHERS

The history of working women is a rich and complex one. You probably haven't learned much about it because most textbooks don't cover it, but if you make the effort to hunt down some reading on women's history, you'll find it worthwhile. As you read, note that the women who stand out for doing "men's" jobs were, most often, actually filling in for male relatives or husbands who died or were called away by war. The point is that women weren't ever *unable* to do men's jobs, they just weren't *supposed* to work.

Pretend for a moment that you are the mother of a 10-year-old who asks you to tell her about some famous American women. How many could you name? Could you give a good explanation of each woman's place in history? How far back in time could you go?

We'll help you out by giving you a sampling of some famous working women both you and your inquisitive daughter should know about. They're known for taking on traditionally male work, for sticking up for what they believe in, for organizing other women, or for generally improving the lives of women in one way or another. To help you locate information on the women with whom you're not so familiar, they're listed in approximate chronological order with a few words about each.

Anne Wilson—ferry operator in North Carolina, c. 1715
Ann Franklin (1696–1763)—Rhode Island Colony printer

Eliza Lucas (1722?-1793)—exporter of first American indigo

Phillis Wheatley (1753-1784)—first American black woman to have work published

Abigail Adams (1744-1818)—equal partner to husband President John Adams, managed his property during the Revolutionary War

Deborah Sampson (1760-1827)—fighter in the Revolutionary War

Margaret Corbin (1751-1800)—fighter in the Revolutionary War

Molly Pitcher (1754-1832)—fighter in the Revolutionary War

Mary Lyon (1797-1849)—founder of Mount Holyoke Female Seminary

Harriet Tubman (1820?-1913)—fugitive slave, rescuer of slaves, Civil War scout, nurse

Clara Barton (1821-1912)—nurse, founder of the American Red Cross

Antoinette Brown Blackwell (1825-1921)—minister, first woman ordained by the Protestant Church

Mary Harris Jones (1830-1930)—known as "Mother Jones"; labor agitator, most famous for her work with coal miners

Sarah Bagley (?-1847)—president of the Female Labor Reform Association

Ida B. Wells (1862-1931)—journalist, lecturer, founder of antilynching societies and Negro women's clubs

Frances Perkins (1882-1965)—social reformer, Secretary of Labor in the cabinet of President Franklin D. Roosevelt

Babe Didrikson Zaharias (1914-1956)—athlete, set more records and earned more medals in more sports than any other twentieth-century athlete

Pearl Buck (1892-1973)—author, won Pulitzer Prize and was the only American woman writer to win the Nobel Prize

Jeannette Rankin (1880-1973)—politician, pacifist, first woman elected to the U.S. Congress

Rosalyn S. Yalow (1921-)—nuclear physicist, second woman to win the Nobel Prize in medicine

Shirley Chisholm (1924-)—politician, first black woman elected to the U.S. House of Representatives

Remember that there were women in your family who lived at the same time as these women, who grew up and grew old, who were working, marrying, having children. What were *your* foremothers' lives like? What roles did they fill? What work did they do? Have you ever asked your grandmothers to describe their early lives? What can they tell you about their sisters, their mothers, *their* grandmothers? Learning about women's history—and discovering your own personal history—can fill you with a sense of excitement and accomplishment. You have a heritage to be proud of.

Remember the old saying, "A woman's place is in the home"? Well, if you have learned anything about the women in the previous section, you now know that's never been the whole truth. Women have occupied many "places" throughout history. Today, especially, a woman's place is anywhere she might want it to be! You think of some new endings for that old saying. Here are some starters.

A woman's place is in space, in a research laboratory, on a farm, on a basketball court, in a classroom, in sales, in construction, in engineering, in science, in the news, on the Supreme Court, in the foreign service, on an oil rig, in a corporation, in electronics, in computer technology, underwater, in the air. . . .

PORTRAITS AND SELF-PORTRAITS

"When I was very young, I half believed one could find within the pages of . . . memoirs the key to greatness. It's rather like trying to find the soul in the map of the human body. But it is enlightening— and it does solve some of the mysteries." The actress Helen Hayes made that comment in her own autobiography, *On Reflection.* Perhaps books like hers can help *you* solve some of the mysteries you face in determining who you are and what you will become. Even if they can't, they're still good reading.

Eleanor Roosevelt traveled the world making friends and influencing people in her crusade for human rights, yet she was painfully shy as a young woman. How did she transform herself into one of America's most eloquent representatives?

Harriet Tubman traveled a different route—the Underground Railroad—and put her life on the line leading slaves to freedom. "No other person, male or female, freed over three hundred slaves and lived to tell about it," commented Judith Nies in her book *Seven Women: Portraits from the American Radical Tradition.* What disguise did Tubman assume that helped her accomplish her mission?

When Florence Nightingale planned her future, what choices did she believe were open to her? What three important things did dancer and choreographer Agnes de Mille learn in college—and what didn't she learn? What made Dr. Alice Hamilton decide to pioneer in the field of industrial medicine? When did Tai Babilonia begin ice-skating?

Biographies and autobiographies are interesting and frequently inspiring portraits of real people. Here's a list of possibilities to get you started:

Anticaglia, Elizabeth. *Twelve American Women.* Chicago: Nelson-Hall Publishers, 1975. Includes biographies of Anne Hutchinson, Rachel Carson, Susan B. Anthony, Dorothea Dix, Jane Addams, Margaret Sanger, and more.

Begley, Kathleen A. *Deadline.* New York: Dell Publishing Co., 1977. Reporter Kathleen Begley writes about her career (which she started at 18 and pursued while attending college), telling exciting and often humorous stories behind news events she covered.

de Mille, Agnes. *Dance to the Piper.* Reprint of 1951 ed. New York: Da Capo Press, 1980. The story of dancer/choreographer Agnes de Mille's college years, marriage, and emergence as a dancer.

du Maurier, Daphne. *Myself When Young: The Shaping of a Writer.* New York: Doubleday Publishing Co., 1977. British mystery author Daphne du Maurier writes about her eventful youth as a member of a famous acting and literary family and traces the experiences and feelings that led to her choice of occupation.

Facklam, Margery. *Wild Animals, Gentle Women.* New York: Harcourt Brace Jovanovich, 1978. Profiles of 11 women who study and work with animals.

Gilbert, Lynn, and Gaylin Moore. *Particular Passions.* New York: Clarkson N. Potter, 1981. Profiles of 46 accomplished women in many fields, who talk about their backgrounds and the fulfillment they find in their work.

Haber, Louis. *Women Pioneers of Science.* New York: Harcourt Brace Jovanovich, 1979. Profiles of 12 women scientists that also provide insight into the development of different branches of science.

Halcomb, Ruth. *Women Making It: Patterns and Profiles of Success.* New York: Atheneum Publishers, 1979. A study of women who work in corporate, official, and professional settings that includes profiles.

Hayes, Helen, with Sandford Dody. *On Reflection.* New York: M. Evans & Co., 1968. Helen Hayes talks about how she became an actress, the strong and sometimes negative influence of her mother, and the important role religion has played in her life.

Higham, Charles. *Kate: The Life of Katharine Hepburn.* New York: W.W. Norton & Co., 1975. This biography includes thoughtful comments from the actress about acting and her philosophy of living.

Hungry Wolf, Beverly. *The Ways of My Grandmothers.* New York: William Morrow & Co., 1980. A Blackfoot (Native American) woman records the histories of many women of her tribe and talks about her own experience as a contemporary Blackfoot woman.

Huxley, Elspeth. *Florence Nightingale.* New York: G. P. Putnam's Sons, 1975. A biography of Florence Nightingale, founder of modern nursing, with many photos, illustrations, and quotes that give a good picture of her era.

Jacobs, Karen Folger. *GirlSports.* New York: Bantam Books, 1978. Fifteen girls from ages 9 to 17 tell about the challenges and rewards of the sports—from jacks to judo—that they enjoy.

James, Edward T., et al., eds. *Notable American Women, 1607-1950: A Biographical Dictionary.* Cambridge, Mass.: Belknap Press of Harvard University Press, 1971. Profiles of 400 women from many different fields.

Jordan, Barbara, and Shelby Hearon. *Barbara Jordan: A Self-Portrait.* Garden City, N.Y.: Doubleday Publishing Co., 1979. Texas-born Barbara Jordan traces her course from childhood through law school and eventually to the United States Senate, exploring the themes of being black and a woman in a nontraditional role.

Jordan, Teresa. *Cowgirls: Women of the American West.* Garden City, N.Y.: Anchor Press/Doubleday Publishing Co., 1982. A nonfiction portrait of the life and work of past and present cowgirls, told through oral histories, literature, songs, and photographs.

Kingston, Maxine Hong. *The Woman Warrior.* New York: Alfred A. Knopf, 1976. Chinese-American writer Maxine Hong Kingston tells about her upbringing as the child of Chinese immigrants, describing her experiences and feelings about growing up in the middle of two cultures.

Kufrin, Joan. *Uncommon Women.* Piscataway, N.J.: New Century Publishers, 1981. Nine profiles of contemporary women in arts-related fields.

LaBastille, Anne. *Woodswoman.* New York: E. P. Dutton, 1976. A wildlife ecologist and writer/photographer on the outdoors and conservation-related subjects, Anne LaBastille tells about her experiences living in the wilderness and discusses survival techniques.

Lloyd, Chris Evert, with Neil Amdur. *Chrissie: My Own Story.* New York: Simon & Schuster, 1982. This self-portrait of tennis professional Chris Evert Lloyd offers an insider's view of the demanding life of a sports professional.

Lynn, Loretta, and George Vecsey. *Loretta Lynn: Coal Miner's Daughter.* New York: Warner Books, 1977. In a natural style, Loretta Lynn writes about her youth and the development of her singing career.

Mirande, Alfredo, and Evangelina Enriquez. *La Chicana.* Chicago: University of Chicago Press, 1979. A study of Mexican-American women that examines their cultural heritage and current way of life; includes profiles of historical and contemporary Mexican-American women.

Moody, Anne. *Coming of Age in Mississippi.* New York: Dell Publishing Co., 1970. Civil rights activist Anne Moody describes the racism she faced while growing up, which later led her to work to help other blacks achieve socially equal treatment.

Morgan, Elizabeth, M.D. *The Making of a Woman Surgeon.* New York: G. P. Putnam's Sons, 1980. From the point of view of a young woman in a predominantly male field, plastic surgeon Elizabeth Morgan recounts her path to becoming a surgeon, giving a detailed picture of the long working hours, critical decisions, and rewards that are part of a career in medicine.

Nies, Judith. *Seven Women: Portraits from the American Radical Tradition.* New York: Viking Press, 1977. Profiles of women who have worked for social change in America, with historical background on the causes they worked for. Also includes a bibliography and suggestions for further reading.

Osen, Lynn M. *Women in Mathematics.* Cambridge, Mass.: MIT Press, 1974. Biographies of 8 women, from Grecian times to the present, who have contributed to the field of mathematics. The book begins with a historical overview of the development of mathematics.

Roosevelt, Eleanor. *This Is My Story.* New York: Harper & Brothers, 1937. Eleanor Roosevelt tells the story of her youth with an honest look at herself and her achievements.

Ross, Pat, ed. *Young and Female.* New York: Random House, 1972. Brief autobiographical sketches and personal accounts of turning points in the lives of 8 famous women, including actress Shirley MacLaine, congresswoman Shirley Chisholm, and athlete Althea Gibson.

Seskin, Jane. *More than Mere Survival: Conversations with Women over 65.* New York: Newsweek Books, 1980. Twenty-two women between the ages of 66 and 97 talk about their continued enjoyment of life. The women also discuss how, in their early and middle years, they developed patterns of living that have given them a positive outlook about aging.

Sicherman, Barbara, and Carol Hurd Green, eds. *Notable American Women, the Modern Period: A Biographical Dictionary.* Cambridge, Mass.: Belknap Press of Harvard University Press, 1980. Profiles of modern and contemporary women from different fields.

Smith, Betsy Covington. *Breakthrough: Women in Religion.* New York: Walker & Co., 1978. Profiles of 5 women of different religious faiths who share a determination to serve as representatives of their religions equally with men.

Sterling, Dorothy. *Black Foremothers: Three Lives.* Old Westbury, N.Y.: Feminist Press, 1979. The stories of 3 lesser-known black women who worked to lessen prejudice and inequality for blacks. Photographs and historical background are presented for each story.

Thomas, Sherry. *We Didn't Have Much, but We Sure Had Plenty.* New York: Anchor Books, 1981. Autobiographical sketches of rural American women.

Uglow, Jennifer S., ed. *The International Dictionary of Women's Biography.* New York: Continuum Publishing Corp., 1982.

Ullman, Liv. *Changing.* New York: Alfred A. Knopf, 1976. Liv Ullman traces her life from her youth in Norway, where she became a stage actress, to her emergence as an international film star. She talks honestly about her feelings of self-doubt, her relationships with others, and acting as a profession.

Women's History Bibliography

If women were absent from the history texts *you* read, books such as the following will help you fill in the gaps.

Agonito, Rosemary. *History of Ideas on Woman.* New York: G. P. Putnam's Sons, 1977.

Baxandall, Rosalyn, et al. *America's Working Women: A Documentary History—1600 to the Present.* New York: Vintage Books, 1976.

Bird, Caroline. *Enterprising Women.* New York: W. W. Norton & Co., 1976.

Brownlee, W. Elliot, and Mary H. Brownlee. *Women in the American Economy: A Documentary History, 1675 to 1927.* New Haven: Yale University Press, 1976.

Davis, Marianna W., ed. *Contributions of Black Women to America.* Vols. 1 and 2. Columbia, S.C.: Kenday Press, 1982.

Decker O'Neill, Lois, ed. *The Women's Book of World Records and Achievements.* Garden City, N.Y.: Doubleday Publishing Co., 1979.

Harris, Janet. *Thursday's Daughters: The Story of Women Working in America.* New York: Harper & Row, Publishers, 1977.

Huber, Joan. *Changing Women in a Changing Society.* Chicago: University of Chicago Press, 1973.

Hymowitz, Carol, and Michaele Weissman. *A History of Women in America.* New York: Bantam Books, 1978.

Lerner, Gerda, ed. *Black Women in White America: A Documentary History.* New York: Vintage Books, 1973.

McCullough, Joan. *First of All: Significant "Firsts" by American Women.* New York: Holt, Rinehart & Winston, 1980.

Noble, Jeanne L. *Beautiful, Also, Are the Souls of My Black Sisters: A History of the Black Woman in America.* Englewood Cliffs, N.J.: Prentice-Hall, 1978.

Rossi, Alice S., ed. *The Feminist Papers: From Adams to Beauvoir.* New York: Bantam Books, 1974.

Wertheimer, Barbara M. *We Were There: The Story of Working Women in America.* New York: Pantheon Books, 1977.

WORKING WOMAN

Marcia Graham

Public Relations Executive

When you think of public relations, do you picture a fast-talking publicity agent who dreams up ludicrous stunts to get a client's name in the paper? Or do you think of a suite of offices on the thirty-fourth floor, where slick "PR" people create sophisticated political campaigns? These images are from opposite ends of the public relations spectrum, which ranges from schlock to chic. There are, however, a whole lot of respectable, hardworking PR professionals who fall in between these two extremes.

Marcia Graham, who works at a 10-person agency in New York City, is one of them. As an account executive, Marcia is assigned one or more clients, and she is responsible for those accounts.

"Our clients are all in travel," she explains. "For example, our firm represents the Australian Tourist Commission. Our job is to publicize Australia, to inform and 'sell' the country to travel editors of magazines and newspapers. We're really a liaison between our client and these members of the press."

Marcia's job has its glamorous side—like escorting members of the press on tours of Austria. Her job also has its drawbacks—like escorting members of the press on tours of Austria. If that sounds contradictory, let Marcia explain it:

"I do a lot of traveling, which I love. For instance, last February I took a group of 10 editors to Austria for a week, to show them the country firsthand. We hiked, rode bicycles, skied. There were so many things going on at once, though. I had to make sure that there was someone to meet us at the airport, that our hotel rooms were all right, and a million other arrangements. *And* that all 10 people were having a good time and getting along with each other. It was all up to me to entertain them and make sure the trip ran smoothly."

Even in the office, the pace is seldom slow.

"You often have a lot of people breathing down your neck," according to Marcia. "Your client is *constantly* calling you. I don't think I have ever sat at my desk for longer than 10 minutes without the phone ringing. Because you are continually selling, you have to exude enthusiasm—which is why I am always so tired at the end of the day."

Marcia was a government major in college, but when she graduated in 1978 she was unsure what she wanted to do with her life. That summer, she got a job as an administrative assistant in a small New York public relations agency.

"I think that the way I entered the field was ideal," she says now. "You do have to be patient. The work was very secretarial at first. I took a few press trips, but not many. In retrospect, though, that experience was very necessary. It might be possible to skip the administrative step by going to graduate school in communications, except I used that time to build up the contacts with travel editors that are so important in my present job."

After a year as an administrative assistant, she was promoted to her present position as an account executive.

Although Marcia majored in government, she says a varied but strong liberal arts education is the best way to prepare for a career in her field.

"All the courses I took—political science, English, art history, etc.—have aided me in some way," she explains. "Good communication skills are important. I didn't take a course in public speaking, but that would help.

"One absolute prerequisite for PR is that you enjoy people—many different kinds and every minute of the day," she stresses. "You're involved with the press, with writers, and with creative people in design and layout. And, of course, with your clients. These can be 'corporate' people, if you're doing product publicity for a company, for example, or they can be people in the nonprofit sector, if your accounts are educational or arts organizations. I enjoy that diversity. One of the reasons I find my job so rewarding is that I'm working with the press, who I find to be a very sophisticated, concerned, articulate group as a whole. As far as the other necessities, I think that diplomacy, enthusiasm, excellent organizational skills, and patience are the most important."

Some people might resent always having to be in the background and seldom getting public credit for their work. Not Marcia.

"In spite of their research, writing, and effort, people in public relations never receive any publicity themselves," she says with a certain amount of resignation. "Their names are never mentioned in connection with an article. To me that doesn't matter. I really don't care whose name is under an article title. Public relations is working *behind* the scenes.

"I am extremely enthusiastic about my work," Marcia concludes. "Public relations is something you, or at least I, can believe in. I find it fascinating to learn about different cultures, to meet people from other countries, and to speak different languages. I really do think that everyone *should* go to Australia *and* Austria."

With that kind of enthusiasm, Marcia Graham has a very bright future indeed—whether it's promoting Australia, radial tires, or her own career.

Drawing submitted by Alice Bendig, 16; Chicago, Illinois
Catalyst Cartoon Competition Winner

WHEN SHE WAS YOUNG

Margaret Mead

The eminent Margaret Mead was a pioneer—both as an anthropologist and as a woman in that field. She traveled all over the world, studying different peoples by living among them and experiencing their cultures. Her sojourns in the Pacific islands are especially well known; in Samoa, Polynesia, and New Guinea she investigated the ways young people of those cultures make the transition to adulthood.

Margaret compared her exposure to other peoples with that of North Americans to make cross-cultural observations that have been widely respected. For example, she believed that men and women in our society need to develop new and diverse ways of sharing the roles and responsibilities involved in marriage and raising children.

The oldest of 4 children, Margaret was born in Pennsylvania in 1901. She spent relatively little time in school. (Although her parents were educators, they seldom allowed their children to stay in school for more than half a day; they felt it detrimental for children to be still for such a length of time.) Once she reached high school, though, as this excerpt from her autobiography reveals, Margaret became somewhat more involved in school life and started thinking about what might follow it.

The next winter we moved to Doylestown, and for two years I went to a quite good small-town high school where the teachers were college graduates, the standards of teaching were high and the books modern, and my parents were far less critical of the education I was receiving. Nevertheless, in my own eyes, there continued to be an odd quality about school. Going to school offered no challenge. No one had to study hard, and if there was good ice and a bright moon, we all went ice skating. But there was something else as well. In all the schools I had attended so far I felt as if I were in some way taking part in a theatrical performance in which I had a role to play and had to find actors to take the other parts. I wanted to live out every experience that went with schooling, and so I made a best friend of the most likely candidate, fell sentimentally in love with one of the boys, attached myself to a teacher, and organized, as far as it was possible to do so, every kind of game, play, performance, May Day dance, Valentine party, and, together with Julian Gardy, a succession of clubs, in one of which we debated such subjects as "Who was greater, Washington or Lincoln?" In all these projects we were given generous backing by my mother and the other mothers she drew into the circle. In the summer of 1915, with the help of a dance and drama teacher Mother brought out from the city, we gave a big Shakespeare festival—with our front porch as the stage—in which we performed the casket scene from *The Merchant of Venice* and sang madrigals. . . .

In school I always felt that I was special and different, set apart in a way that could not be attributed to any gift I had, but only to my background—to the education given me by my grandmother and to the explicit academic interests of my parents. I felt that I had to work hard to become part of the life around me. But at the same time I searched for a greater intensity than the world around me offered and speculated about a career. At different times I wanted to become a lawyer, a nun, a writer, or a minister's wife with six children. Looking to my grandmother and my mother for models, I expected to be both a professional woman and a wife and mother.

Flight 89

Airports are lonely
Strangers too hurried to buy
Pretty flowers from the lady.
Mentally, I make a note to
Buy you some on my
First visit home.
Yes, Ma I know
Atlanta's 2000 miles away
And law school's a big step,
But just one of many
On my way to
Independence.
Yes, Ma I know
A country girl can't
Trust everybody,
People aren't always
What they seem.
Yes, Ma I have
Enough change to call
"Right when I get there, mind you,"
My favorite recipes,
Your tried-and-true advice,
The knowledge you'll be there.
I have to go now
Flight 89 is ready to fly
And so am I.

Poem submitted by Anastasia Angelos, 15;
Conrad, Montana
Catalyst Poetry Competition Winner

9

Introducing the World of Work

Autonomy means moving out from a world in which one is born to marginality, to a past without meaning, and a future determined by others—into a world in which one acts and chooses, aware of a meaningful past and free to shape one's future.

—Gerda Lerner, *educator and writer*

When you were 4 years old and someone asked you, "What do you want to be when you grow up?" you probably thought about it for 5 seconds and said, "Wonder Woman." Or "a mommy." Or teacher, doctor, nurse, clown, or Big Bird on Sesame Street. After all, when your life revolves around your parents, your teacher, other tots, the park, the doctor's office, and television, you tend to develop a somewhat limited view of the world.

Alas, as you got older, things became more complicated. (Have you noticed they rarely seem to get simpler?) Becoming Wonder Woman is probably out now that you know the pay is terrible and the fringe benefits are worse. Just the *thought* of trying to decide what you want to be when you "grow up" may make you wish to scurry back to childhood. But, before you begin to yearn for graham crackers and Kool-Aid, take some comfort from the fact that you have already begun to plan your future. There's still a lot of work ahead, though.

What kinds of occupations will meet your needs and goals? Where can you best use your skills? What do you demand from a job and what will it demand from you? The work world's rule is quid pro quo, Latin for "something for something." You not only have to consider your own requirements, but the requirements of the workplace as well.

If you're still not convinced of the necessity of *working* at learning about work, here is something else to think about. When you choose an occupation, or even a specific job, you are also choosing a life-style: where you'll live, the types of people you'll be with almost every day, the amount of money you'll have to spend, the kinds of clothes you'll wear, even the amount of leisure time you will have. This isn't some isolated, small-potatoes decision that affects only one aspect of your life.

20,000 AND COUNTING

How many different occupations can you name? A couple dozen? Well, there are literally millions of jobs and thousands of occupations in the United States. Over 20,000 occupations are listed in the U.S. Department of Labor's *Dictionary of Occupational Titles*, or "DOT" as it's affectionately known. (The DOT, a standard reference work found in many libraries, is an important source of information for career exploration. More on this later.)

Just for fun (and to whet your appetite for making good use of a valuable resource), see how many of these DOT job titles you can correctly identify. In case you get stuck (which is unlikely), you'll find the answers at the end.

1. A Boring Machine Operator is
   a. the opposite of an interesting machine operator.
   b. the worker who sets up and operates the machinery that bores holes in wooden parts.

2. A Vulcan Crewmember is
   a. a character on *Star Trek* named "Mr. Spock."
   b. a member of the military who operates multibarrel rapid-firing weapons and support equipment.

3. A Wrinkler Chaser is
   a. a medicinal beverage that smooths away facial wrinkles.
   b. a worker who irons wrinkles from shoes or shoe parts.

4. A Frit Coater is

   a. a person who coats frits.

   b. an electronics worker who assembles cathode-ray tubes for television receivers and display instruments.

5. A Stove-Bottom Worker is

   a. a worker who has let herself go to pot.

   b. a person who works machinery that processes floor-covering material.

6. A Retort Unloader is

   a. someone who always answers back.

   b. the worker who unloads kilns after the charcoal-making process.

7. A Sweet Potato Disintegrator is

   a. an "explosive" vegetarian.

   b. a worker who tends the machine that grinds sweet potatoes into a semifluid state to facilitate the cooking process.

8. A Shrinking Machine Operator is

   a. someone who'll make you smaller—for a big fee.

   b. a worker who tends the machine that shrinks the cone sections of felt hats to the proper size.

(The correct answers were all "b.")

These jobs are only the tip of the iceberg, and they are hardly representative of the broad spectrum of opportunities in our country. It's impossible for any one individual to be familiar with every single job that exists. Fortunately, you don't have to research all 20,000 occupations. (Relieved?) Just find out as much as you can about those that match your unique interests, values, and abilities. And that takes some investigation.

Generally, people learn about various occupations from books, television, magazines, films, and other people. Sometimes people choose a job simply because they know somebody who works in that job. Obviously, this can cut out a lot of possibilities. Nobody knows 20,000 people—in 20,000 *different* occupations.

Where you live can also be a factor that limits your knowledge of job options. If you live in an urban area, you may have only fuzzy notions of what a forester or farmer does. If you live on a farm, you might be unaware of the vast array of jobs available in a big city—everything from bartending to bookselling. The point is that you can't just leave your career choices to chance. You have to stretch beyond your immediate world in order to learn about other possibilities.

Even if you have some idea of what you'd like to do, your exploration still isn't over. Suppose you're interested in architecture. The obvious choice: Study to become an architect. But what *kind* of architecture are you interested in? Maybe you'd prefer marine architecture, designing and overseeing the construction and repair of ships, barges, submarines, and torpedoes. Maybe you'd be a superb landscape architect, planning the layout of outdoor areas for parks, airports, hospitals, or homes. Other possibilities include architectural drafting and landscape drafting.

Seeking a Frontier?

In a world where there is so much to be done, I felt strongly impressed that there must be something for me to do.

—Dorothea Dix, *social reformer*

Throughout much of our country's history, the American people have felt a yearning for the frontier, the raw edge of civilization, the wilderness to be explored. What was over the next ridge? What was beyond that distant river? The continent seemed limitless.

Well, although most of those frontiers have been conquered and civilized, there are uncharted places left. They are the challenges that must be met on this shrinking planet.

Will we learn how to prevent disease? Cure the cold, stop cancer, prevent birth defects? Will we develop energy sources that are clean, cheap, accessible, and renewable? Will we manage to dispose of chemical waste so that it will not poison the earth?

Are there other planets that could support human life? Are there other humans out there somewhere? Who will pilot that first starship sent, like the Enterprise in *Star Trek*, "to seek out new life and new civilizations"?

Will we stamp out illiteracy? Provide fulfilling work for everyone? Learn to live peacefully and cooperatively with the rest of the human race?

There is no shortage of frontiers. The real question is this: Who has what it takes—the foresight, intelligence, creativity, determination, faith, and guts—to do what needs to be done? Who will be the new pioneer?

Why not you?

Or maybe you'd like to work in the aviation industry. Does that mean being an airline pilot or a flight attendant? An airport manager or a test pilot? How about an air mechanic, a navigator, an air-traffic controller, or an airline representative?

You're getting the picture. One of the basic rules of career exploration is to look beyond the obvious. And lest you be tempted to narrow your focus to a single occupation too soon, learn always to ask yourself this question: If for some reason I couldn't do this, what other things would I want to do?

Have you ever looked into a kaleidoscope? As you shift and turn it, the colors and patterns change. Like a kaleidoscope, the work world changes too—sometimes slowly and sometimes with dramatic speed—as people and technology and the economy shift and turn.

During the past fifty years, the United States has experienced a rapid growth in its number and kinds of occupations. New technology and new ways of doing business create new jobs and make others obsolete. Changes in the size and the tastes of the population create demands for different goods and services, leading to employment for some people and unemployment for others.

Learning about possible occupations can be an overwhelming task, but it needn't be. Just take it one step at a time. A good first step is to get an overall picture.

HOW THE WORK WORLD IS ORGANIZED

Work can be organized in many ways. In highly complex industrial societies like ours, work isn't organized the way it is in countries that are still developing. Capitalist countries organize work differently than socialist countries do. Further variation occurs from region to region, city to city, employer to employer. But for all the differences in the world of work, there are similarities that bind the whole picture together. To make sense of the complex work world in this country, it is necessary to devise some broad systems that divide "work" into smaller segments. Let's start with how the Bureau of Labor Statistics divides up the work world: by industry and by "occupational cluster."

Industry

Our economy has two basic kinds of industry: those that produce goods and those that provide services. Making a distinction between industries that produce goods and those that provide services helps divide the world of work into two simple units. It clarifies the nature of industries. And that might help you make a career choice.

The goods-producing industries supply everything from gasoline to drill presses to lamb chops. These industries employ less than one third of U.S. workers. Major goods-producing industries include

- Agriculture (farming, food and fiber processing, and manufacturing of farm tools and fertilizers, to name a few elements of a basic industry)
- Mining (industries producing most of the basic raw materials and energy sources that industry and consumers use, including coal mining, metal mining, and oil exploration and processing)
- Contract construction (industries that build, alter, and repair roads, bridges, and structures such as factories)
- Manufacturing (industries that manufacture goods ranging from miniature computer circuits to textiles to spacecrafts)

The service industries either provide services (medical care or haircuts, for example) or maintain and distribute the goods listed above. More than two thirds of U.S. workers are employed in these major industrial groups. They include

- Trade (industries involved in the distribution and sale of goods from producers to consumers, such as restaurants, wholesale textile dealers, and department stores)
- Finance, insurance, and real estate (industries that provide financial services, protection, and property to businesses and consumers; among those in this group are banks, consumer credit agencies, insurance companies, and real estate brokers)
- Services (industries engaged in providing a personal service to consumers, such as private hospitals, private schools, hotels, and the Girl Scouts)
- Government (public schools, the postal service, police and fire protection, the Army)
- Transportation, communication, and public utilities (industries grouped together because they provide a public service and are regulated and sometimes owned by public agencies; examples are telephone companies, power companies, airlines, and truckers)

Each of these major industry divisions is briefly profiled in the Bureau of Labor Statistics' *Occupational Outlook Handbook* (OOH), which is updated and published every two years.

The service industries employ the largest portion of today's work force, and that portion is growing. Not only are more workers employed in this sector, but job opportunities have been increasing at a faster rate in service industries than in goods-producing industries.

As incomes rise and living standards improve, people demand more schools, better health care, better police and fire protection, and more financial services. The result: more jobs, especially in the service industries. With the increasing number of single-parent households and families in which both parents are employed, there is a growing need for high-quality child care and timesaving services such as providing restaurant meals and housecleaning. And, as the *Occupational Outlook Handbook* points out, "because many services involve personal contact, fewer people have been replaced by machines in service-producing industries."

While the service segment of the work force has expanded rapidly, employment in the goods-producing industries has remained fairly constant since World War II. New technology and sophisticated machinery have automated production, sometimes reducing or eliminating the demand for certain groups of workers. But that doesn't mean that the job outlook in these industries is necessarily bleak. There will always be a need for creative talent. There will always be a need for managers. And robots can never replace all the people who die, retire, or leave to take other jobs.

Keep in mind that none of these industries, in either the goods or services group, exist as isolated islands within the work world. Industries, like people, are highly dependent on each other. For instance, the trade industry depends upon the manufacturing sector to provide the goods it sells, and it depends upon the finance, insurance, and real estate industries for the loans needed to buy goods and to expand, for insurance, and for the land and buildings needed for warehouses and stores. The trade industry also depends upon public utilities industries for transportation, electricity, telephones, and so on.

Occupational Clusters

Dividing jobs by industry is one broad way of organizing the work in our economy. But work can be further divided into even more distinct units called *occupational clusters*, which group jobs on the basis of their similarities. The 1982–83 edition of the *Occupational Outlook Handbook* identifies twenty clusters of occupations. (Other career literature might vary the categories somewhat, but the OOH clusters are fairly standard.) These are

1. Administrative and Managerial Occupations
2. Engineers, Surveyors, and Architects
3. Natural Scientists and Mathematicians
4. Social Scientists, Social Workers, Religious Workers, and Lawyers
5. Teachers, Librarians, and Counselors
6. Health Diagnosing and Treating Practitioners
7. Registered Nurses, Pharmacists, Dietitians, Therapists, and Physician Assistants
8. Health Technologists and Technicians
9. Writers, Artists, and Entertainers
10. Technologists and Technicians, Except Health
11. Marketing and Sales Occupations
12. Administrative Support Occupations, Including Clerical
13. Service Occupations
14. Agricultural and Forestry Occupations
15. Mechanics and Repairs
16. Construction and Extractive Occupations
17. Production Occupations
18. Transportation and Material-Moving Occupations
19. Helpers, Handlers, Equipment Cleaners, and Laborers
20. Military Occupations

Each cluster encompasses many individual occupations within its general heading. For instance, the Administrative and Managerial Occupations cluster includes bank officers and managers, health service administrators, city managers, purchasing agents, school administrators, hotel managers, and a number of other administrative and managerial occupations.

Every job in our economy can be classified by industry and by occupational cluster. Let's try an example.

Your community needs to build a new public high school. The local Board of Education arranges with a *real estate broker* to buy the land. An *architect* is hired to design the school building and a *drafter* begins to prepare the blueprints, based on the architect's specifications. Once the bids are in and the *general construction contractor* is hired, work begins on the structure.

Meanwhile, school officials have been talking with *manufacturers' sales representatives* so the officials can draw up specifications for desks, chalkboards, and other school equipment. The officials and the school board have also been busy hiring the staff for the school: *teachers*, a *principal*, *counselors*, a *librarian*, a *nurse*, and *secretaries*.

Since high school students are occasionally known to be hungry, a *school lunch service staff* is hired as well. To maintain the building and surrounding grounds, the board lines up a *school custodian*.

Once the building is finished, a *government contract inspector* makes sure it complies with building codes, contract specifications, and zoning regulations. The board also checks with *insurance agents* before deciding what insurance protection to buy. Finally, after pouring so much money into the project, the board may decide to protect its investment by hiring a *security guard* to patrol the grounds at night.

That's a simplified version of "This is the school your board built." Even so, it illustrates how goods/services and occupational clusters operate. Each worker mentioned has his or her place in the larger scheme of things. With the help of the OOH, we have prepared Chart 1; this lists the workers mentioned in the example and classifies them according to industry and occupational cluster.

Chart 1
Industry and Occupational Cluster Classifications for Workers Involved in Building a New High School

Worker	*Industry*	*Occupational Cluster*
real estate broker	Finance, insurance, and real estate	Marketing and sales occupations
architect	Services	Engineers, surveyors, and architects
drafter	Services	Technologists and technicians, except health
general construction contractor	Contract construction	Construction and extractive occupations
manufacturers' sales representative	Trade	Marketing and sales occupations

Chart 1. Industry and Occupational Cluster Classifications for Workers Involved in Building a New High School (continued).

Worker	Industry	Occupational Cluster
teacher	Government	Teachers, librarians, and counselors
school principal	Government	Administrative and managerial occupations
school counselor	Government	Teachers, librarians, and counselors
school librarian	Government	Teachers, librarians, and counselors
school nurse	Services	Registered nurses, pharmacists, dietitians, therapists, and physician assistants
secretary	Services	Administrative support occupations, including clerical
school lunch service	Government	Service occupations
school custodian	Government	Service occupations
government contract inspector	Government	Service occupations
insurance agent	Finance, insurance, and real estate	Marketing and sales occupations
security guard	Services	Service occupations

What About Plaid?

You've seen how jobs can be classified by industry and by occupational clusters. They can also be classified by collar color.

You've probably heard the terms "white-collar worker" and "blue-collar worker." These terms originated when many people who worked mostly with their "hands" (that is, did manual labor) wore (you guessed it) blue work clothes, while those who worked mostly with their "heads" worked in offices and wore white shirts and ties. In time, the terms "blue-collar" and "white-collar" came to stand for more than a worker's clothes. Blue-collar frequently meant work that some people considered dirty, boring, or lacking in prestige; the white-collar label, on the other hand, seemed to add instant status to an occupation.

Attitudes have changed somewhat and the distinctions are not quite that simplistic. Besides the obvious fallacies (not every manual worker wears blue, and not every office worker wears a white shirt and tie), there are other inaccuracies. For example, creativity and cleanliness are not the exclusive province of white-collar workers, and a white-collar worker can get just as dirty or bored as a blue-collar worker. What color collar do you think the majority of college graduates wear? Look at Chart 2 below. If you guessed that most college grads are now in professional and technical positions ("white-collar" work), you were right—but notice that the figure has gone from 67 percent to 55 percent in just ten years. The number of graduates entering all of the other occupational groups grew during that period— and the trend is continuing.

The "heads work" versus "hands work" distinction isn't reliable either. Surgeons and artists, for instance, work with their hands as much as their heads. Electricians certainly use their hands; they'd also

Chart 2
Occupational Employment Pattern of
College Graduates, 1970–1980

| *Employment of college graduates* | *Percent distribution* | |
	1970	*1980*
Professional and technical workers	67.0	55.0
Managers and administrators	16.6	19.5
Sales workers	5.3	6.8
Clerical workers	6.3	9.0
Craft workers	1.8	3.3
Operatives	1.1	1.4
Laborers	0.2	0.8
Service workers	1.1	3.3
Farm workers	0.6	0.9

Source: *Occupational Outlook Quarterly,* Summer 1982.

better use their heads or the occupants of buildings they wire will get a *real* jolt.

Another factor that used to separate blue-collar and white-collar work was unionization. A union is a group of workers who have joined together to bargain for better working conditions, job security, and higher pay. Originally, blue-collar workers such as steelworkers, factory workers, and miners were the only ones organized into unions. Today, white-collar unions are also common. There are teachers' unions, actors' unions, police and fire fighters' unions, and journalists' unions, to name a few.

There's still another collar color we haven't talked about yet—pink. The term "pink-collar" has come into use recently to refer to jobs that have traditionally been labeled "women's work"; examples are waitresses, beauticians, secretaries, elementary school teachers, and salesclerks. Pay in these jobs has been consistently lower than in other types of jobs--blue-collar or white-collar—and still is. (You'll sometimes hear it said that many women are stuck in a "pink-collar ghetto." That means they're concentrated in low-status, low-paying, traditionally female jobs.)

Why classify jobs by collar color? In occupational literature, it's just another way to group occupations according to similarities. Mostly, it makes it easier to write about them. In the end, it's not the color of your collar that's important, it's whether you're using *your* skills to the best of your ability.

Public, Private, and Nonprofit

There's a fourth way of organizing work. Every employee in this country works in one of three sectors: public, private, or nonprofit.

The public—or government—sector employs more workers than either of the other two. Federal, state, county, municipal, and quasi-governmental agencies are all under the public-sector umbrella. Its workers range from the mayor of Chicago to the toll collectors on the Golden Gate Bridge.

Competition and profits are the hallmarks of the private sector. A private business is just that—one owned by a private individual or group of individuals. (In this case, private doesn't mean "confidential" or "unknown"; it just means it is not owned by the government.) Examples of specific private-sector employers are department stores, banks, airlines, hotels, and multinational corporations.

Like a platypus, the nonprofit sector is neither fish nor fowl. It exists to perform some kind of public service, not to make financial profits that benefit individuals. Yet it is not governmental. Nonprofit organizations can vary from a two-person office to a huge bureaucracy. Catalyst is a nonprofit organization, as are the Girl Scouts, the American Cancer Society, the Ford Foundation, and the American Civil Liberties Union.

Workers in most occupations can choose to work in any of the three sectors. For example, a lawyer might work for the U.S. Attorney General's office, for a private law firm, or for the American Civil Liberties Union.

Data, People, and Things

Okay, you've now mastered goods and services, clusters, collars, and sectors. But you're not through. There's still another concept: "Data, People, and Things." Call it "DPT" for short. DPT is a way of looking at what people actually do on a job.

Every job requires a worker to deal with data (numbers, words, ideas), people, and things (tools, machines, vehicles, nature). But the degree to which any job requires a worker to be involved with the three elements varies. Both plumbers and librarians deal with data, people, and things. But plumbers use wrenches, reamers, pipe benders, and other tools on the job more often, and more skillfully, than librarians do. The librarian's work, on the other hand, involves a lot of data-related tasks (selecting and purchasing library materials, classifying publications, helping people find information they need), which also call for specialized skills.

Much of the occupational literature uses the DPT concept. All jobs listed in the *Dictionary of Occupational Titles* are coded to show how the worker functions in relation to data, people, and things. The DOT also explains this concept in greater detail.

Most people tend to prefer one element over the other two. Remember that girl in your fourth-grade class who was forever taking things apart and putting them back together? She was a "things" person in the making. Remember the boy who was perpetually collecting baseball cards and telling anyone who'd listen the batting averages of all the major-league players? A budding "data" personality. Recall the kid who was always starting up a club, selling lemonade, or organizing everyone on the block into a neighborhood talent show? A "people" person if ever you saw one.

The DPT concept can help you figure out what you prefer in a job and which occupations fit your preferences. When using this concept, however, it's important to keep in mind that the jobs are classified based on an *average* profile of what people in that job do. In reality, jobs are rarely as rigid as they might seem on paper. That's because each worker is a unique person and uses his or her own personality to shape the work. Suppose you're interested in becoming a life scientist. (In case you're not, life scientists study all aspects of living organisms, placing particular emphasis on the relationship of animals and plants to their environment.) As a university professor, you'd probably deal more with people than with data or things; but if you decide to go into research, you could be dealing more with data (and things) than people. Whether you're a "D" person, a "P" person, or a "T" person, there's a place for you somewhere!

People Environments

Another way to organize the work world is by the type of "people environment" a job involves; that is, the types of people one is likely to encounter working in a particular occupation.

No one, except a hermit meditating in the Andes, works entirely alone. Jobs bring us into contact with any number of people—clients, customers, patients, colleagues, superiors—all of whom are part of the people environment of an occupation.

Dr. John L. Holland has conducted probably the best-known research on this aspect of work. In Chapter 6 we applied Holland's categories (realistic, investigative, artistic, social, enterprising, and conventional) to your interests. The categories also correspond to people environments at work.

Dr. Holland's basic premise is that different types of people have different interests, skills, and personalities, and we should try to match our characteristics with compatible jobs and similarly inclined coworkers. When a group of compatible people join together in a work setting, they create an environment that reflects the sort of people they are.

Holland has grouped the 456 most common occupations in the United States according to their people environment. You might want to turn back to Chapter 6 and reread the categories, looking over the sample occupations listed. If you want to find out more about Holland's theory and see how he classifies other occupations, take a look at his book *Making Vocational Choices: A Theory of Careers* (Englewood Cliffs, N.J.: Prentice-Hall, 1973).

Now that you've learned different ways of looking at today's work world, maybe you should think a little about the future. You probably won't be retiring until something like 2033—if "retirement" isn't just another outdated concept by then. During your work life, some jobs will become obsolete while new ones will appear. And the face of the workplace—be it office, shop, classroom, or wheat field—may be changed beyond recognition.

Here are some of the visions from the futurists' crystal balls:

- More and more robots, and not cute little human-looking ones either. Instead, these will be mechanical "arms" programmed by computers to perform tasks that are too precise, rapid, monotonous, or hazardous for people. There are a number of such robots in use already, doing things like spray-painting cars and handling uranium.

- More workers staying at home, and not because of the flu. Computer terminals in their living rooms will allow them to perform their jobs at home and avoid the rush-hour traffic. They'll also use their terminals to shop from catalogs, gain access to their bank accounts, and decide whether to whip up a spinach quiche or a cheese soufflé from their electronic cookbooks.

- Good-bye pencils, good-bye books, good-bye teachers' dirty looks. Students will receive their day's lessons via their home computer system, thanks to a teacher who programs the lessons from his or her own home. (At least a computer can't give you a dirty look.)

- Flexible work schedules that increasingly replace the standard 9-to-5 hours. Part-time and flexitime will become conventional patterns, an obvious boon to parents who are struggling to find time for both baby and boss. Other patterns will appear, like one already in existence at one company allowing workers to negotiate a level of daily production and letting them go home as soon as that level is achieved.

And you may need that watch they give you for twenty-five years of distinguished service to help you get to your next job on time. As Americans live longer, alternatives to quitting at age 65 are being developed. You might retire from your post as a college president and take over as recreation director on a cruise ship. Why not? You will have earned it.

WORKING WOMAN

Claudette Fourchtein

Small-Business Owner/Manager

Put yourself in this scenario: You are a young woman with a master's degree in English, several years of teaching experience, and a yen to try something different. You decide to move to New York City, where your father has just purchased an interest in a small graphics and printing business. The business has had financial troubles, but your father believes it is basically sound. He asks you to assume his partnership role in managing the business. That troubles you a little because you like to do things on your own, and you worry that your father has simply bought you a job.

But you make the best of things. You dutifully try to learn the business, and one thing you learn is that business is getting worse. It gets so bad, in fact, that less than a year after you became a partner you arrive at work one day to discover that your two partners have bailed out. There you are, standing in the middle of a couple thousand square feet of office space, with one employee, no partners, and lots of creditors. Yipes!

Well, you *said* you liked to do things on your own. But what do you do next? Ask Claudette Fourchtein, who was the real-life star of this drama several years ago.

"I learned all kinds of things I didn't *want* to learn," she says, "including dealing with angry creditors and confronting people to whom I owed money when I had none in the bank. Still, it wasn't a bad education."

Claudette was scared when she first learned that her partners had bailed out, but she was relieved, too; "It was like having a big yoke taken off."

There were plenty of problems the first year. She had no experience running her own business. She acquired all the debts the other partners had run up, in addition to losing clients they had run out on. Like Alice in looking-glass land, it took all the running she could do to stay in the same place.

"Everything the first year was a surprise," Claudette recalls. "I think the toughest thing was pricing. I had no idea of how to price myself in the market. I just had to jump in and find out for myself when I was making money and when I was losing it."

Her father gave her some financial backing, which meant she could afford a gamble. She went deeper into debt so she could hire additional help and free herself to do more managing and less scurrying. "The trap you can get into," she explains, "is finding yourself doing the routine stuff and not making the long-range planning decisions that you should be making. You get tied up in routine instead of looking at the overall picture."

Eventually, when she thought she'd reached the break-even point but discovered she was still losing money, she called in a consultant to straighten things out. "When you're doing something wrong and don't know how to figure out what it is, you need outside help," she advises.

Claudette also joined a typographers' association and a group of women business owners. "It's good to affiliate yourself with a group," she feels, "both for sales—members can sell to each other—and to locate people who have expertise in any area in which you don't. That outreach is a big part of running a business: finding people who know what you don't know."

Moral support from relatives and friends also helped Claudette survive during her tough initiation. Raised in a close family, she particularly credits her father for avoiding stereotyped notions of what girls should—and should not—do.

"My father didn't treat me particularly as a woman, but as a person," she recalls. "I also had a very traditional mother, so I had a chance to evaluate: do I want to do that or do I want to do what my dad is doing? I was always fascinated with things boys could do that I could do too."

Managing a business is traditionally something that "boys do," and Claudette has faced some difficult challenges because she is a woman.

"I wouldn't have joined the Women Business Owners if I didn't think it was quite different being a woman business owner," she explains. "But I don't know if it's a question of discrimination or of not being taken seriously. Occasionally I have to remind someone I'm doing business with that I don't want to be called 'honey' or 'sweetheart.' But if I tell them firmly that I don't like it, they back right off.

"It's more a problem of fighting a lot of things that are built into my understanding of myself, rather than of external pressures. It's trying to fight the passivity that's built into a woman's role, fighting my own attitudes about what women should and should not be doing. For me, management was very, very difficult and still is. Bossing people around, taking a hard line and sticking to it, and confronting people are all things that I was taught not to do. That's the hard part.

"You must sit down somewhere along the line and decide what you're good at—and what you're not good at. Everybody's not good at several things. Then you try to get someone else to do those things. The sooner you do that, the less you bring your own liabilities into your company."

There are some advantages to being a woman in business, Claudette has discovered. Her company is listed by the government as a "minority" subcontractor, so contractors seeking to meet federal quotas sometimes hire her for that reason. She's also profited from affirmative action programs in private industry. "That will help get you in," she cautions, "but it won't keep you in."

Even now that her business is humming along smoothly, Claudette still puts in many 12-hour days. This schedule has a definite effect on her social life.

"Your good and old friends will stick with you, but you also need to find other people who have the same kind of involvement in what they're doing," she recommends. "Then they don't think you're crazy when you work late and think about it all the time. There are other people who won't understand why you're not writing them letters anymore or calling them once a week."

She compares running a business to playing a game—a totally absorbing sort of game with very high stakes.

"There are, of course, a lot of disadvantages to being in business for yourself," she concedes, "especially in the beginning—like insecurity about your own income and never knowing whether you're going to be able to pay yourself or how much. For over a year I took home less pay than my secretary. When you're self-employed, you lose that financial security. If you make a really wrong move, you pay for it directly."

Claudette believes that her company's future is bright. With increasing experience, she's found that her clients want her to do more designing and editing for them. She plans to open a new division that will be devoted solely to editing, fulfilling her longtime goal of becoming an editor. And she's discovered that one of the greatest joys of management is tapping the talents of others.

"When I was going through school I turned up my nose at business," Claudette concludes. "I thought it was all figures and finance— a lot of dull stuff. But I have much more human interaction all day long now than I did when I was a teacher."

Drawing submitted by Emily Diane Ehrlich, 13; Ann Arbor, Michigan
Catalyst Cartoon Competition Winner

WHEN SHE WAS YOUNG

Kate Gleason

A pioneer in a "nontraditional" job, Kate Gleason was born in Rochester, New York, in 1865. Her father, a machinist, encouraged his daughter to be active and independent. This resulted in her playing more often with boys than with girls, although she had to prove herself before being accepted.

> " 'They didn't want me,' she recalled. 'But I earned my right. If we were jumping from the shed roof, I chose the highest spot; if we vaulted fences, I picked the tallest.' "

When Kate's older brother died, she began to work in her father's shop. Here she remembers her first day.

> " 'I walked down to the shop, mounted a stool and demanded work. At the close of the day he handed me one dollar, my first pay. I had no pocket, so I tucked it in my dress, and lost it on the way home. My mother and grandmother made a terrible fuss.' "

Kate went on to become the shop's salesperson, traveling all over the country and later the world to sell Gleason Works products to the automobile and other industries.

The Baker's Apprentice

*My father just took me under his wing; I'm his apprentice, what a wonderful
thing.*

*What does he do? My father, you mean? Well he's the best darn baker you've
ever seen!*

So I'd be ready to work and be paid, he taught me every trick of his trade.

*Finally that wonderful day arrived; I took all my tests and through them
I'd glide.*

*I popped out those muffins like I was a pro; Dad was so pleased, you could never
know!*

*The very next day Dad came up to me, said "It's time you should solo and
receive a fee."*

*"I'll leave you alone in charge of the store. You're in command once I walk out
that door."*

*He smiled at me while he lifted his racket, standing there in his "Chris Evert"
jacket.*

"Gonna play a few sets to pass the time," said Dad as he put up the "open" sign.

I stood there a minute watching him go; I was so scared and stunned you know.

*My first sign of life that returned you see, was my stomach starting to growl
at me.*

*Since I'm not one to argue, and prefer not to fight, I gave in to my stomach by
grabbing a bite.*

It started with cookies (chocolate chip), and next a crispy cheddar cheese nip.

*A cinnamon danish, some chocolate mousse; with my stomach I begged for
a truce.*

I had some brownies, just a bit; I was beginning to think I was a bottomless pit!

*The next thing I knew, I looked around, but not a morsel of food was left to
be found.*

So I finally snapped out of it; I slowly drifted back to earth,

Although I must have gained a ton and looked like I'd soon give birth.

*Then in walked Dad, he started to grin; I pulled in my stomach and tried to
look thin.*

*I awaited my fate like a prisoner his sentence; I was perfectly willing to pay up
my penance.*

I shut my eyes and held my breath, awaiting a dark and painful death.

*"My daughter," said he, "I go out for some fitness; I return and can't believe
you did so much business!"*

Poem submitted by Laura Ciolkowski, 15;
Great Neck, New York
Catalyst Poetry Competition Winner

155

10

Matchmaking

"But once I had set out, I was already far on my way."

—Colette, *novelist*

Up until now, you've learned about the work world in very broad terms. In this chapter the focus will narrow to help you begin thinking about specific occupations.

You already know a lot about certain occupations, of course. But even an occupation like teaching, which seems to hold no mysteries, should be thoroughly investigated if it's a field that interests you. You'll want to know what the educational requirements are, what examinations must be passed, what licenses must be obtained. You'll want to know the future job outlook, the different types of employers that hire teachers, and the salary ranges for teachers. It's also important to be aware of the personal characteristics that are common to most successful teachers.

In making realistic career plans, it's a mistake to rely on vague notions about occupations, although they're helpful as a starting point. It's not enough to know that an accountant "works with numbers," or that a manager "manages a business," or that an architect "designs buildings." You need a comprehensive, accurate picture of an occupation so you can avoid investing time, energy, and money in preparing for a field that will turn out to be wrong for you.

Making sure you know a lot about your occupational choice is especially important if you'll be looking for a job immediately after high school graduation. You probably won't have an extensive work history to show a prospective employer. So the employers who interview you will make their hiring decisions, in part, on the basis of your knowledge of the occupation. They'll want to see that you've taken the job (and yourself) seriously enough to know what you're getting into.

How do you find out more about specific occupations? Do you begin with occupations that start with A and work your way through to the Z's? Well, you can. But when you finish you'll be handing in your first job application form at age 50 or so. If you can't wait that long, save some time by looking first at the occupations that might suit you best. That's why self-awareness is critical; you have to know what you're looking for before you can begin your search. (This would be a good time to review your answers to the exercises in Part I that helped you explore your needs, values, skills, and interests.)

There are lots of ways to begin your occupational research. If there's a subject in school that especially interests you, you could begin by researching occupations related to that subject area. If you come alive in biology class, consider the jobs held by biochemists, anatomists, biological oceanographers, pathologists, ecologists, microbiologists, zoologists, and medical writers. If art is more your thing, look into architecture, commercial art, photography, industrial design, and other occupations that call for artistic ability.

Remember the ways the work world can be organized: by industry, occupational cluster, "people environment," and the "data, people, things" concept. You could also use any one of these categories as a starting point. If a certain people environment appeals to you, investigate occupations related to it. Or if a particular industry interests you, begin there. Turn to the Appendix, Matching Yourself with the World of Work, and read down the lists of occupations. Jot down the ones that appeal to you. Your list will provide a base for beginning research.

Fixing on a starting point will help get you going, but before you begin you need to know

1. What type of information to look for
2. Where to find this information
3. How to evaluate the information you get

And that's what this chapter covers.

One last thing before you start: Don't expect your research to yield one sure-fire answer to all your career questions. Research will

---

Testing

Uncertainty, risks, change, hard work—planning and developing a career involves plenty of these things. It's no wonder many people wish they could somehow bypass the anxiety and effort. If told that vocational counselors can give them tests developed by experts to help them plan their careers, many people believe they've found the magic fulfillment of their wish.

These tests include aptitude tests (which define talents or capacity for learning specific skills), intelligence tests (which measure a person's relative mental capacity), interest tests (which help assess interests), and personality tests (which focus on attitudes and feelings rather than measuring performance).

A test isn't quite a crystal ball, however. No test can tell you what you're "meant" to be. But if you're looking for information or insight to help you plan your career, tests can be helpful. What's more, you *can't* fail them; there are no right or wrong answers, except on intelligence tests. Many factors, though, can affect your score, like how you're feeling on the day of the exam, your attitude toward tests in general, and your educational background.

The tests themselves aren't perfect. Some might contain items that show racial or ethnic bias, asking questions oriented toward one particular culture—a custom, tradition, or piece of literature—rather than something more generally known. (Imagine yourself taking an intelligence test in China and you'll get the picture.) Being a woman might also have an effect. For instance, you may be excellent at math and be told that teaching is for you. But why not engineering or computer programming?

So if you take any vocational guidance tests, do so with a grain of skepticism. Look at the questions and consider also how your answers and scores will be interpreted. Discuss them with someone who thoroughly understands the tests, someone who knows their value as well as their limitations and can help you get the most from them. That "someone" is a trained career counselor or psychologist at a reliable testing service or counseling center.

Your school guidance counselor may be able to tell you more about vocational testing and where to find a good testing service. You might also look in your library for *A Directory of Counseling Services.* This publication is issued annually by the International Association of Counseling Services and describes testing services in each state that have been accredited by the association.

produce *additional information,* both facts and insights. But *you* have to take it from there and put the pieces together. And it's possible that the pieces will fit together in several ways. That's fine. It just means you have several options to choose from.

KNOW WHAT YOU NEED TO KNOW

That may sound contradictory, but it's really not. You have to have a clear idea of the kind of information you'll need *before* you can go out and find it. Here are some of the more important "need to knows":

- *Job title.* Too obvious? Try the next one.

- *Nature of the job.* Translation: What do these workers *really* do? What specific tasks fill their day? What skills do they need to do them? What tools, machines, or materials do they use? Are the tasks varied, or is one repeated over and over? Are the workers closely supervised, or do they work independently? Alone or in a group? What are some typical entry-level, middle-level, and upper-level positions?

- *Education/training.* How do you get to be a full-fledged holder of this job title? Do you need a high school diploma? A college degree? A doctorate? A certificate from a professional school? A license? Must you serve an apprenticeship or go to technical school? Will you earn while you learn? Whether you will or not, what are the costs of preparation, in time as well as in money? Must you pass written or physical exams to qualify? Are there opportunities for on-the-job training? Once a worker is trained and on the job, what about continuing education—in classes or through independent study—to keep up with changes in the field?

- *Pay and benefits.* What will the tangible rewards be? What is the pay range for the occupation? Do workers receive an annual salary, an hourly wage, a wage plus commission? Do earnings vary with geographical area? How great is the variance? What are some of the fringe benefits (such as insurance, pension, tuition reimbursement, vacations)? In general, how rapidly and how much does a worker's pay increase?

- *Personal rewards.* Aside from money, what does the job offer? What you consider a personal reward is tied to your own value system, of course. The chance to spend a lot of time at home is a reward for some people; the chance to travel is a reward for others. Other possible personal rewards include prestige, challenging assignments, interaction with other people, having a great deal of free time, and a star on the dressing-room door.

- *Disadvantages.* Every occupation has its drawbacks. In evaluating an occupation, look at some of the unpleasant duties. Check on whether the work is steady, seasonal, or irregular. Look into health and safety hazards. (Sure, there are federal and state laws designed to eliminate or minimize occupational hazards, but hazards remain. A fire fighter runs more risks than an office worker and so do people who work around machinery, explosives, toxic substances, or radiation.)

- *Related occupations.* Years ago, when the buggy factories shut down, the people who made the upholstery were better able to find work than the people who made the whip sockets. Find out if the skills needed for your planned occupation can be used in a variety of companies or organizations and if they're useful in different occupations. Learning about related occupations—those requiring similar skills or background—gives you more flexibility and can broaden your options if you find yourself dissatisfied or if technology forces you to change occupations. For example, a chemist could consider selling pharmaceutical products, doing public relations work for a chemical manufacturer, or writing technical material or textbooks.

- *Places of employment.* Who hires workers in this occupation? Government agencies? Private businesses? Nonprofit organizations? Will you have to open your own business? Will you work indoors or out? Will there be unusual locations? Will you work in cramped quarters, a noisy factory, a large office? Are most jobs in the field concentrated in urban areas or on farms or in small towns? Are most in a few parts of the country?

- *Employment outlook.* What are your chances of finding a job in this occupation? Are employment prospects improving, declining, or remaining fairly stable? What are the prospects in the places you'd like to live? (As the section below on employment prospects explains, this isn't always predictable; still, you can keep up with current trends and make the best guess possible.)

- *Physical demands.* Are there age, height, weight, or other physical requirements? Do you have to lift, push, or use heavy machinery? Do you have to stand, sit, or bend for long periods? Must you work at high altitudes? Do you have to travel a great deal?

- *Coworkers.* What types of people generally enter this occupation? (If you hate sneaky sorts, you may not wish to get into the covert operations division of the CIA.) Are there males and females in about equal numbers? Will there be a variety of age groups? Will you work mostly with high school graduates, college graduates, technical school graduates, or a mixture? Will you work mostly with others in the same occupation, or will you have frequent contact with persons in different fields?

- *Advancement opportunities.* Does the job offer a chance to take on more and increasingly challenging responsibilities? To learn new skills? To make more money? What are some of the top positions open to a person with basic training in the occupation? Would you need additional education or training to move from entry-level jobs to higher positions?

All that is what you need to know. Acquiring the information may not be easy, but it's not nearly as difficult as the life of a person who gets into the wrong field through ignorance and stays in it through lethargy. And once you make a start, getting the information you need may not be as tough as it seems at first.

And Now for Our Employment Forecast . . .

Employment forecasters aren't like some of the weather forecasters you see on television—daffy "Dr. George" or starry-eyed "Tammy." They're more like the serious government weather statisticians who compile reports, study satellite pictures, and forge a forecast that is broad, complicated, and, frequently, wrong.

Sometimes those predicted upper-level lows turn out to be lower-level highs. Changes in the work world can be just as hard to predict. One reason is that the labor force is composed of a great number and variety of individuals, all of them making individual decisions about their lives and work. And those individuals don't give a hang if their choices follow the forecasters' predictions.

But if you take the forecasts with a grain of skepticism, you can learn to use them as a guide. The projections include which kinds of workers will be in the greatest demand, which industries will offer the best job opportunities, and what earnings might be like a few years ahead.

Employment forecasts are prepared by government agencies, universities, businesses, trade associations, and labor unions, among others. You'll find them in newspapers, in trade journals, on TV news, and in government publications such as the *Occupational Outlook Handbook,* which discusses the employment outlook for more than 200 occupations and trends in basic industries.

The most important thing to remember is that employment forecasts aren't meant to tell you exactly which occupation will be a sure bet for you. You also must take into account your own goals and skills, your ability to acquire training and education, and your pocketbook.

What the forecasts *can* do is give you a broader picture of the world of work. You can find out which fields are likely to grow (or decline), where competition is likely to be stiffest, and what your earnings might be. All these factors can affect your career-related decisions.

Remember to evaluate employment predictions with these things in mind:

- It's important to get the most up-to-date information you can find.

- Know that sources can sometimes be biased. Occasionally, for example, it's in the interest of a labor union or professional association to paint an unfavorable picture of job prospects. The idea is that the fewer workers there are in a field, the less competition there is for jobs and the higher the wages are. Use more than one source.

- Check local and state forecasts as well as national ones. Visit your local state employment office to get information on the job outlook for your area.

- Don't let "supply and demand" estimates overwhelm you. Suppose you read that there will be an oversupply of workers in a field you're very interested in. Well, that's certainly something to consider. But even in a crowded occupation, there's room for someone with talent and top qualifications. And virtually every occupation has to replace workers who leave, retire, or die. If you're thinking about entering a crowded occupation, though, it's wise to have some backup plans.

- Employment forecasts can't measure the intangibles that can act in your favor—things like personal initiative, talent, perseverance, and plain old luck. If you think, realistically, that you've got what it takes to succeed in a particular occupation, that might be the most accurate forecast of all.

SEEK AND YE SHALL FIND

There are three basic ways to learn about an occupation: reading, talking to others, and actually doing the job.

Whether you are interested in animals or animation, forestry or fashion, paleontology or plastic surgery, you can probably find some books, pamphlets, or newspaper or magazine articles that will tell you a good deal about the occupation. Whether you live in a small town or a large city, you have access to all kinds of occupational literature.

The best place to start your search is your high school guidance office. Although the variety of material may be limited in some schools, most counselors have at least a few basic guidebooks, occupational leaflets, and counseling magazines on hand. Some schools also have films, slides, and computerized counseling systems available for student use. Your counselor can probably tell you where to find additional information as well. So be sure to make this office your first stop.

Collections of career-related materials can also be found in public libraries. Some large libraries even have special career centers. The amount of material will vary with the size and budget of the library, but even the smallest library is likely to have a number of the helpful reference books you'll be reading about in this chapter.

You might also find collections of vocational guidance materials in nearby community college counseling centers, the adult continuing education divisions of some colleges and school districts, college libraries, and college placement offices. Local women's groups may have such materials available too. Some of these sources may restrict use of their materials to their own students or members, but give them a call anyway. They may be open to the public.

If you don't find what you need in any of these collections, never fear—there are other sources to mine. You'll just have to do the mining yourself.

The government is a gold mine. All kinds of free or inexpensive materials are available for the asking. And since your tax dollars (or your parents') are paying, you might as well start asking. Many government publications are also available in public libraries. Some of the more pertinent career-related materials are probably in your school's guidance office. Here are some basic publications of the U.S. Department of Labor that all researchers should look at. (None of these are free, and we've mentioned some of them before, but they're worth a reminder.)

1. *Dictionary of Occupational Titles* (DOT) provides definitions of more than 20,000 occupations in the American economy. The definitions include information on the industries in which an occupation is found as well as descriptions of each job's tasks and responsibilities. Moreover, each occupation is coded according to how the worker functions in relation to data, people, and things.

2. *Occupational Outlook Handbook* (OOH) includes descriptions of job duties, education and training requirements, employment outlook, earnings, and working conditions for over 200 occupations. Each description lists other occupa-

tions that require similar abilities, interests, education, and training.

3. *Exploring Careers* is a more general guide that aims to increase students' awareness of the world of work and their own skills, abilities, and interests. It includes narratives of workers in fourteen different occupational clusters, as well as activities and career games to help readers assess their interests and abilities in order to make career choices.

4. *Guide for Occupational Exploration* groups thousands of occupations by interests, abilities, and training required for successful performance.

5. *Occupational Outlook Quarterly* is a magazine that contains up-to-date information on occupations and employment developments. Subjects covered include how to look for a job and how to match personal and job characteristics.

6. *Jobs for Which You Can Qualify If You're a High School Graduate; Jobs for Which You Can Qualify If You're Not a High School Graduate; Jobs for Which You Probably Will Need Some College or Specialized Training; Jobs for Which You Probably Will Need a College Education; Jobs for Which You Can Train Through Apprenticeship.* This series of booklets, available from the Bureau of Labor Statistics and written specifically for young people, explores different careers with informative descriptions and information on educational or training requirements.

The Department of Labor publishes useful leaflets as well, and it has broken down the sections of the OOH into small occupational briefs that may be ordered separately. To find out about the materials that are available, write to the U.S. Department of Labor, Room 1539, GAO Building, 441 G Street, NW, Washington, D.C. 20212.

The Women's Bureau, a separate division of the Department of Labor, publishes material on career opportunities, education and training, women workers, and legislation affecting women—much of it free. For a list of its publications, write for "Leaflet No. 10" to the U.S. Department of Labor, Office of the Secretary, Women's Bureau, 200 Constitution Avenue, NW, Washington, D.C. 20210.

The same materials are also available from regional offices of the Department of Labor and its Women's Bureau. To find the office nearest you, look in the section of the telephone directory devoted to "U.S. Government Offices."

Two warnings: Uncle Sam can be slow about sending out information; rather than waiting several weeks or more for your order to

165

arrive, you'll often do better to get the material from your counselor or library. And government budget cutbacks may reduce the number of occupational advice freebies Uncle offers.

Many corporations and other private businesses publish career guidance and educational material that ranges from brochures on specific occupations to general vocational advice. It is useful to pick a few companies in an industry or field that interests you and ask their public relations department for any career materials or recruiting literature they may have published for the general public. (To get names and addresses, look in your library for such directories as *Standard and Poor's Register of Corporations, Directors and Executives, Foundation Directory, Thomas Register of American Manufacturers,* or the *American Hospital Association Guide to the Health Care Field.*) If you find a particular company especially interesting, ask its public relations department for a copy of the company's annual report, which tells stockholders how good or bad business has been and explains why it will be better next year. You might also ask for copies of any employee magazines or newsletters. Some companies are reluctant to give these materials to outsiders, but if you stress that you are researching career options and are particularly interested in the company you're writing to, you may find your mailbox stuffed with its publications.

Trade associations, professional organizations, and labor unions are also good information sources. And just about every occupation has one of each. Most publish newsletters or journals, and many publish career-related materials, some written specifically for young people. Also check into professional women's organizations.

Names and addresses of associations, organizations, and labor unions can be found in the *Encyclopedia of Associations* or the *National Trade and Professional Associations of the United States.* Check for these reference volumes in your library. In these books you can find addresses of groups ranging from the American Association of Zoo Keepers to the American Association of Women Dentists, from the Vacuum Cleaner Manufacturers Association to the American Association of Owners and Breeders of Peruvian Paso Horses, from Clowns of America to the Solar Energy Institute of North America. There's a place for everyone in this world.

You can also find names of relevant organizations after each entry in the *Occupational Outlook Handbook.*

Many of these organizations publish a magazine or journal, but trade magazines, newspapers, and journals pertaining to specific fields are also published by commercial publishers. These range from *Publishers Weekly* (which covers news of book publishing) to *Variety* (a newspaper that reports on the entertainment world) to *Fishermens News* (the title says it all). Trade publications generally carry in-depth articles, research reports, book reviews, and news of people and trends in an occupational field. Many also contain ads for job openings, and these can give you an idea of types of positions and salary ranges. Some of the material in these journals is technical and specialized, since they're written for people with training and experience in the field, but glancing through the technical articles and reading some of the others can give you a real feeling for what's happening in an occupation.

To find the names of periodicals in your field of interest, consult *Ulrich's International Periodicals Directory* or the *Ayer Directory of Publications* in your local library. Many trade publications can be found in libraries or at newsstands.

No doubt about it, careers are a hot topic these days. Many general-circulation magazines and newspapers run regular features on career-related topics. Subjects can range from job interview tips to sexual harassment in the workplace to interviews with working women. Many "women's" magazines are now specifically geared to working women. Some magazines you might look at include *Savvy, Working Woman, Ms., Self, Glamour, Mademoiselle, Seventeen,* and *Essence. Money* magazine also contains career-related articles fairly regularly. You can find these publications at newsstands or libraries.

Your local newspaper probably runs career features as well. (If not, maybe it's time you wrote a letter to the editor.) One national newspaper you should be familiar with, especially if you're considering the business world, is the *Wall Street Journal.* The *Journal* is much more than a list of stock market prices. It summarizes general news, offers some distinguished investigative reporting, provides news of current economic trends, and reports on the work world in general. Other business publications that can be good research tools include *Fortune, Forbes,* and *Business Week.*

Commercial publishers haven't ignored the subject of careers, which ranks not far behind astrology and dieting as a subject of general appeal. Check your library's card catalog—and if necessary, the librarian—for books on specific occupations, career planning, and job hunting. You should also find in your bookstore or library some recent books dealing specifically with career concerns of working women.

Want to do a little more reading? If you're a glutton for information, your local Chamber of Commerce can bring you up to date on business, economic, and employment trends in your community. Call and inquire about their literature; they'll be in the phone book.

Speaking of phone books, the Yellow Pages can be useful for more than just looking up phone numbers. By glancing through the Yellow Pages, you can get an idea of the many different varieties of businesses, industries, and employers in a given area—an indication of the types of employment opportunities available. And, as you'll see later on, the Yellow Pages are also a handy tool for getting the names of people working in different occupations.

Another way to research occupations is by reading want ads. By studying ads for both entry-level and experienced personnel, you'll get a general idea of salary ranges in an occupation, the skills employers are looking for, the responsibilities different jobs entail, and even the kinds of occupations in demand in a given area. For instance, if your local paper advertises fifty job openings for engineers and only one for a graphic artist, then an engineer would be much more likely to land a job in your area than would a graphic artist.

Finally, by reading biographies and autobiographies of well-known people who've worked in various fields, you can visualize what a lifetime spent in an occupation might be like. These books can be informative and pleasurable reading, but be careful when it comes to using them as occupational research tools. Most are about "superstars," those who have experienced exceptional success—monetary or otherwise—in their careers. But few people rise to the pinnacle of any profession. (In other words, don't fall into the trap of measuring yourself against everyone else or expect that your career will be like Madame Curie's or Barbra Streisand's.) Keeping this in mind, turn to page 124 for suggestions of books to read.

Reading occupational literature is a good way to find out about different jobs, but it shouldn't be your only source of information. For one thing, print materials can become dated rather quickly. For another, it just isn't possible to cover all the variables in working conditions, pay, and responsibilities within each occupation. That's why you'll find that in a lot of literature (including this book), many qualifiers are inserted. For instance, you'll read that a worker "generally" performs a certain duty, or "often" or "usually" possesses certain qualifications or characteristics. Working conditions in an occupation can vary greatly from one employer to another or from one geographical area to another. So written information about occupations must be fairly general.

This inherent limitation can result in your getting a very broad and sometimes superficial view of an occupation. It's like looking at a painting when only the preliminary brushstrokes have been sketched in. You can get an idea of what the artist is trying to do, but you're missing the details. When you read about an occupation, you see only the preliminary brushstrokes. You must fill in the details yourself.

GETTING IT FROM THE SOURCE'S MOUTH

One of the best ways to get the details is to talk to people who are working in the field. It's like being a reporter, because you have to interview one or more "sources" to make sure you get the information you need—and to check the views of different people against each other. You don't end up with a newspaper article, but you do get a clearer picture of what an occupation is really like.

Not only does this research technique give you something close to an insider's view, it also provides some side benefits: you get used to meeting people, you acquire some interviewing skills (they will come in handy when you're the one being interviewed by a prospective employer or a school admissions officer), and you may even become friendly with someone who can help you find a job someday.

Don't start cold, though, or things may get even chillier. Prepare for the interviews carefully and systematically. Start by doing as much preliminary library research as possible. Interviewing should be a supplement to that research, not a substitute for it. Don't waste time by asking for information that can be found in publications like the *Occupational Outlook Handbook.* People are flattered by a genuine interest in them and their work, but if you ask too many elementary or general questions, the interviewee is likely to suspect your interest is shallow or nonexistent. A doctor, for example, will open up and talk more—and provide more useful information—if, instead of asking how long it takes to get through medical school, you ask, "What pressures do students in medical school experience?"

After you've done the preliminary research, you must come up with a list of people to interview. Easy—just ask around. Start with your family. Then go to neighbors, friends, friends' parents, teachers, and guidance counselors. Any of them might know people who work in an occupation that interests you. So might your yoga instructor, your track coach, you violin teacher, your dentist, or the people at your church or synagogue. When asking for names of "contacts," stress that you're doing career research, are enthusiastic about a particular occupation, and want to learn more. It's a good idea, too, to ask if you can use the name of the person who suggested a "contact" when you introduce yourself.

But if you want to talk to geophysicists and your mother, your aunt, and the corner grocer all give you a blank look when you ask for help in finding some, don't give up. Reference librarians can help in such a crisis. And if you're looking for jewelers or French horn players or printers, there are lots of ways to find them:

- Read local newspapers and magazines to get names of nearby business owners, tradespeople, and professionals.
- Check with college or university public information offices.
- Let your fingers do the referring. If you're interested in photography, for example, look up "photographers" in the Yellow Pages and pick out a few names.
- Write or call a professional organization or union (if the occupation you're researching has one), and ask to be referred to local people.
- Call local women's organizations for names of women employed in fields you're researching.
- Community service organizations such as the Rotary Club, Kiwanis, Lions, Business and Professional Women, veterans' groups, and the local Chamber of Commerce may help.

Don't be intimidated by the prospect of talking to all these strangers. You may suspect that "busy" or "important" people will not have the time or desire to talk to you, but you will be surprised to discover how many are flattered by the chance to expound at length on a subject that fascinates them: themselves and their work. If one or two give you a fast brush-off, move on to the next person on the list. You may have found someone who's having an especially busy or awful day. You may have found a grouch. You can be sure other people will be willing to share time and information if you just take the initiative and ask.

When you go to the interview, let the person talk as much as she or he wishes—don't take it upon yourself to draw out the interview too long. A busy person, especially one giving you part of a workday, will appreciate a respectful approach that doesn't waste time. Here are some guidelines to help in conducting an interview in a professional manner.

Write or call to arrange the interview at least a week ahead of time. Identify yourself and clearly state the nature of your research. Make sure people understand that you want information and not a job; it may mean the difference between being treated as "The Future of the Nation" or a nuisance. Tell the person the approximate time you'll need. (A half hour is a pretty safe estimate; some may give you more time, but others may balk at spending more than 15 minutes.)

Whatever you ask, take what you're given without argument. Try to set up the meeting at your contact's workplace and during the workday so you can get a clearer picture of the occupation. But if that's not possible, arrange the interview at a time and place that are mutually convenient. If you're worried about getting tongue-tied in the telephone conversation requesting the interview, write out your "speech" in advance and rehearse it with friends or family.

Arrive for the interview on time and dressed appropriately. A skirt and blouse are usually a good bet. If you're going to be late (and you shouldn't be for any reason short of a natural disaster), call as soon as possible and explain. If the person you'll be interviewing wishes to reschedule the interview, agree.

Always address the person by title and surname unless told otherwise (Ms. Brown, Mr. Jones, Dr. Smith). In the course of a conversation you can call a doctor "Doctor" (but not "Doc"). When you meet, take the initiative and shake hands. When you're invited to sit, do so.

Take a small notebook and pencil; you can't expect to remember everything you're told.

Be aware of your body language. If you're nervous, take a few deep breaths before the interview begins. Don't hum, chew gum, or smoke, even if the person you interview does all three. Don't wear dark sunglasses; most people like to make eye contact (but don't get into a who'll-blink-first contest). Don't slump, fidget, or fiddle with notebook, hair, or earrings. Don't worry about all this advice, either. Relax.

Prepare a list of questions for the interview. The more, the better. You aren't obligated to ask them all, but if your mind goes blank during the interview you can throw Number 39 at Ms. Brown and she'll never know that you've forgotten your own name. If your mind has never been known to go blank, prepare the questions anyway. They'll be a useful guide for the interview. Put a check by the most important questions and ask those first. Other questions are likely to be answered without your having to ask them, but if they haven't been and time allows, you'll have them there to ask. Also, what Ms. Brown says is likely to suggest questions you didn't think of in advance.

Try to draw out your subject. Your aim is to get as much information as possible. If you find that someone constantly answers only "yes" or "no," ask, "Why?" Or say, "Can you give me an example?" Or, "In your opinion, why is this so?" Look over your list of questions and give preference to ones that can't be answered yes or no, or try to phrase them so they elicit more information. "What do you like about your work?" is a better question than, "Do you like your work?"; "What do you think are the most important personality traits for someone interested in engineering?" is a better question than, "Are you glad you became an engineer?"

Be a good listener. It's natural to worry about what you're going to ask next, but don't let that worry cause you to miss the answer to the question you've just asked. And don't worry about asking dumb questions or, conversely, about impressing the person you're interviewing with the depth of your knowledge. Your goal is to learn more, and all you need impress your subject with is your desire to learn. If a point needs clarification, incidentally, it's a good idea to underline it as you jot it down. Then when the person has finished answering the question, you can ask about whatever was unclear. But try not to interrupt.

When do you end the interview? Take your cue from the person you're interviewing. Be alert for glances at a clock or watch or for signs of impatience or fatigue. Don't overstay your welcome.

Ask for names of other contacts before you go. You may get names of people who can provide a quite different viewpoint or a great deal more information.

Always write a thank-you letter promptly after the interview, and tell the contact how the conversation has helped you. If you meet with someone who has been especially helpful and supportive, you might wish to keep that person informed of your progress. (You never know what may come of it in the future—maybe a job.)

Finally, just as a journalist avoids a one-sided story, you shouldn't form a one-interview opinion. Talk to several people—men and women, old and young—to get an accurate picture of an occupation.

Now that you know *how* to do the interviews, exactly *what* do you ask? That depends on what you want to know. Word your questions carefully. You'll get more information if you break up very long questions into shorter ones. Here are some sample questions:

1. How did you get started in the field?
2. What kinds of interests do you have? Did your interests help you decide what occupation might be best for you?
3. What school subjects do you use in your work, and how?
4. What would you recommend in education, work experience, and internship programs?
5. What is a typical workday like for you?
6. What do you like most about your job? Least?

7. What pay range and benefits can one expect in this occupation? (Note: *Never* ask a person how much money he or she makes. It's rude. Anyway, salaries can vary considerably from employer to employer. Always ask for a general salary range in the occupation. If your contacts decide to volunteer information about their salaries, that's fine; but never ask.)

8. What personal traits do you think are required in your occupation?

9. With your present skills and background, what other jobs could you pursue if you wanted to make a change within your field?

10. Could you use the knowledge and training you've acquired in another occupational field?

11. If you were starting all over to launch your career today, what steps would you take? (Or would you pick a different occupation? Why?)

12. Would you say that your field is a growing one or a closing one? What explains that? Do you think that new technology or social developments could dramatically change the field in the near future? (What ones do you have in mind? What will the changes be? How will career possibilities in this field be affected?)

13. Are there any other people you know of in the field who you'd suggest I might talk with about it?

Don't limit yourself to this list of questions or ask them in exactly this way. Divide your list into two groups. In the first group, place the most important questions; put in the second group the questions you'll ask if you have time. And keep in mind that you want the people to provide information but not to make your decisions for you. So there's not much point in asking, "Should I be a carpenter (or auto mechanic or lawyer or nurse)?" That's a question that, finally, only you can answer.

TRY IT ON FOR SIZE

If you want to know what a chocolate mousse tastes like, you can read about it in *Gourmet* magazine. You can talk to people who have eaten one. You can taste one yourself. All three approaches would give you some idea of what chocolate mousse tastes like. But which do you think would give you the best idea? (And which is the most fun?)

The same principle applies, just as richly, in learning about occupations. Library research and talking to people add to your storehouse of occupational knowledge, but if you really want to know what an occupation is like, you must heed the call of the wild mousse and taste it. You can do that in cooperative education programs, internship programs, or volunteer programs.

In many colleges and some high schools, there is a growing trend toward providing a more comprehensive, career-oriented educational program that combines on-the-job work experience with traditional classwork. These programs, usually referred to as *cooperative education*, give a student the opportunity to learn about an occupation, earn money, *and* take related courses in school. Co-op education programs are usually coordinated by teachers who work with both students and the participating employers.

How does co-op ed work? Suppose you're interested in a career in journalism. You might be assigned to work part-time as a copyperson (known in the old, more sexist days as a "copyboy") for a local newspaper while you take journalism courses. If science is your interest, you might work part-time as a laboratory assistant while continuing your science studies in school. In co-op ed, the learning process is based on a strong interaction between the school world and the work world. (See page 221 for more on co-op education.)

Internships are not necessarily tied into a formal course of study, although they may be. Many schools offer internship programs, but students may also be able to arrange their own internship. An internship (sometimes called "experiential education") is a formal opportunity offered by an employer to students desiring experience in an occupation or with a particular organization. Just about any internship will give a useful taste of life in that corner of the work world, but some employers are far more serious than others about making sure that interns get a well-organized look at a possible occupation. (As a journalism intern, you might spend most of your time sharpening pencils and delivering coffee at one newspaper; at another paper, the interns may be encouraged to help with research, to write stories, to cover meetings at the side of skilled reporters, and to serve a stint working with wire service stories and writing headlines.) High school or college credit may go with the internship, but the experience—even in the worst internship—is worth more than the credits.

Few internships are open to high school students or even to college freshmen. But a multitude of *volunteer* positions can be taken by students of high school age. Actually, there is a pretty fine line between internships and volunteer programs. Volunteerism can take the form of participating in a formal program run by a social service agency, for example, or it may be just an informal arrangement for after-school help by a student interested in a particular organization or cause. The difference between interning and volunteering is often not in responsibility but in pay or credits. Interns usually receive academic credit, and they may also receive a stipend or salary. Volunteers aren't paid, but the nonmonetary rewards can be considerable.

Internships and volunteering also differ in that internships are specifically designed to educate while volunteer work is not. A volunteer is expected to donate labor for the good of the organization, not for the good of the volunteer. But just as the educational needs of interns are sometimes ignored by employers, so some volunteer work turns out to be highly educational. Volunteers may do more filing or envelope stuffing than interns, but that won't necessarily be the case. Different volunteer opportunities vary in the amount of structure, supervision, and responsibility they have—and they can be just as educational and rewarding as a formal internship or co-op program.

As an intern, volunteer, or co-op ed student, you'll have a chance —in addition to whatever good works may be involved—to

- Experience the fun, the "glamorous" side of the job—and its daily drudgery
- Gain work experience that demonstrates your motivation and initiative to possible employers
- See which subjects in school or college may be especially relevant and plan your course schedule accordingly
- Learn skills you might not acquire in school or in other activities
- Be exposed to a range of human experiences beyond those available in a classroom
- See how people behave and dress on the job
- Test, define, or focus in on your occupational options, interests, skills, and talents

What kinds of things could you do as a volunteer or an intern? You could visit young patients in a hospital, conduct tours at a museum, cover news stories for your local paper, help conservation efforts in a national park, campaign for a state or local politician, write press releases for a community dance company, teach a craft or read to an elderly person, work with people who have physical disabilities, help out in a crisis intervention center—you name it!

Are you ready to try the work world for yourself? The place to begin your search for a co-op ed program, internship, or volunteer position is in your guidance counselor's office. There you can find out if your school has any formal programs, and your counselor might also be able to tell you about other internship and volunteer opportunities in your community.

Local libraries also sometimes maintain listings of volunteer opportunities or can tell you how to find a volunteer assignment in your community. In addition, some professional associations publish directories of volunteer and internship programs in their fields. Write to an organization in a field that attracts you and ask for information. There are also several good directories that you can look for in your library. Or you might want to get in touch with the National Society for Internships and Experiential Education (124 St. Mary's Street, Raleigh, N.C. 27605). This organization exists to promote internships as a means of education and publishes several directories that might help you locate an internship.

Volunteer opportunities can be found in any community in the country. Hospitals, local government agencies, and public welfare organizations offer the most conspicuous opportunities, but there are others.

ACTION, an agency headquartered in Washington, D.C., sponsors many volunteer programs around the country and the world. The best-known are the Peace Corps and VISTA, but you have to be over 18 for these, and they require full-time commitment for one or two years.

Volunteer opportunities need be limited only by your own imagination and willingness to help others, however. You might wish to get in touch with ACTION's National Student Volunteer Program. It helps high school and college students set up volunteer activities in their own communities and acts as a liaison between young volunteers and causes in need of their services. You can find out more about these programs by writing to ACTION, Room P-314, 806 Connecticut Avenue, NW, Washington, D.C. 20009. (You can also call a toll-free number for general information on ACTION programs: 800-424-8580.) ACTION puts out a handy booklet called "High School Student Volunteers." It covers all the hows and whys of volunteering, and it's available for a small price from the Superintendent of Documents, U.S. Government Printing Office, Washington, D.C. 20402.

Other national organizations you could write to for additional information on volunteering and volunteer opportunities in your area include

American Red Cross
17th and D Streets, NW
Washington, D.C. 20006

VOLUNTEER: The National Center for Citizen Involvement
P.O. Box 4179
Boulder, Colo. 80306

Volunteers of America
National Headquarters
3813 North Causeway Boulevard
Metairie, La. 70002

If you don't find a formal volunteer or internship program that suits you, create your own! Here are a few ideas:

- Ask family, friends, and your parents' business associates for names of other people you might talk to about volunteering or interning.

- Look around your community and make a list of groups and community service agencies that work with problems and issues that concern you. Call or visit them and see how you can help.

- Read your local paper to see who's running for legislative office and what the important issues are. Pick a candidate you respect and visit campaign headquarters. Find out what kinds of help the candidate needs and then figure out how you could put your talents to use. Don't expect to be asked to write campaign speeches or plan rallies on your first visit. You're more likely to be asked to type labels or stuff envelopes with brochures. But political campaigns are chronically under-staffed and often underfinanced. Your best talents are likely to be put to use eventually if you prove to be a sincere and willing worker at the more mundane tasks.

- Pick a few local businesses you'd like to learn more about. Call or write. Explain briefly what you're trying to do. Say why you're especially interested in working there. Employers are rarely offered free labor; one might jump at the chance to get some. If you'd like to learn the ins and outs of retailing, volunteer to work at a small shop. If you dream of becoming a professional cook, set up an informal internship with a chef in a nearby restaurant.

Whether you work as a volunteer or participate in a formal internship program, the quality of the experience will depend in great part upon what you put into it. The more clearly you know your own goals, the more worthwhile the experience will be.

So, when you're shopping around for an internship or a volunteer position, ask yourself questions like these: What do I hope to gain from the experience? What do I like to do? What skills do I want to learn? How will this internship or volunteer position benefit me? How much time can I devote to it? (Some internship and volunteer programs stipulate a specific time commitment—so many hours a week, perhaps, or full-time for a semester—while others leave the time spent entirely up to the participant; it's important to decide *in advance* how much time you can give and how much you wish to give.)

One recent trend is the drawing up of a formal agreement between the interns or volunteers and the organization they work for. These agreements typically state

- The objectives of the internship/volunteer program (for both the employer and the participant)
- The duration of the service/work schedule
- The on-the-job responsibilities of the intern/volunteer
- The class credit, if any, to be granted
- The stipend or salary, if any, to be paid

Drawing an agreement ensures that both sides are clear about their goals and expectations. The employer knows what you expect to get out of the experience, and you know exactly what the employer expects of you.

Internships and volunteer positions should not be taken lightly. You will be expected to conduct yourself like a professional and to make a strong commitment to your work. In other words, treat it as if it were a salaried position. Here are some tips on being a good intern or volunteer:

- Be reliable and punctual.
- Notify your supervisor if you are unable to work as scheduled.
- Dress properly.
- Recognize your own limitations. You probably won't be assigned a lot of the work done by salaried employees simply because you lack the training and credentials. (If you're a hospital volunteer, don't expect to do brain surgery!) Both you and the employer should be clear ahead of time on what you can and will be allowed to do.
- Prove your ability to handle assigned tasks before asking for greater responsibility. (After a while, however, if you find yourself stuck with what you consider only "lowly" tasks, have a talk with your supervisor. Explain the problem and discuss other ways you could put your talents to work in the organization.)

- Finally, get all the experience you can by asking questions, contributing ideas, and generally taking an active interest in your work.

It's possible that after your internship or volunteer experience, you'll be positive that this is the type of work you would like to do. That's great! It's also possible you'll decide that you want to do a different type of work. And that's fine too. After all, not everybody likes chocolate mousse.

A POTPOURRI OF WAYS AND MEANS

Reading. Talking. Doing. Those are excellent ways to find out about different occupations. If you use your imagination, you can probably think of quite a few more. Here are some additional suggestions.

- *Take a tour.* No, not of the Caribbean. Arrange to take a tour through a business, newspaper office, or manufacturing plant. Some employers regularly conduct tours for "interested by-standers" and others will let you visit if accompanied by a company representative. Some schools can arrange "class" trips for students to make on-site visits. You could also arrange for tours on your own. (Get together with a group of interested friends and write or call a company's public relations department. Explain that you're in the process of exploring career options and would welcome an opportunity to see workers "in action.")
- *Visit colleges, technical schools, or other educational institutions* that offer courses or programs in fields that interest you. Many schools permit outsiders to visit classes with the permission of the instructors. Although you might not understand everything that's going on, a class visit gives you a general picture. Such a visit will also give you an opportunity to talk with students about their own career plans and about how they chose their school.
- *Volunteer to work in the guidance office of your high school.* A harried guidance counselor might welcome help with gathering and filing career brochures—and you'll get first crack at the latest stuff. You'll also benefit from the work experience.
- *Talk to retired people in your community.* Older people can be living career encyclopedias. Mr. Higgins down the block might have thirty-five years as an engineer under his belt and be delighted to tell you what they were like. It's possible he may talk more candidly than persons now in the field about

179

the obstacles he faced, about the obstacles women face, and about career possibilities in the field. While there may have been numerous changes in the field since he retired, he may have kept up with many or all of them. Even if he hasn't, you can benefit from his experience and advice. Give him a try.

- *Go to summer school.* Summer school isn't just for making up bad grades. It's also an ideal time to explore interests and learn skills as you take courses you can't fit into your regular school schedule, like public speaking, chemistry, typing, and ceramics. Some colleges also allow high school students to attend summer classes. Write to nearby colleges or universities for information.

- *Do some temporary work during the summer.* Check with a local employment agency that specializes in temporary work assignments. If you can type or handle phone work, you can work as a "temp" in various offices. You'll be earning money while you get an inside view of different work environments.

- *Do an independent study project for school.* For instance, you could prepare reports on topics such as how job opportunities for women have changed since World War II, discuss the arguments for and against affirmative action, or write profiles of people you interview who work in various fields. Perhaps your school paper would be interested in publishing your reports in upcoming issues.

- *Join a club.* Many schools offer a variety of extracurricular activities and clubs. Some clubs (math and science clubs, for example) are closely related to vocational interests. Some schools also sponsor local chapters of national clubs for high school students, and some of these can provide a great opportunity for career exploration. If agriculture is one of your interests, consider joining a 4-H Club or the Future Farmers of America. If business is your bag, why not join Future Business Leaders of America or Junior Achievement? For students interested in engineering, science, or technology-related occupations, a club called JETS (Junior Engineering Technical Society) might be just the thing.

  Many other clubs that are not so strictly vocational in nature—Girl Scouts and Girls Clubs, for example—often have their own career awareness programs and activities. But even if you join a club that's strictly for fun, the experience can have long-term advantages for your career.

  In a vocational club, you might become acquainted with people working in the field, receive assistance in appraising your interests and abilities, and maybe even get some "hands-on" experience at working in an occupation. But in any club, you can develop some important life skills as you learn to work harmoniously with others. Club activities also give you the opportunity of seeing projects through to completion and of learning the responsibilities of contributing to and conducting meetings.

Stop by your school's guidance office to see what clubs your school has. You can find the names of other clubs by looking in the *Encyclopedia of Associations* in your library. If your school or town doesn't have a local chapter of a club you'd like to join, write to the national headquarters. Many clubs will send you a "starter kit" and help you organize your own chapter.

There are other ways to explore career options. Here are some activities that you and your classmates can do for a career unit in school, as a special project in a general-interest club, or on your own:

- Ask professional women's groups if some of their members would give talks about promising job opportunities for women.
- Set up a referral service between students who want to do volunteer work and agencies in the community that need volunteer workers.
- Arrange trips to local businesses, manufacturing plants, or newspapers to see how they operate.
- With the cooperation of your librarian, arrange a special "career information" session to acquaint class or club members with career guidance and reference materials available in the library.
- Compile a list of professional organizations in various occupations that students can get in touch with for career information.
- Compile a list of standard reference books useful to career researchers. (You could start with the ones mentioned in this book.)
- Arrange an educational fair. Invite representatives from local colleges, universities, trade and technical schools, and the military to come and discuss training and admissions policies.
- Conduct mock information interviews to practice interviewing techniques.
- Hold a career film festival.
- Visit a local union to see how it operates.
- Begin your own career information "library" by collecting free materials available from the government, trade and professional associations, labor unions, etc.

- Make a list of your hobbies and your friends' and think about ways to get paid for doing them. For instance, someone who really loves to paint and hang wallpaper might start up a small neighborhood decorating service. Someone who loves to do graphic design might design personalized party invitations and greeting cards for clients. See how many of those "just for fun" activities can be turned into possible future jobs.

- Arrange a monthly or weekly bulletin board display of notable American women in various fields.

- Hold a résumé-writing workshop. Invite several local employers to come and discuss what impresses them about some résumés.

- Conduct a survey and compile a list of employers in your community who are interested in hiring high school graduates for entry-level jobs.

- Organize a career day and invite representatives from several different local industries to come and speak. They may be able to bring movies or filmstrips to show or informative materials to hand out.

MAKING SENSE OF IT ALL

Any one or several of the research techniques we've discussed in this chapter can yield a lot of information about an occupation. But as you gather more and more information, you might find yourself in something of a predicament. Some of the information might be contradictory, some might seem wrong, and some might sound totally outdated. The work world changes so fast and so frequently that occupational information is especially prone to mistakes and inaccuracies. That goes for information from both print and "live" sources. So how do you know what to believe? How do you reconcile seemingly contradictory statements about an occupation?

In researching occupations, you have to learn to be a critical consumer. Whether you are consulting written material or people, there are four questions you should ask yourself when evaluating the information you get:

- Is it accurate?
- Is it thorough?
- Is it up-to-date?
- Is it biased?

Accuracy. The best way to ensure accuracy is to check and double-check, and that means consulting more than one person or publication. If you're in doubt about something you've read or heard, look it up somewhere else or ask someone else. The more sources you consult, the more likely you are to arrive at the truth. Also check the qualifications of the writer or speaker. What makes this person an expert on this occupation?

Thoroughness. Does the information contain specific, solid facts about an occupation? Does it say earnings are "good," for example, or does it give actual figures? What about nonmonetary aspects—workers' life-styles, their sense of accomplishment, the importance of the work to society? Are the negative aspects of an occupation discussed as well as the positive ones? You can check any information you gather against the occupational checklist in this chapter (see the next page for an explanation).

Currency. Because technological and social change can come swiftly, printed information about occupations tends to be outdated quickly. Between the time information is gathered and the time it is published in a magazine article or book, a month to a year may elapse. Check the publication date of any printed source that you consult, and try to get the most recent material available. Published salary figures are especially questionable, since the amount workers earn in any occupation is continually fluctuating. Interviews with persons working in the field are often the best source of salary information. Generally speaking, if the material is more than five years old, then its information on employment outlook, earnings, and training requirements may be obsolete.

Bias. This can be the hardest to detect because it can be very subtle. In evaluating printed material, ask youself why it was written. Was it intended to recruit workers into an occupation, for example? Was it written to persuade students to undergo a certain kind of training? Often the identity of the publisher provides a clue. Company recruiting brochures, materials published by trade associations and labor unions, and technical and vocational school publications may be designed to sell people on a particular occupation or type of training. They might present only the most favorable aspects without discussing the drawbacks. Even a good department in a respectable university may not be above issuing a brochure that colors the prospects its graduates will enjoy. It's not so much that all these publications lie as that they don't tell the whole truth. Be vigilant.

Occupational literature can be sexually biased as well. Be skeptical of any material that presents people in stereotypical roles based on age, sex, color, or other arbitrary categories. You might, for example, find a brochure on health-related occupations that presents women only as nurses, men only as doctors, and minorities only as orderlies. If you do, don't let it limit your options or your thinking, but *do* point it out to the librarian or counselor you got it from.

Printed information isn't the only source that can be biased. The people you interview can have a slanted perspective. Each person will give you information based on personal experiences and opinions, and the information will probably vary depending on such factors as age, temperament, and sense of satisfaction. If you interview a young person who is fairly new to an occupation, you might get a report of unlimited opportunities. A veteran who has weathered a few storms might paint a picture with a few clouds. A person who hasn't been as successful as he or she wishes might discourage you because of his or her own dissatisfaction. People's views of an occupation can also differ depending on where they are employed. A lawyer in a small town may be discouraged by a relatively modest income—or exhilarated by the opportunity to handle all kinds of cases, from writing contracts to defending persons charged with crimes to representing victims of negligently manufactured products. A lawyer in a large city may enjoy a large income, and that enjoyment may be reflected in the conversation you have—but he or she may also be disturbed by the pressure of work in a large firm or may resent the specialization forced on the firm's lawyers.

So one source is never enough. Occupational information is gathered, analyzed, written, and spoken by mere mortals—all of whom perceive subjects in different ways, and all of whom are occasionally guilty of distorting pictures of reality.

FINALLY ...

You can start your own occupational file for occupations that appeal to you and that you research. Include magazine articles, newspaper clippings, pamphlets, and notes from information interviews. To improve your chances of having all the basic facts, fill out an Occupation Fact Sheet for each occupation you research. There's a sample one in this section that you could photocopy or adapt to suit your own needs.

Getting good information about occupations requires plenty of concentrated digging. But it can be fun, and it provides an opportunity to make friends and discover more about the multifaceted world both inside you and outside you.

Occupation Fact Sheet

Job Title: _____

Industry(-ies)*: _____
_____

Occupational Cluster*: _____

Data/People/Things Relationship*: _____
_____

People Environment*: _____

Nature of the Job: _____
_____
_____

Education/Training: _____
_____

Pay and Benefits: _____
_____

Personal Rewards: _____
_____

Disadvantages: _____
_____
_____

Related Occupations: _____
_____

Places of Employment: _____
_____

Employment Outlook: _____
_____

Physical Demands: _____
_____

Coworkers: _____

Advancement Opportunities: _____
_____

Your Sources (publications you've consulted; names and addresses
of people or organizations you've written to or interviewed for information): _____
_____
_____
_____

*See Chapter 9 for explanation.

WORKING WOMAN

Nancy Heinaman

Bank Titling Secretary and Receptionist

Banks can be an entrancing place for a child, with the cool marble, the pens with curly cords, the pads of deposit slips, the ashtray sand, the vaults and chambers.

"And the lollipop when you leave!" laughs Nancy Heinaman, who grew up to fulfill her childhood fantasy of working in a bank. Now she's the one handing out the lollipops in her position as a titling secretary and receptionist for the loan department in a Billings, Montana, bank.

After graduation from high school in a small town near Billings, Nancy enrolled at a business college in Great Falls, about 200 miles away. She took regular business classes during the day—secretarial, math, accounting, and English—and also managed three nights a week of airline and travel course work.

"I was 18, and I thought a career with the airlines would be really exciting and mean a lot of travel," she says. "I chose the Great Falls Commercial College because it was small, only 300 students, just far enough away from home, and offered the airline program. I wasn't interested in attending a big university.

"After graduation a year later, I discovered that the airline job market was really tight. It was very disappointing; the few people they did hire were older and experienced."

Nancy got married the summer of her graduation. She went with her husband to Helena for six months while he finished at a trade school. Then they found themselves back in Billings, diplomas in hand, and no jobs in sight.

"We were desperate," she recalls. "I signed up with the state job service. I had to take lots of tests for different secretarial positions. Fortunately, my business classes gave me good training. I checked back daily. Finally, they called to tell me about this job at a bank. As a kid I had always wanted to work in a bank. I got the job six years ago, and I'm still there and still happy about it."

Nancy says she finds her job interesting because of the people she works with and the people she meets.

"Although we have our dull days, especially in winter, it's pretty exciting normally," she says. "You really see extremes in human behavior when you work in a loan department. People are often at their very nicest—if they need a loan. Or at their very worst—if they can't talk you out of repossessing their car.

"Sometimes the place is a madhouse, with the phone ringing and people showing up at my desk who want to tell me their life stories while my work stacks up. In a job like this, it's very important to be able to work well despite a lot of interruptions. It's stressful.

" 'Feast or famine' is another factor. Days can go by with nothing happening; other weeks there'll be a holiday and we'll have to do five days' work in four."

Her duties fall into two sections: titling and being a receptionist.

"In my role as titling secretary, I make sure that people who have car loans with the bank follow through and show the bank as lien holder on their papers," she explains. "I check serial numbers and license numbers and make sure they match up. If someone defaults on a loan, I order the repossession title for the bank.

"Meantime, I'm also the receptionist for the 14 members of the loan department. I'm the first person people see when they come in, then I route them to the appropriate person. I also answer two phone lines—and that's a job in itself!"

During the slower winter months, Nancy's bank has a practice of "cross-training" employees, who try out another "desk," or job, for a month.

"Among the jobs in my department are setting interest rates, deciding if a loan will be granted, dictating letters about delinquent payments, doing computer work, and organizing insurance coverage," Nancy explains. "Cross-training gives you a taste of what these other jobs are like. After a month with the computer, for example, I learned that I found that work very frustrating."

In the past, she recalls, the supervisors were always men. That's begun to change in the half dozen years she has worked at the bank.

"Our bank is funny," she comments. "They tend to bring in outsiders rather than promote from within. But they're trying to do better. Out of the blue, for example, I was offered a promotion when a job opened up in another department. It made me feel good that they singled me out, but I turned it down because the work didn't interest me."

At 26, Nancy says she's planning to stay at her bank, but eventually she'd like to move to another position in the loan department. She's analyzed her own interests and abilities to help her determine what a new job should involve.

"I know that I don't like working with figures," she says. "I much prefer the secretarial end. But I *really* enjoy the people here. We're a unit; we pitch in and help each other, and we like each other."

Drawing submitted by Rochelle Ritchie, 17; Bothell, Washington
Catalyst Cartoon Competition Winner

WHEN SHE WAS YOUNG

Hannah Senesh

Hannah Senesh was born in Hungary in 1921. At the age of 18, she left Europe to live in Palestine. She returned in 1944 as a member of a unit of specially trained Palestinian Jews intent on rescuing Hungarian Jews from Hitler's forces. Captured and tortured by the Nazis, Hannah refused to reveal any information and was killed by a firing squad.

As a young girl, Hannah kept a diary. In these excerpts, she muses about her dreams of a future career as a writer.

June 15, 1936

I have had such strange thoughts lately. I would like to be a writer. For the time being I just laugh at myself; I've no idea whether I have any talent. I've been inspired by the success of *Bella Gerant*—everyone likes it. But even so, I don't think I would write plays. I would rather write novels.

August 3, 1936

I still long to be a writer. It's my constant wish. I don't know whether it's simply a desire for praise and fame, but I do know it is such a marvellous feeling to write something well that I think it is worth struggling to become a writer. . . .

July 14, 1938

Mother wrote to say that she showed some of my poems to Alkalay, a journalist and translator, and that he was surprised and favourably impressed by them. I'll hear all the particulars when I get home. He mentioned someone to whom I could take the poems, and I shall do so. I now need honest and serious criticism, not just the praise of family and close friends.

I feel that writing isn't difficult for me, and if something turns out well it gives one such a great feeling. The other day, in a weak moment, I recited for Lisbeth the farewell poem I wrote for George. I think it's good because of its simplicity and informality. Whereupon she remarked how nice it is when a person can write a poem when he wants to, and she wrote her last poem when she was twelve, but since then hasn't felt like writing poems. I could have used greater discrimination in my choice of audience, but sometimes the overwhelming need to share and confide gets the best of one.

Trying Writing

"Hello, I'm calling from the campus newspaper and I would
    like to... Excuse me?... Yes, I'll hold."
This week I'm assigned another boring story.
My beat has no news for me today.
I'm transferred and put on hold endlessly.
My sources send me to more sources.
I sit for hours in the lobby waiting for an interview;
An afternoon wait is ended with an "I don't have time."
My typing ribbon tangles as I attempt to decipher my notes.
I lean back in my chair pondering my career choice—
The constant movement, challenges, and deadlines—
And I pause to ask myself if it's worth it.
The editor's forehead wrinkles as I grin and begin to bang
    thunderously on the typewriter.

Poem submitted by Stephanie Helminiak, 17;
Largo, Maryland
Catalyst Poetry Competition Winner

11
Getting Skills and Credentials

> Training is everything. The peach was once a bitter almond; cauliflower is nothing but cabbage with a college education.
>
> —Mark Twain, *writer and humorist*

Up until your high school graduation, your life is pretty much programmed by your schooling. You probably went to a certain school because you happened to live in the neighborhood. Once enrolled, you and your classmates were dutifully "all in your places with bright shining faces" from about 9 until about 3, with a prescribed time out for lunch and a stint on the sports field. You didn't have much to say about all this.

Now things are finally up to you. After graduation, you'll have to decide what direction to take next, whether it's studying engineering at a four-year college or becoming an apprentice carpenter. Maybe you'll train to be a broadcast technician by attending a technical school. Perhaps you'll even take six months off and trek to Italy to soak up the culture, the language, and the spaghetti sauce.

The tools you need to make a good decision are knowledge and awareness. You've been honing your self-awareness throughout this book, and in this chapter you'll get some of the specific knowledge you need to help you make the decisions ahead.

HIGH SCHOOL DIPLOMA: MORE THAN A PIECE OF PAPER?

Schoolwork overwhelming? Social or family pressures too great? Bored? Want to be out in the "real" world?

These are among the reasons teenagers give for dropping out of high school, and drop out they do. According to the U.S. Bureau of Labor Statistics, 668,000 high school students left school in the 1981–82 school year.

What happens to the teenagers who leave school without getting their diplomas? Most end up in jobs that are low paying, dead-end, and temporary—if they're lucky enough to get jobs at all. In 1982, according to the Bureau of Labor Statistics, over a million high school dropouts under age 25 were unemployed.

Why? For one thing, automation has eliminated many of the jobs that were commonly filled by teenagers who lacked training and more sophisticated skills. Meanwhile, a high school diploma has become a "given" in our country, so employers can afford to be choosy. Preemployment tests, which are given to job applicants by many employers, can pose another problem. People who haven't learned to take tests in high school may find them difficult. And, fair or not, many employers have stereotyped images of teenage workers, believing them to be unreliable and lacking basic skills, so they prefer to hire older workers.

What it all means is that in an increasingly competitive, specialized society like ours, the adage "To get a good job, get a good education" is truer than ever.

Are you thinking about dropping out of high school? The best advice we can give you is this: don't do it. Try to figure out why you are unhappy in school. For example, are you getting such bad grades that you feel you'd better drop out before you flunk out? Do you need to earn some money? Are family or social problems pressuring you? Leaving school is rarely the only way to solve any of these problems. If there is something troubling you, find someone you can talk to about it, or look around your community to see what services are available to help you work it out. If you are falling behind in your studies, for example, you could do one of the following:

- Talk to the teachers whose courses are giving you trouble. (They may not be aware of your difficulty, and, once they are, they may be able to help.)

- See if you can switch to classes that move less fast and allow you to work at your own speed.
- Arrange to have a fellow student or a teacher tutor you in exchange for a small fee or a favor you can do for him or her.

If your problem is the opposite—your schoolwork isn't challenging—take the initiative. Again, speak to your teachers first. Then,

- Ask to do outside work—special projects that you and your teachers design together—for extra credit.
- Find other students who could use your help as a tutor.
- If your high school has an Advanced Placement Program, enroll in that. Or study on your own to take the tests offered by the College Board. (See page 206.)
- Look into the accelerated programs offered in some communities. (For further information, write the National Association for Gifted Children, 217 Gregory Drive, Hot Springs, Ark. 71901, or the National Association for Creative Children and Adults, 8080 Springvalley Drive, Cincinnati, Ohio 45236.)

Maybe you're leaving school to find a job so that you can help out financially at home. Find out first whether your community offers social service programs that could help, such as food stamps, unemployment benefits, and aid to families with dependent children. As an alternative to leaving school altogether, you might also investigate such things as job-training programs that allow you to continue to study for your diploma and night courses (if you have daytime commitments) that offer regular high school classes to help you make up credits needed for graduation. To find out more about these and other education-related programs, call your local Board of Education; to find out about other types of assistance you or your family might need, look under "city listings" in the phone book.

If personal pressures are causing you to leave school, dropping out may create more pressure than it relieves. It would be best, again, to find someone you can talk to—a parent, teacher, guidance counselor, or member of the clergy. If you do not feel comfortable talking to the people around you, there are others who can help. Most communities have low-priced or moderately priced clinics offering personal and family counseling. Your school guidance department can refer you. Or look in the Yellow Pages of your phone book under "counseling," "clinics," or "marriage and family counselors." Some of these groups will suit your needs better than others. Many communities have "hotlines" (often advertised on radio or TV) offering advice to dropouts or people with personal problems.

Have you already left school? If you are finding it difficult to get a job or regret cutting short your education, there are several things you can do. The most obvious, of course, is to go back to school. If this is impossible, however, there are other options.

Dropout Outreach programs, which are available in many communities, offer services (often free of charge) such as personal or academic counseling, course work, and job training.

In addition, most communities offer adult education programs that can help you in a number of ways. While services and requirements for eligibility may vary from one program to another, in general most provide

- Counselors offering educational, vocational, and personal guidance, as well as information about other community resources
- Remedial tutoring in basic skills
- Training in basic business skills
- Career and occupational training to prepare you for entry-level jobs in trade and technical areas
- Job development and placement counseling

You can call the local Board of Education for further information about these resources as well.

If going back to school for a regular high school diploma is not possible for you, you might want to consider getting a high school equivalency certificate. This certificate, issued by the General Educational Development (GED) program, is recognized as equivalent to a high school diploma by most employers, directors of apprenticeship and training programs, and colleges and universities. To earn the GED certificate, you have to pass a series of standardized examinations that test your skills in five subject areas: writing, social studies, science, reading, and mathematics. The tests are designed to evaluate the skills you have acquired through experience outside of the traditional learning situation of high school and to measure your ability to think clearly about ideas and concepts rather than just your knowledge of facts. GED programs are operated by local school systems, so information about the testing procedures, when the tests are given, and classes you can take to help prepare for them can be obtained from the superintendent of schools in your community. For general information about GED programs, write to GED Testing Service, One Dupont Circle, NW, Washington, D.C. 20036.

Why get a diploma? Even if you don't want to go on to college, you will find a lot of doors closed to you if you don't have a high school diploma. Studies have shown that the success of young people in the job market is strongly related to their level of education, with those less educated less likely to find employment. It's no secret that there are many people out of a job in this country today, and it makes sense to have as much on your side as possible when looking for a job in a market that is growing increasingly competitive. A high school diploma tells prospective employers that you have completed certain requirements and possess certain fundamental skills, that you are responsible and have the capacity to work hard to achieve something for three or four years. Your high school diploma *is* more than just a piece of paper. In today's world, it is a first step toward opening up your future.

A GLANCE AT THE JOB MARKET

It's important that you have a realistic idea of what's required to get you from Point A (high school student) to Point B (career woman). You may have decided at age 3 that your true calling in life was for the profession of an osteopathic physician. But did you know that after high school it could take from ten to fifteen years of additional education to reach your goal? Take a look at the following list of occupations and the *usual* education required for each. These specific occupations were chosen because their opportunities for growth are as good as or better than average. Check to see that your sense of educational requirements for the job market is on target.

Accountant: Bachelor's degree is usually required, master's degree sometimes preferred. Accounting courses from colleges, universities, accounting and business schools, and correspondence schools.

Architect: To qualify for the licensing exam, a degree in architecture, either a bachelor's (five-year curriculum) or a master's (six-year curriculum), plus three years of acceptable practical experience in an architect's office.

Computer Programmer: College degree with courses in data processing or completion of special training programs.

Construction Inspector (government): High school diploma plus several years' experience as a construction contractor, supervisor,

195

or craft worker; an apprenticeship program; or two years of college-level engineering or architectural courses.

Dietitian: Bachelor's degree with a major in food and nutrition or institution management. For professional certification, completion of an approved dietetic internship or coordinated undergraduate program (six months to one year).

Dispensing Optician: Several years of on-the-job training, completion of a training program, an associate degree (two-year program), or an apprenticeship program offered by optical dispensing companies (two to four years).

Drafter: Training in technical institutes, junior and community colleges, university extension courses, and vocational and technical high schools; on-the-job training programs with part-time schooling; or an apprenticeship program (three to four years).

Economist: Bachelor's degree with a major in economics is sufficient for many beginning research, administrative, management trainee, and business sales jobs. Graduate training is increasingly required for advancement in the field.

Engineer: Bachelor's degree in engineering (any of the specialties).

Forestry Technician: One to two years postsecondary education, from a technical institute, junior or community college, or university, plus work experience.

Geologist: Bachelor's degree in geology or a related field. Advanced degrees are recommended for advancement.

Health Services Administrator: Master's degree in hospital administration, health administration, or public health. Degrees in business, personnel administration, or public administration are also applicable. (Educational requirements vary with the size of the organization and the amount of responsibility involved in the job.)

Lawyer: To qualify for admission to a state bar, applicants must pass a written examination, have completed at least three years of college (usually requires a bachelor's degree), and have graduated from a law school approved by the American Bar Association (total required education usually takes seven years).

Market Research Analyst: Bachelor's degree, or a graduate degree for specialized positions and advancement within the field.

Medical Laboratory Technician: Four years of college plus completion of a specialized training program in medical technology (two years).

Occupational Therapist: Bachelor's degree in occupational therapy or a bachelor's degree in another field plus a master's degree in occupational therapy. Some states require a license.

Physical Therapist: To be licensed (required in all states), a state examination plus a degree from an accredited physical therapy educational program. This can be a bachelor's degree in physical therapy (four years), a bachelor's degree in another field and a second bachelor's degree in physical therapy, or a bachelor's degree in another field plus a master's degree in physical therapy.

Physician: Bachelor's degree, graduation from an accredited medical school (four years), supervised practice in a graduate medical education program (three-year residency), and a licensing examination.

Psychologist: Doctoral degree (three to five years). Qualifies for a wide range of research, clinical, and counseling positions in universities, private industry, and government.

Radio and Television Announcer and Newscaster: Formal training in college or technical school is helpful. Applicants submit taped auditions. Graduates usually start as production assistants, researchers, or reporters and then move on if they show aptitude.

Real Estate Broker: For the required license, college degree preferred, formal training (90 hours) and experience selling real estate (one to three years) or a bachelor's degree in real estate, and an examination.

Registered Nurse: For the required license, a degree from a state-approved school of nursing (a two-year associate degree, a three-year diploma, or a four- or five-year bachelor's degree) and a state board examination.

Securities Sales Worker: College education with courses in business administration, economics, and finance.

Systems Analyst: College graduate; graduate degree sometimes preferred. Familiarity with programming languages.

Technical Writer: College degree recommended, reflecting writing skills and appropriate scientific or technical knowledge. Knowledge of graphics, communications technology, and computers also helpful.

Urban and Regional Planner: Usually a master's degee in planning, but for some positions a bachelor's degree in city planning, architecture, landscape architecture, or engineering is sufficient.

Veterinarian: For the license, a minimum of two years of preveterinary study (usually four), a Doctor of Veterinary Medicine degree from an accredited college (four-year program), and an examination.

FIRST, A CAVEAT

No, a caveat isn't a witty talk-show host. A caveat is a warning—from the Latin phrase "caveat emptor," meaning "let the buyer beware." And there are some unscrupulous people in education just as there are in any other business. They're happy to take your money and give you a meaningless diploma in return. Sometimes they'll enroll you in classes that never meet; or, if they do meet, they're taught by unknowledgeable frauds. Remember—you don't get something for nothing. You're not going to get a college degree by writing off for it and enclosing the necessary "handling" fee. You're not going to master a complex skill overnight. And you're not going to become Norman Rockwell because you can copy the drawing on a matchbook cover.

Sure, you say, but I'm just a teenager, not the FBI. How can I tell what's legitimate and what's not?

Whenever you invest money or time in something, you want to know beforehand what you can expect to get in return. The same is true of your education. Find out as much as possible about an institution before enrolling. Write for the catalog, talk to recent graduates if possible, and see what your guidance counselor knows about the school.

Then find out if the college is accredited. Accreditation isn't a guarantee of a better-quality education, but it does mean that the school has met basic requirements established by a regional or professional accrediting association. These are private, voluntary organizations that set certain standards for the institutions they review. Basically, a college that's accredited has been judged to have

- A competent faculty
- Educationally sound and up-to-date courses
- Facilities to support the courses offered
- Reasonable tuition charges
- Financial stability

FOUR-YEAR COLLEGES AND UNIVERSITIES

If you are planning to attend a four-year college or university, you'll be joining the majority of students graduating from high school today.

In 1982, 12.4 million students were enrolled in American colleges, according to the National Center for Education Statistics. If you'll be among them in a year or so, probably your biggest dilemma is zeroing in on one of the almost 2,000 four-year colleges and universities in America. Careful thought and research will help you make the best decision possible.

First, think about why you want to go to college at all. Be honest with yourself. Are you going mostly to get away from home? To meet new people? To explore a field of interest? To please your folks? Because your friends are? To prepare for your career? To broaden your general knowledge? These are all sound—though some are more sound than others—and knowing your reason(s) will help you determine what to look for in a college.

If you decide that college is your next step, start with one of the guides to four-year colleges that are available in bookstores and libraries, such as Peterson's *Guide to Four-Year Colleges. Everywoman's Guide to Colleges and Universities* is a valuable reference for learning about aspects of college life of special concern to women. Another very helpful resource is *The College Guide for Students with Disabilities,* by Elinor Gollay and Alwina Bennett, which addresses the special information needs of students with all types of disabilities. Narrow down your choices of schools according to factors that are important to you. Consider these things:

- *Liberal arts colleges vs. specialized schools vs. universities.* Colleges emphasizing liberal arts studies generally offer bachelor's degree programs leading to the Bachelor of Arts (B.A.) degree. At these institutions, students take a broad four-year program, studying the arts, humanities, social sciences, and sciences, eventually majoring in a subject area of one of these disciplines. If you already have a definite idea of what you want to study, you might want to go to a specialized college or school, where less emphasis is placed on liberal arts and more is placed on a specific field—education, law, music, art, engineering, or agriculture, for example. Universities usually combine a liberal arts college with several specialized colleges and offer both undergraduate and graduate degree programs.

- *Curriculum.* Does the college specialize in any areas of study —agriculture, languages, or arts, for instance? What majors does it offer? Does each department have enough courses to give you a thorough education in your chosen specialty? Another consideration is the academic calendar. Some colleges operate on a trimester basis, others have a mandatory summer term, others offer independent study between semesters. Find out, too, about study options such as internships, semester exchanges with other colleges, foreign study, and independent study programs.

- *Location.* Have you thought about living at home and commuting to a local college? Or perhaps attending the state university, which is usually closer and less expensive but still offers the experience of campus life? If money and homesickness aren't considerations, you might decide it's time to try living on your own and learning about another part of the country. Remember this, however: The farther you go the more costly and inconvenient it is to travel back and forth. As eager as you may be to get off on your own, be sure that an occasional long-distance phone call won't devastate your savings account or that you can get home for a weekend break once in a while.

- *Costs.* College is expensive. Don't assume, however, that you can't afford further training or education after high school. Whatever kind of college you go to, there are numerous financial aid programs and scholarships available from many sources. For more information about them, see page 236. If you *are* going to need help, find out about aid and deadlines for applying for it when you first investigate a college. Often financial aid applications must be turned in several months before the admissions applications, and the information needed can be quite detailed.

- *Faculty.* What credentials, advanced degrees, and backgrounds do the faculty members have? Are there professors with expertise in the areas you are thinking of studying? What is the ratio of faculty to students? A high ratio means better chances for individual attention. This information is usually listed in the college's catalog.

- *Accreditation.* The general discussion of accreditation at the beginning of the chapter certainly applies to colleges and universities. You can find out if a college is accredited by looking in its catalog. Do be aware that even at accredited institutions not all departments are equal in quality. In most colleges, some departments are more outstanding than others.

- *Student body.* The influence your fellow students will have on you is considerable, so it's important to find out about the student body of a college. How many students are there? Does the college tend to attract people of similar backgrounds or those from one particular region? You may prefer a varied student body—one in which people come from diverse backgrounds and areas and have different skills and interests. Perhaps you think you'd like to go to a small college where there are fewer students in a course and where your chances for individualized instruction are greater.

- *Student life.* How many students live on campus? In urban colleges especially, there may be a high proportion of commuters. If only a small minority of the student body lives on campus, this may limit the cultural and social life. If the college is far from a city, is it a "suitcase school"? Does almost everyone pack up and take off on Fridays? This can be dreary for students who live far from home or who don't have friends nearby to visit. They can find themselves hanging around an empty campus every weekend.

- *Extracurricular activities.* College is more than just classes and studying. What opportunities are there for attending cultural events—plays, dance concerts, art exhibits? What about lectures and debates? If you are interested in sports, how are the athletic facilities? Are there teams and intramural (within the college, not against other colleges) activities?

- *Affiliations.* A college's affiliation—whether it is public, private/independent, or private/church-related—can affect the campus life of the students. A church-affiliated college may have more rigid codes of conduct, although the degree of influence may range from required attendance at religious services to a required one-semester course on comparative religion.

- *Admission.* Admission is usually based on your high school record, recommendations from teachers or employers, your answers to one or several essay questions, and your scores on one of two standardized admissions tests: the Scholastic Aptitude Test (SAT) or the American College Testing Program's exam (ACT). (See the next section for information about these and other tests.) Find out specific procedures and requirements from each college you apply to. The selectivity of colleges varies from those that accept as few as 15 or 20 percent of their applicants to colleges with an open admissions policy that accept almost everyone who applies. Competition can be fierce. To get a realistic idea of your chances for admission, compare your academic background and SAT or ACT scores with published figures on the makeup of the average freshman class of the colleges you're interested in. If there's a significant difference, you may want to reconsider your application. However, if you *really* want to attend a particular college, go ahead and apply, even if you think your chances of acceptance are slim. A variety of factors influence the decision to accept a student; the fact that you're extremely enthusiastic about the college, come from a far-off state, or play the bagpipes might cause the decision to swing in your favor.

Glossary of Terms in College Catalogs

Academic probation—Trial period for students not making satisfactory academic progress.

Admissions counselors—Often recent graduates of an institution, these people do much of the traveling and interviewing for admissions committees. They may also have interviewing responsibilities for a specific region. They are the people you encounter most frequently in the admissions process.

Advanced standing—Credit for college-level courses given on the basis of tests or previous work experience.

Applicant pool—The total number of students who are applying to a given college or university in a particular year.

Associate degree—The degree awarded for successful completion of a two-year program, either terminal (occupational) or transfer (the first two years of a liberal arts program).

Audit—To attend a course without getting credit for it.

Automatic transfer—A plan in which a two-year branch of a larger educational system allows students in good standing to go on automatically to a bachelor's degree program on the main campus.

Bachelor's degree—The degree awarded upon successful completion of three to five years of study in the liberal arts and sciences, which sometimes includes preprofessional work necessary for a career in law, medicine, and other fields.

Barrier-free campus—A campus that provides access for the handicapped to all buildings and facilities.

Bursar—College or university treasurer and accountant.

Candidate notification date—The date by which an institution will announce its decision on a student's application.

Candidates Reply Date—The date by which students must notify each college that has accepted them whether or not they plan to attend that college in the fall.

Class rank—An indication of a student's approximate standing in his or her high school graduating class. Rank is based on grade point average and is expressed either in percentiles (e.g., top quarter, top 5 percent) or in rank order (e.g., 51st in a class of 240).

College—An individual institution that offers undergraduate education only, or an educational division of a larger university, such as a College of Arts and Sciences. Colleges of the first kind tend to be small and emphasize teaching and undergraduate education over research, since graduate programs are not usually offered.

College viewbook or prospectus—A pictorial brochure produced by colleges and universities to publicize themselves to prospective students. A viewbook usually provides succinct information on entrance requirements, campus life, courses of study, costs, etc.,

College viewbook or prospectus (cont.)—and is a good clue to an institution's image of itself.

Consortium—A group of colleges that have joined to offer certain advantages to themselves and their students. Often colleges in a consortium share a common application and offer students the opportunity to take courses on each other's campuses.

Cooperative education plan—A program offered by many colleges that enables a student to alternate periods of full-time study with full-time work. In most such programs, it takes five years to earn a bachelor's degree.

Credit—Official certification that a student has successfully completed a course.

Credit hour—Unit of measurement for credit.

Dean/director of admissions—The person in charge of the admissions office. In some cases there will be a dean and a director in the same office. Usually the director will have responsibility for office procedures, and the dean will have broader policymaking responsibilities. Deans and directors will often have little to do with the actual processing of students' applications but will lead the committee that makes the final decisions.

Deferred entrance—An admissions plan that allows accepted students to postpone their college entrance date for one to three years, with a guarantee of enrollment at the time they choose.

Early action—An admissions option allowing students to learn of the decision on their application before the standard April notification date. Early action is distinguished from early decision in that students are not required to accept admission or withdraw other applications if accepted, and they have until the May 1 Candidates Reply Date to respond.

Early admission—A program in which a college accepts high school students to begin college work before they graduate from high school. Admissions standards are more stringent for early admission candidates.

Early decision—A plan in which students apply in November or December and learn of the decision on their application during December or January. This plan is suggested only for students who are academically superior. Accepted early decision students are usually required to withdraw their applications to other colleges and to agree to matriculate at the college that accepts them.

Early notification—This program is similar in purpose and process to the early action option. Under the early notification program, applicants must file their papers by December 1 in order to receive an admission decision by February 1. In contrast to the rule in early decision programs, an applicant is not obligated to attend if admitted.

Elective—A course not required in the curriculum but contributing to the total number of credits needed for graduation.

Enrollment deposit—A nonrefundable deposit required of accepted students at many colleges and universities to reserve a space in the incoming class.

Family contribution—The amount an outside agency estimates that you and your family should be able to contribute to the cost of your college education, as determined by such factors as your parents' income, assets, and debts; your earnings and savings; and the number of children in your family currently in college.

Grade point average—A system of scoring student achievement used by many colleges and universities. A student's GPA is computed by multiplying the numerical grade received in each course by the number of credits offered for each course, then dividing by the total number of credit hours studied. Most institutions use the following grade conversion scale: A = 4, B = 3, C = 2, D = 1, and E and F = 0.

Honors program—Unusually challenging program for superior students.

Independent study—An option offered by many high schools and colleges that allows students to pursue independent research or undertake a creative project, usually with minimal faculty supervision.

Individualized major—A plan that allows students to design their major based on individual interests.

Liberal arts—Courses in humanities, social sciences, and natural sciences as opposed to technical or professional subjects.

Major—Subject in which a student chooses to concentrate.

Matriculation—Enrollment at a college or university to begin work toward an academic degree.

Midterm—Halfway point in a semester or trimester.

Midyear or January admission—An option some colleges are now offering to candidates who do not receive fall admission, allowing them to start classes in January of the second semester rather than in the fall.

Minor—Subject in which a student may take the second-greatest concentration of courses.

Open admissions—A policy adopted by a number of institutions— mostly public—that allows virtually all applicants to be accepted, without regard to such traditional qualifying criteria as test scores, class rank, grades, etc.

Pass/fail grading system—An alternative to traditional letter or numerical grading systems in which course credit is indicated simply by a pass or fail notation.

Prerequisite—Basic course or courses needed for preparation to take a higher-level course.

Quarter—A period in the academic calendar equivalent to approximately ten or eleven weeks. Students enrolled at institutions operating on the quarter system usually attend for three quarters a year, unless they wish to accelerate their program by studying the year round.

Registrar—College or university official who keeps records of enrollment and academic standing.

Residential life—This term has replaced "housing" in many colleges and universities. The office of residential life is responsible for housing assignments and maintenance and for student life in the dormitories and other campus residences.

Rolling admissions—A program adopted by many colleges through which admissions applications are evaluated upon receipt and applicants are immediately notified of the decision.

Semester—A calendar period equivalent to approximately half of the academic year (seventeen to eighteen weeks).

Standardized admissions tests—Tests such as the SAT and ACT designed to provide college admissions offices with a national comparative standard for rating a student's academic aptitude and thus predict likelihood of success in college.

Syllabus—Outline of a course.

Three-two program—This entails three years of liberal arts study followed by two years in a professional program at the same college or another institution, resulting in two bachelor's degrees or a bachelor's plus a master's degree.

Transcript—A record of a student's courses and grades.

Trimester—An academic calendar period equivalent to approximately fifteen weeks. Students enrolled at colleges operating on the trimester system usually attend classes for two trimesters each year, unless they wish to accelerate their program by attending the year round.

University—A large educational institution comprising a number of divisions, including graduate and professional schools. Universities are geared toward research, and therefore less emphasis may be placed on undergraduate teaching. In fact, graduate student assistants may teach some undergraduate courses. Academic offerings are usually more comprehensive than at smaller colleges.

Waiting list—A list of students who were not initially accepted by an institution but who will be accepted at a later date if space becomes available. In many cases, waiting list candidates are not notified of the final decision until late in the summer.

ETS, SAT, ATP, TSWE, ACH, AP, ACT:
What Do All Those Initials Mean?

Most colleges and universities in this country require applicants to take a standardized admissions test as part of the admissions process. There are two programs with two different series of tests: the Admissions Testing Program offered by the College Board (a nonprofit organization with a membership of 2,500 colleges, schools, school systems, and education associations) and the American College Testing Program, which sponsors the ACT Assessment Program. The tests you will be required to take depend on the schools you apply to.

The purpose of these tests is to show both you and the college how well you are prepared for its particular study program. Accordingly, the tests are designed to measure abilities that are related to successful academic performance at college. Bear in mind, however, that your score on these tests is not the only thing the college is interested in when considering your application. Although different colleges place varying amounts of weight on the tests, you can be sure that your high school record and other personal and academic information will also be considered. You should, of course, prepare for these tests by reading the booklets available from their sponsors and by taking practice tests. But don't feel that the entire course of your future will be determined solely by how you score on them.

The tests of the Admissions Testing Program, developed and administered by the Educational Testing Service for the College Board, include the Scholastic Aptitude Test (SAT), the Test of Standard Written English (TSWE), and the Achievement Tests (ACH). A college may require one or all of these for admission.

SAT. The SAT consists of four sections: two verbal and two mathematical. The verbal sections measure your ability to understand what you read and the extent of your vocabulary. The math sections measure how well you solve problems involving arithmetic, algebra, and geometry. The SAT is offered seven times a year at test centers around the country. A booklet called "Taking the SAT," published by the College Board, provides a detailed description of the tests as well as a sample practice test. Most schools should have this booklet, or you can get it by writing directly to College Board ATP, Box 592, Princeton, N.J. 08541.

TSWE. Administered with the SAT, the TSWE is a 30-minute multiple-choice exam. It measures your ability to read and write standard, college-level English. Its function is to identify students who may need special help in English and to place others in courses suited to their skills. More information about this test can be found in "Taking the SAT."

ACH. Achievement Tests measure knowledge of particular subjects and the ability to apply that knowledge. Fifteen different tests, each lasting an hour, are available in such subjects as American history, English composition, literature, French, mathematics, biology, physics, and chemistry. Not all colleges make you take these exams, but those that do generally require one test in English composition or literature, one in a foreign language, and a third in history, science, or math. The tests are used both in admissions and in course placement. It's best to take an Achievement Test soon after you've completed the corresponding course at school. They are offered five times a year and you may not take more than three on one day, nor may you take them the same day as you take the SAT. For more information about Achievement Tests, write to College Board ATP, Box 592, Princeton, N.J. 08541.

AP. Advanced Placement tests are also offered by the College Board. These tests measure a student's achievement in a specially designed college-level course taken in high school. Tests are offered in thirteen subjects corresponding to AP courses. Credit for the tests, determined by each college individually, may exempt you from a course requirement as well as give you academic credits. Take—and pass—enough AP exams and you may even be able to enter college as a sophomore, saving yourself a year of college and a lot of money. Check the catalogs of the colleges you are interested in for information on AP credit. AP tests are offered only once annually (in May). You should start preparing for them at least by the preceding January. For more information, write to the AP Program, Box 977, Princeton, N.J. 08541.

CLEP. The College-Level Examination Program, like the AP test, allows you to earn college credit for what you already know. CLEP consists of a series of exams divided into two parts, general and subject. The general exams cover five basic areas of study—English composition, humanities, mathematics, natural sciences, and social science/history. The subject exam measures your knowledge of an area that would be offered as a particular college course, for instance, American literature, trigonometry, or microbiology. Hundreds of colleges and universities around the country grant credit based on CLEP scores; credit earned from successfully completing the entire series is comparable to a full year of college. For more information, write to College-Level Examination Program, Box 1822, Princeton, N.J. 08541.

PSAT/NMSQT. The Preliminary Scholastic Aptitude Test, which is the National Merit Scholarship Qualifying Test, is offered to students in their junior year of high school. Although shorter than the SAT, it is similar in format and is good practice. This is the qualifying test for students who want to participate in the two nationwide competitions sponsored by the National Merit Scholarship Corporation: the National Merit Scholarship Program and the National Achievement Scholarship Program for Outstanding Negro Students. For information about the test, write to PSAT/NMSQT, Box 589, Princeton, N.J. 08541. For information about the scholarship programs, write to the National Merit Scholarship Corporation, One American Plaza, Evanston, Ill. 60201.

ACT. The ACT Assessment is offered at least five times a year throughout the United States and at about 200 test centers in seventy foreign countries. It consists of four academic tests (covering English, mathematics, social studies, and natural sciences), a Student Profile Section, and an Interest Inventory. To register, see your school counselor, who will give you a four-page registration form. This is returned to the American College Testing Program along with the registration fee. If your counselor does not have the registration materials, write directly to the program yourself (ACT Registration, P.O. Box 414, Iowa City, Iowa 52243). When you take the tests depends on the deadlines of the colleges you are interested in or scholarship agencies. If you are applying for early decision, you may want to take the tests during the spring of junior year. Since ACT scoring is adjusted to the educational level of the student, taking the tests earlier won't put you at any disadvantage.

The emphasis of the ACT Assessment is on the abilities and knowledge you have acquired over the years and not on specific facts, so studying for it won't do much good. But it's smart to be familiar with the format on the tests and to be used to taking standardized exams. You should practice on the sample test questions included in the booklet "Taking the ACT Assessment," which is usually available through your guidance office. Or you can send for it (along with a copy of an old filled-in test form as well as further information including testing dates, current fees, and publications) by writing to the American College Testing Program. P.O. Box 168, Iowa City, Iowa 52243.

COED VS. WOMEN'S COLLEGES

One option to consider in choosing a college is whether you want to go to a coed institution or an all-women's institution. Women's colleges were founded mostly in the last century as an alternative to a higher education system dominated by men. There used to be many more single-sex colleges; in the past twenty years, however, many colleges that formerly accepted only men or women have opened their doors to applicants of either sex.

There are still about 75 two- and four-year colleges in this country that accept only women, and enrollment in them is increasing. Students who choose an all-women's college often feel that these institutions will better meet their particular academic and career needs, are more sensitive to women's changing roles in society, and are more flexible in accommodating the life-styles of older women returning to college or women who work.

One of the advantages in attending a women's college seems to be less sex stereotyping. According to a recently completed survey of women's colleges conducted by the Women's College Coalition, "Women's college freshmen at four-year institutions are more likely than freshman women in general to plan majors in such non-traditional majors as the biological sciences, management, economics, and political science." Additionally, according to the survey, graduates of these schools are more likely to choose such nontraditional occupations as business executive, lawyer or judge, doctor, foreign service worker, writer, and journalist.[1]

Women's colleges provide an opportunity to develop strong friendships with other women and encourage you to take on leadership positions in student government and management of the college. You'll find more role models, too, since women are usually well represented on the faculty and in the administration.

Perhaps the strongest disadvantage of any all-women's college is that, even as your confidence in dealing with men on all levels is strengthened, your actual experience with dealing with them is limited. Another obvious problem is the odd social situation. Most of your time is spent with women, except for weekends reserved for socializing with "imported" men from other colleges or making trips to other colleges yourself. This is especially true of colleges in isolated locations. Many colleges resolve these problems by encouraging their students to take advantage of the facilities of other colleges nearby by attending classes on each other's campuses, engaging in informal social or sports activities, or jointly sponsoring cultural and academic programs.

APPLY YOURSELF!

The decision to go on for further schooling is not one you should make lightly. It's a commitment of time and energy that shouldn't hinge on the fact that your mother went to this college or your boyfriend's going to that one. Study directories and college catalogs and talk with college representatives when they visit your area or with recent graduates, as well as with your parents, your guidance counselor at school, and friends who have already made some of these decisions. If possible, visit the campuses yourself and speak with professors, staff, and students; read the campus newspaper, the yearbook, the bulletin boards—anything to give you an idea of what daily life there is like. Most colleges welcome visits from prospective students and some even require on-campus interviews as part of the admission process. Use the interview to ask questions about the college.

After gathering all the information you can and taking into account your own instincts and other people's advice, you're ready to apply to the colleges you feel best satisfy your needs. The number of colleges you apply to will depend on your energy and financial resources, since applications can be lengthy and can cost as much as $75. It may also depend on your high school, since some limit each student's number of college applications to reduce the paperwork involved.

College application forms are fairly standard in the basic information they require: names and occupations of parents or guardians, secondary schools attended, work experience, extracurricular participation. Some ask about your activities and interests. And often you'll have to write a personal statement about why you want to go to college, why this particular college interests you, and what your goals are. This essay is your opportunity to stand out as an individual.

Everything on the application is important, so give it all careful thought. Make two or three drafts on scratch paper before marking the application form. (Practicing on a photocopy of the form is a good idea.) Legibility is essential; if you have access to a typewriter, use it. Pay attention to special instructions and deadlines.

Most application forms are self-explanatory. Following are some tips on how to fill out the sample application that begins on page 212. The numbers given correspond to numbers placed in the relevant spots on the form.

1 Ask your college adviser what the number is that is assigned by the College Board to your high school.

2 Include both school and community activities.

3 This can be a club, an athletic team, a course—whatever you feel provided your most important high school activity. Describe it and explain why it was important to you.

4 You are not committed to whatever you fill in here; it just gives the committee an idea of what your interests are and how they compare to those of other applicants.

5 Include hobbies, sports, and other passions, such as collecting antique quilts, hang gliding, etc.

6 Include volunteer as well as paid jobs, level of your responsibility, and duties.

7 How did you hear of the school? From a school adviser? Literature distributed by the college? Recent graduates? Current students? Parents? This helps the college evaluate its program of reaching prospective students.

8 This is probably the most important part of your application (some ask for autobiographies, others simply say, "Describe yourself"). Have a little fun. It's your chance to talk about yourself. Think about what you would like the committee to know about you. What things from your personality, your background, your interests, and your goals make attending this particular school right for you? Also show that you've been interested enough to find out more about the college by referring to specific programs and specializations or its educational philosophy and relating them to your own particular interests. If you had a personal interview, you may want to include any relevant remarks the interviewer made.

This essay is also a chance for the committee to evaluate your writing skills, so be as careful about writing this as you would any school assignment. On second thought, be more careful. Don't ramble; know what you want to say. Make an outline first if it helps, show it to your friends and family for comments, and be sure all punctuation, spelling, and grammar are correct on the final draft.

It's a good idea to make a copy of the application before you mail it—both in case it gets lost and to refer to later if you need it.

<table>
<tr><td colspan="3" align="center">Application for Freshman Admission
to Cramdon College September 19___</td></tr>
</table>

☐ Regular Admission ☐ Early Decision Plan	

Mr ☐
Miss ☐
Name Ms ☐

Permanent
Address

Mailing Address
(if different from above)

To be used
until (date)

Home Telephone: (   )   Soc. Sec. No.:

Date of Birth: yr: mo: day: Place of Birth   Citizenship

Are You Interested in College Housing? ☐ Yes ☐ No

Father's Name Living?	Mother's Name Living?
Home Address	Home Address
Education	Education
Occupation	Occupation

Applicant's Guardian & Address

Brothers & Sisters	Sex	Age	Education

Relationship, Class, and Maiden Names of Relatives
Who Are Cramdon Alumni or Former Students

Secondary Schools in Order of Attendance

Name of School (most recent)	❶ CB Secondary School Code	Street	City & State	Zip Code	Dates of Attendance (From–To)

Other Secondary Schools Attended

Please check one: ☐ regular graduate ☐ early graduate
Date of secondary school graduation: _____

| Other Colleges Attended | | Dates of Attendance | |
Name & Address of College	Credits Earned	From (Mo.–Yr.)	To (Mo.–Yr.)

Are you applying for financial aid? _____
(Those who wish to be considered for financial aid must file a Financial Aid Form with the College Scholarship Service as well as a financial aid application with Cramdon.) An application for financial aid does not in any way affect a candidate's application for admission.

2 In what extracurricular activities have you participated? Please list in order of interest, noting any school office you have held.

_____

_____

_____

_____

_____

_____

_____

_____

3 What school activity has most benefited you? Please explain. _____

_____

_____

_____

_____

Have you traveled in this country or abroad? Where? _____

_____

_____

4 What area of concentration do you think you will choose in college? ____

_____

What are your possible career interests after college? _____

_____

_____

5 Please list and describe your current interests. _____

_____

_____

_____

6 Please describe your activities during the past several summers (e.g., jobs, travel, etc.). _____

_____

_____

_____

6 Have you ever held a job during the school term? If so, please describe.

_____

_____

_____

What books have you most enjoyed reading during the past year? Please include author and title. _____

_____

_____

_____

_____

What movies, plays, concerts, or exhibitions have you most enjoyed during the past year? _____

_____

_____

_____

_____

7 What was the source of your interest in Cramdon? _____

_____

_____

_____

_____

8 PERSONAL STATEMENT

The members of the Committee on Admissions seek to gain an understanding of you as a person. Please use this page to give us any information you think would be helpful to us as we consider your application. You may be certain that your statement will be kept in strict confidence. Do not hesitate to attach additional pages if the space provided is insufficient.

Signature_____

Date_____

Please complete and return this form, not later than January 15 for regular admission applicants or November 15 for candidates under the Early Decision Plan, to the Office of Admissions, with the following:

> Perforated College Card
> White application card
> School card
> Fee receipt
> $25 application fee

All information, reports, and recommendations submitted to Cramdon College by or for the applicant are strictly confidential and will not be released by the College to anyone.

Now the wait begins. Although the ball is out of your hands, you should continue to weigh your choices and think about your goals and plans. You may have to choose between colleges if accepted by more than one or apply to others if accepted by none.

Once you've been accepted, don't think that you can glide aimlessly through the rest of the year. Most colleges accept applicants on the condition that they finish high school in good academic standing; colleges reserve the right to change their minds about admitting you should your grades suddenly plummet.

Even with 750 test scores and straight A's, you may be rejected by a college you apply to simply because of the number of other applications. Many colleges receive applications from more students than they can accept; some, therefore, must be rejected. Keep in mind that it's not a rejection of you as a person, but a result of the intense competition to get into some colleges. Remember, too, that luck plays a role. Often students get screened out because too many people from the same geographic area—or too many who play the drums, or are math wizards, or are tennis champs—are all applying to the same college. Colleges look for a mixture in their student body. If you're rejected by a college, don't look at it as a setback to your future career plans. The college you go to is not as important to your future as the quality of work you do there. It's even possible that the admissions committee was right in turning down your application. Perhaps you aren't suited to the academic demands and emphasis of their college.

There is no *one* right college for you. If you don't get into your first-choice college, chances are you'll be equally happy at your second or third choice. And, no matter what college you go to, there's always some cause for complaint, whether it be your roommate, the food, or the quality of the biology lab mice. But college is a place to acquire more than textbook learning. Change, adjustment, acceptance of others, and growth are all important parts of your college experience. Many students, despite their complaints, develop strong and lasting ties to their college, becoming faithful "alums" and contributing to fund-raising drives, poring over the alumni newsletter, going to football games, and eventually urging their own children to go to the same place.

COMMUNITY AND JUNIOR COLLEGES

Perhaps your career plans don't require a full four years of study. In that case, you might consider one of the 1,200 two-year community and junior colleges across the country. The programs offered by these institutions include occupational and liberal arts programs leading to associate degrees, as well as short-term training courses leading to specialized certificates and diplomas. Many utilize such innovations as credit by examination, cooperative education, multimedia instruction, volunteer service programs, and individualized instruction. In some two-year programs, you can qualify for a degree in a job-oriented field such as accounting, law enforcement, or dental hygiene. Of course, you can also decide to go on for further study at a four-year institution.

One advantage of studying at a community college is that costs are much lower than at a private four-year institution. You may be able to save even more money by attending night classes and holding a job during the day or by living at home and attending a community college nearby. Another advantage is the open admissions policy practiced by many of these colleges; almost all applicants are accepted whether they did well in high school or not. It's one of the few places where your past mistakes aren't held against you.

These colleges are accredited through regional accrediting commissions. Most are also evaluated by state agencies, and those offering specific programs (nursing, for example) may seek accreditation from professional organizations as well.

Much of the information on choosing and exploring the options of a four-year institution also applies to these schools. You can obtain further information by writing to the American Association of Community and Junior Colleges (Suite 410, One Dupont Circle, NW, Washington, D.C. 20036), by writing directly to the colleges you're interested in, or by using one of the published guides to two-year colleges, such as Peterson's *Guide to Two-Year Colleges.*

NOT SEPARATE—BUT NOT QUITE EQUAL

More women are attending college than ever before. However, according to Dr. Bernice Sandler, Director of the Project on the Status and Education of Women, "Women's educational experiences often differ considerably from those of men attending the same institutions because faculty often treat men and women students differently."[2] As a result of this and other influences of family and society, many women college students

- Continue to shy away from fields that are traditionally considered "masculine"
- Experience a decline in their academic and career aspirations while in college

- Feel less confident than their male peers about their preparation for graduate school

A 1982 report issued by the Project on the Status and Education of Women entitled "The Classroom Climate: A Chilly One for Women?" brings together the results of several studies in an attempt to show that teachers' behavior in the classroom can have a very definite effect on students. This can include such things as

- Calling on the men in the class more often than the women
- Addressing the entire class as if it included only men, by saying things like, "What if your wife..." or "When you were a boy..."
- Giving men more time than women to answer questions before going to another student
- Interrupting women students more often or allowing them to be interrupted by other students
- Asking men more challenging, "thinking" kinds of questions
- Giving credit to men for their comments ("As Joel just said ...") and not doing the same for women
- Not taking women's career aspirations seriously, believing they'll only get married anyway
- Referring to doctors, scientists, and supervisors as "he" and secretaries, patients, and assistants as "she" when giving examples
- Making "helpful" comments like, "I know you girls have trouble with figures; I'd be glad to help you after class"

Just as harmful, but less obvious, are nonverbal behaviors such as

- More frequent eye contact with male students
- Nodding, gesturing, and looking more attentive when men are speaking
- Seating students of the same sex together
- Sitting closer to the men than to the women in the classroom

Chances are teachers who do any or all of these are not even aware of it. "Most faculty want to treat all students fairly and as individuals with particular talents and abilities," says Roberta M. Hall, author of the report and assistant director for special programs at the Project. "However, many professors—men and women alike—may inadvertently treat women and men differently in the classroom and in related learning situations."[3] It is this unintentional behavior that can do the most harm. With neither the teacher nor sometimes even the student aware of the problem, nothing is done to correct it.

Why do some professors—consciously or unconsciously—respond differently to their male and female students? Some may have been making sexist remarks or jokes for so long that they no longer hear how hurtful and insulting such remarks are. Others may feel uncomfortable with women students, especially if they teach in an area where women are relative newcomers. They may resort to sexist language or humor to relieve their anxiety. And some professors may genuinely believe women are intellectually inferior or belong at home raising a family.

Unfortunately, these attitudes can have some serious consequences. With no encouragement or feedback from their teachers, women students may stop participating in class discussions or feel reluctant to seek extra help should they need it. They may subsequently drop the class or switch majors entirely. When women are not encouraged to develop a good rapport with advisers and teachers, they also lose possible mentors. All of this can result in feelings of helplessness, anger, frustration, and self-doubt. As women lose confidence in their abilities, they may lower their career goals and close off future options.

Women are not the only ones who lose out. By inhibiting women from participating in class, the contribution of half the students is lost. The men in their classes suffer further by having stereotyped ideas of women reinforced by their professors, which can make relating to women difficult for them. In addition, when women are discouraged from majoring in fields labeled "inappropriate" for women, other students, professors, and the department stand to lose potentially valuable colleagues.

If you find yourself in a class where you feel your presence isn't welcome, your participation isn't expected, and your contributions aren't important, don't despair. There are several things you can do to try to correct the situation.

- When making a comment in class, give credit to your fellow women students by saying something like, "As Phyllis said ..."
- If your professor makes an effort to be fair—frequently using "she" instead of "he" when making a general reference, for instance—let him or her know you appreciate it. Smile or nod or mention it after class.

- Keep track of the number of times women are interrupted versus the number of times men are interrupted. If the number for women is substantially more, draw the professor's attention to this.

- Talk with other students. Have they noticed different attitudes toward men and women in the classroom? If they have, speak to the professor.

- If you're asked to write a course evaluation, use this opportunity to comment positively or negatively on the way women are treated in class.

- Encourage student publications such as the campus newspaper to write about the issue.

Awareness is the first step toward change. Once teachers are aware they may be treating men and women students differently and causing harm, they can try to change. And once the women students are aware that they really are being treated differently, they can pinpoint why they've been feeling frustrated and angry and do something about it.

ALTERNATIVE ROUTES

Once in college, it's not mandatory that you go straight through, remaining on the same campus for the full two or four years. You may find that, for a variety of reasons, you're dissatisfied or unhappy and would prefer to do something else. Perhaps you've changed your mind about what you want to study, or maybe you've decided formal schooling just isn't for you right now, if ever. Or you may just need a change of scene. Consider spending a semester or year attending another college, transferring to a different college, working for a while, or pursuing independent study.

Transferring

Many students transfer to another college. Whether transferring from a two-year college or from one four-year school to another, you'll usually need to be in good academic standing with the institution you're leaving behind before you can be considered by another one. Transferring can be like starting the college search all over again. It should be easier the second time around, though, since you will probably have a better idea of what you want and what is available. Start with the catalog of the college you want to transfer to and check to see that you fulfill its general educational requirements. If your original college is accredited, chances are most other colleges will accept your credits. You may have to repeat some courses that the new college does not consider equivalent to the ones it offers. Requirements and prerequisites may differ too. It's best, therefore, to talk with the registrar of the new college. You may discover that you'll lose too many credits to make transferring worthwhile.

Your chances of being accepted as a transfer student will depend on the policy of the individual college. Colleges with more transient student bodies accept larger numbers of transfer students than those —usually smaller—whose student population is fairly stable. Some students, however, find that they do better in the second round of college applications. They've clarified their goals and improved their grades, two things that can help a lot in getting admitted to college.

Cooperative Education

Cooperative education is a way for students to finance their education while gaining knowledge of the work world. It supplements classroom learning with practical, on-the-job experience and helps make a necessary part-time job relevant to a future career. Under the cooperative education program, offered by more than 1,100 colleges and universities across the country, students are allowed to spend one semester attending class on campus and one semester working full-time in a job related to their field of study. With the help of their faculty advisers, nursing students find work in hospitals, journalism students with newspapers and magazines, and engineering students with technical firms. In this way, students discover if they really like their chosen field, learn some practical skills, and make some good contacts. Both work and studies become more meaningful as one reinforces the other. An additional benefit is the possibility of employment with the company after graduation. Although a job is by no means guaranteed, many students are offered a permanent position after finishing school. General Electric, an enthusiastic participant in the program, hires almost 50 percent of its co-op ed students.

In a 1981 survey of cooperative education, Arthur D. Little, a research and consulting firm, reported that "cooperative education also provides unique opportunities for both the prospective employer and the prospective permanent employee to evaluate each other...." In effect, the survey concluded, the program is like "trial employment."[4]

Participating in a co-op ed program means that it will probably take you an extra year to get an undergraduate degree. At the same time, however, you will be earning enough money to pay for most or all of your education, as well as acquiring on-the-job experience that will help you in a future career. Cooperative education is an option offered by a limited but increasing number of colleges. The National Commission for Cooperative Education (360 Huntington Avenue, Boston, Mass. 02115) can supply you with a list of colleges and universities that offer these programs.

Stopping Out

What happens if, once in college, you find that after a dozen or so years of formal schooling you've had enough and need a break? Or that you are unsure of your goals and want a taste of the "real world"? Or perhaps you simply find that you've overloaded yourself, taking on too many obligations—a job, college, family, or other commitments. "Stopping out" either before or during college is an option that increasing numbers of students are choosing. Feeling a need for a breather from education, they take time off to work or travel before returning to their studies. These students differ from those who drop out of school completely in that most have a good idea of what they plan to do during their year or so off and intend to return to college to finish their degree. Stopping out can help you clarify your career goals; by holding a job in a field you are thinking of entering after college, you'll get a realistic picture of what a career in that field would be like and what training you need to enter it. It will give you a better idea of courses to take once you're back at college, and will put your studies in a "real-world" context.

Most colleges and universities are flexible in allowing their students to take time off; some even give academic credit for the experience. If you do want credit, be sure to talk it over with your adviser and other college officials beforehand to get their approval. Often some kind of "real-life" experience will give you an edge when job hunting later on. It is a good idea, however, to have a definite plan of what you hope to accomplish to present to your college as well as to future employers. Before you decide to leave college, make sure it is the best answer for you and that you wouldn't be better off transferring to another college.

There are a few other things to consider when contemplating stopping out:

- Possible loss of financial aid for your schooling when you return
- Loss of contact with friends
- Loss of access to social and extracurricular activities

- Availability of employment or travel opportunities
- Interruption of studies—especially if you've chosen your major
- Parents' reaction, particularly if you rely on their financial support

College is not for everyone. There may be any number of reasons not to go on to college after high school: you may not be ready for more study right away, perhaps you are unsure of your goals and feel it would be a waste of time (and money), you may feel a need to check out the "real world" or to earn a living for a while, or you may have career goals that are best satisfied through a different kind of training. Whatever your situation, there are still many choices open to you, whether you decide to work for a while and then go back to school, to work and attend some classes at the same time, or to go full-time to a school other than the traditional two- or four-year institution.

VOCATIONAL EDUCATION

Have you been building skateboards and tree houses since you were 5? Is your thumb so green you can grow a tomato out of concrete? Does your sister trust you to cut her hair? These are the kinds of skills and talents you can turn into a career. And vocational education can help you do it. Interest in this kind of training has increased significantly, while the old snobbish attitude that vocational education is only for those who "can't hack" college is on the wane. It's also an area that is increasingly attractive to women, who want a share of the good salaries, benefits, and challenges vocational training can bring.

Training is available at public or private vocational schools, community colleges, adult education and extension programs, correspondence schools, and private trade, technical, and business schools. Although these schools vary in curriculum, their basic goal is the same: to teach you in a relatively short time a specialized skill or trade. You can select from a wide variety of courses, ranging from acting to computer programming to electronics.

Narrowing down your goals will help you to pick the program that suits you best. When you have decided what field interests you, the next thing to do is to check job opportunities in that field. Are there openings in your community for the job you want? Is the pay good? Look in the *Occupational Outlook Handbook* for long-range forecasts of job prospects. Check, too, with local employers in your field. Are they hiring people? Do they anticipate continued hiring within the next few years? Another thing to ask employers is whether they've hired graduates of vocational schools in the past and, if so, if they were satisfied with them. Did graduating from the program make any difference in their salaries? You may find that you could receive the same kind of training on the job—and earn a salary at the same time.

When you're satisfied that your job goal is a realistic one and that vocational education is the best way to attain it, find out which schools in your area offer the program you want. The employers you talk to or your high school's guidance counselor may be able to suggest some. Consult the *Handbook of Trade and Technical Careers and Training* for a list of accredited schools in nonbusiness subjects (published annually and available free from the National Association of Trade and Technical Schools, Suite 315, 2021 K Street, NW, Washington, D.C. 20006). The Yellow Pages of your phone book list private schools offering training in a variety of fields. You could also write or call professional organizations and local community colleges.

Here are some things to look for as you investigate various schools:

- *Accreditation.* Schools are accredited by state bureaus for vocational schools (check local state government listings in the phone book under "Department of Education"), regional agencies, or—for private schools—independent accrediting agencies, such as the Accrediting Commission of the National Home Study Council (1601 18th Street, NW, Washington, D.C. 20009), the National Association of Trade and Technical Schools (Suite 315, 2021 K Street, NW, Washington, D.C. 20006), and the Association of Independent Colleges and Schools (Suite 600, 1730 M Street, NW, Washington, D.C. 20036). Another way to check on private schools is to ask the Better Business Bureau if there have been any complaints lodged against them. Professional organizations also sometimes offer accreditation to schools specializing in training for their particular field.

- *Dropout rate.* Ask the director of admissions what the school's dropout rate is. If it is higher than 50 percent, this may indicate that the program is not good or that it accepts students who are unable to do the work.

- *Teacher turnover.* A school that can't hold on to its teachers may have other problems as well. In addition, having a succession of teachers instruct the same course can result in inconsistency and discontinuity in your studies.

- *Job placement services.* Not all schools offer such services. If you are applying to a school that does, find out exactly what the services include. Do counselors offer advice, guidance, and help in arranging interviews? Or do they just hand you a list of possible employers and shove you out the door?

- *Refund policy.* Find out if you can get your money back should you change your plans or have to drop out due to an unexpected emergency. Most schools will refund at least some of your money—but be sure you understand the terms.

Try to speak to some graduates of the school as well. Ask the director of admissions to give you names of recent graduates living in your area. No reputable school should refuse to do this. Call some and find out what they are doing now. Did their vocational training help them get a job and move ahead? Would they recommend the school?

You should also try to visit the campus and attend a class. This gives you a chance to see the facilities. Are they adequate? If machinery is involved, is it up-to-date? Do people seem happy and serious about their work? Are instructors helpful and concerned?

Beware of hard-sell ad campaigns, fancy brochures, and slick sales pitches. While most schools are reputable, there are some that will try to lure you with promises of a job they can't really guarantee. This may be especially true of private institutions that pay the recruiters a commission for every student they sign up.

Vocational education can be an excellent way to learn a skill. Just be sure your decision to get vocational training is based on a knowledge of your own goals and the requirements of a particular field.

APPRENTICESHIPS

Through an apprenticeship, you can learn to become a skilled worker in one of the 450-plus occupations recognized by the Department of Labor as "apprenticeable." Cooking, bricklaying, plumbing, commercial art, watchmaking, bookbinding, public health, TV repair, and aircraft maintenance are only a few examples.

Why become an apprentice? It's a good way to develop a recognized skill that will allow you to find a job almost anywhere. A career in the skilled trades provides good pay and benefits, job security, and rewarding work.

Apprenticeships are formal arrangements involving employers, unions, schools, and individuals who want to master a skill. Apprentices work in their chosen field while receiving a combination of on-the-job training from an experienced craftsperson and related classroom instruction. The programs last between one and six years, depending on how long it takes an individual to meet the requirements. During this time, apprentices receive 40 to 60 percent of a trained worker's salary, with regular pay increases. Apprentices are expected to learn all aspects of their trade, not just one part of it, so you would probably be moved to different jobs and sites during an apprenticeship. This is also a test of your ability to get along with people and a test of your flexibility. Like most beginners, apprentices are on the bottom of the heap and can expect to be assigned some work no one else wants to do. When you "graduate," you'll receive a certificate and journeyworker's (sometimes referred to as "journeyman's") card, signifying that you are skilled and ready to be employed in the trade.

The apprenticeship system in this country is administered by the Bureau of Apprenticeship and Training (BAT), an agency of the Department of Labor, which sets up and promotes work standards protecting the welfare and rights of apprentices. Through its ten regional offices and its field representatives in each state, the Bureau works with employers, labor unions, schools, and other interested groups to improve the quality and availability of apprenticeship training.

Apprenticeship programs can be sponsored by individual employers or jointly by a union and an employer. Requirements vary, with some accepting only high school graduates and others accepting applicants with a grammar school education. In general, you are required to be between 17 and 26 years old. Application procedures vary also. Some programs accept applications all year; more often, however, there are set recruiting periods lasting thirty, sixty, or ninety days. Information on specific procedures and openings can be obtained from the BAT regional office nearest you or an Apprenticeship Information Center.

When you have decided on a program, you must first file all the necessary information with the sponsor. Next, you take a qualifying test. This can be a short aptitude test or a longer test covering a wide range of subjects. If you pass this, you are interviewed to assess your attitude, interest, and motivation, as well as your knowledge of the field. Following acceptance into a program, apprentices must work a probationary period lasting up to six months. During this period you can be asked to leave the program without your employer having to explain why.

But what if you don't know the difference between a monkey wrench and a monkey? Were you handed dolls and tea sets while your brothers were using tools and taking shop classes? If so, you're at a disadvantage if you want to work in the skilled trades. But you can overcome your "deprived" childhood by signing up for some classes like these:

- Weight training, to develop strength for lifting, pushing, and pulling
- Basic math, to brush up on fractions, decimals, ratios, percentages, and spatial relations
- Shop classes, for obvious reasons; if you're still in high school, take woodworking, metalworking—whatever's offered. If you're not, check into nearby community colleges and adult schools.

As a woman apprentice, you will probably find yourself one of a minority. You may also find that some employers, unions, and male coworkers (not to mention relatives and friends) regard this as "man's work." This attitude can make you uncomfortable and generate self-doubt. Especially if you've never worked before, you may feel unsure about your ability to handle any job, let alone one in which women aren't fully accepted.

If you're in this kind of situation, it might be helpful to investigate special programs available to women in nontraditional jobs. They provide counseling, support, orientation, and even direct experience for women who are hesitant about entering an apprenticeship. To find these programs, check with state employment agencies, job service centers, community colleges, technical and vocational schools, and the Yellow Pages of the phone book.

For further information about apprenticeships, write to your state employment service or regional BAT office (see next page) or talk to an employer or union representative in a trade that interests you. We've also included a list of publications that tell you more about being an apprentice.

INDUSTRY TRAINING

The rapid change wrought by modern technology and the increasing complexity of industrial skills means that even long-term employees may have to learn new tricks. To provide for this, many companies offer on-the-job training for their veteran as well as new employees. This can include company courses during and after work, courses offered by other institutions during working hours, and paid tuition for courses outside of work.

Taking on the additional responsibility and commitment of training while simultaneously holding down a job can put you under a lot of pressure. But the increased chances for promotion, a raise, and expanded career options can be worth it. For descriptions of numerous programs offered around the nation, check the *Directory of Career Training and Development Programs* (Santa Monica, Calif.: Ready Reference Press, 1979; first supplement, 1981).

Bureau of Apprenticeship and Training Regional Offices

Region I: Connecticut, Maine, Massachusetts, New Hampshire, Rhode Island, Vermont

Room 1001, JFK Federal Building, Government Center, Boston, Mass. 02203

Region II: New Jersey, New York, Puerto Rico, Virgin Islands

Room 3731, 1515 Broadway, New York, N.Y. 10036

Region III: Delaware, Maryland, Pennsylvania, Virginia, West Virginia

P.O. Box 8796, Philadelphia, Pa. 19101

Region IV: Alabama, Florida, Georgia, Kentucky, Mississippi, North Carolina, Tennessee

Room 700, 1371 Peachtree Street, NE, Atlanta, Ga. 30309

Region V: Illinois, Indiana, Michigan, Minnesota, Ohio, Wisconsin

230 South Dearborn Street, Chicago, Ill. 60604

Region VI: Arkansas, Louisiana, New Mexico, Oklahoma, Texas

Room 858, 55 Griffin Square Building, Griffin and Young Streets, Dallas, Tex. 75202

Region VII: Iowa, Kansas, Missouri, Nebraska

Room 1100, Federal Office Building, 911 Walnut Street, Kansas City, Mo. 64106

Region VIII: Colorado, Montana, North Dakota, South Dakota, Utah, Wyoming

Room 16440, Federal Building, 1961 Stout Street, Denver, Colo. 80202

Region IX: Arizona, California, Hawaii, Nevada

Room 9008, 450 Golden Gate Avenue, P.O. Box 36017, San Francisco, Calif. 94102

Region X: Alaska, Idaho, Oregon, Washington

Room 8014, Federal Office Building, 909 First Avenue, Seattle, Wash. 98174

FOREIGN STUDY

Perhaps you've decided to sample another culture and live in a foreign country for six months or a year. Living abroad can be exciting and an eye-opener. Your outlook will broaden as your accent improves.

Bibliography on Women and Apprenticeship

"The Blue Collar Scholar: Vocational Schools," *Consumer Survival Kit.* March 1978. (Available from Maryland Center for Public Broadcasting, Owings Mills, Md. 21117.)

Directory of Accredited Private Trade and Technical Schools. (Available free from the National Association of Trade and Technical Schools, Suite 315, 2021 K Street, NW, Washington, D.C. 20006.)

McCormick, Dale. *Against the Grain: A Carpentry Manual for Women.* Iowa City: Iowa City Women's Press, 1977. (Available from Iowa City Women's Press, 1801 Stevens Drive, Iowa City, Iowa 52240.)

Mitchell, Joyce Slayton. *The Work Book: A Guide to Skilled Jobs.* New York: Sterling Publishing Co., 1978.

O'Sullivan, Judith, and Rosemary Gallick. *Workers and Allies: Female Participation in the American Trade Union Movement.* Washington: Smithsonian Institution Press, 1978. (Available from U.S. Government Printing Office, Washington, D.C. 20402.)

Wetherby, Terry, ed. *Conversations: Working Women Talk About Doing a "Man's Job."* Millbrae, Calif.: Les Femmes, Celestial Arts, 1977.

Wider Opportunities for Women. *Getting Ready for Work.* 1978. (Available from WOW, 1649 K Street, NW, Washington, D.C. 20006.)

Wider Opportunities for Women. *National Directory of Women's Employment Programs.* (Available from WOW, 1649 K Street, NW, Washington, D.C. 20006.)

Women's Educational Equity Communications Network. *Apprenticeship and Other Blue Collar Job Opportunities for Women.* 1978. (Available from WEECN, 1855 Folsom Street, San Francisco, Calif. 94103.)

Women Working in Construction. *Blue Collar Trades Handbook for Women.* 1977. (Available from Women Working in Construction, 1854 Wyoming Avenue, NW, Washington, D.C. 20009.)

You could take advantage of a university-sponsored year or semester program or of similar private programs, or you could arrange your own program, applying directly to schools in the country of your choice. Consider these factors:

- How independent are you? Organized trip programs take care of travel arrangements, accommodations, meals, and enroll-ment. Going on your own, while providing a chance to test your wings, can also be a supreme test of your patience as you struggle with train schedules, foreign money, and your 150-pound trunk.

- Do you want to live with a family? If you are truly interested in learning about another country—its people, customs, habits, food, and language—there is no better way than total immer-sion in family life.

- Can you get academic credit for study abroad? If you want credit for your studies, be sure you participate in a program whose credentials are accepted by your American college.

Most U.S.-sponsored programs don't require language fluency. To appreciate your experience fully, however, it will help if you have *some* knowledge of the language. You should at least be able to ask a price or the location of the restroom. A short-term crash course can help you get off to a good start. Your lack of a foreign language shouldn't scare you away from study abroad, however. Even if you arrive in total ignorance, you *can* survive, as Claire found out when she studied in Denmark for a year:

"I'd never spoken a word of Danish, but my college had a Scan-dinavian exchange program that I was interested in. We flew to Den-mark about three weeks before we were to start school and lived on a school campus where we had intensive language classes all day long. After three weeks, we split up and went to live with our families. The family I stayed with lived out in the country with two small children. None of them spoke any English and, even with the intensive study, my Danish was pretty shaky. I was really scared about how I'd get along—both with them and at the school I was going to go to. But it's amazing how fast you can learn when you really *have* to. There was some gesturing, acting out, pointing, and a lot of laughing in the be-ginning. But by Christmas I was having no problems!"

Why study abroad at all? First of all, living and studying in another country provide an education you can't get inside a classroom. No matter how much you've read about the Ashanti tribe, Aztec civi-lization, or Renaissance art, it becomes more real when you actually see the places where it exists or existed. Living in another country helps you understand its history, its people, and its place in the world today. It's also the best way to learn a foreign language. You're much more apt to remember the word for cheese when forgetting it means going without lunch! Beyond lunch, learning another language may help you get a job. Also, a recent survey of major U.S. businesses conducted by the Modern Language Association showed that employees who speak a foreign language improve their chances for promotions, top salaries, and overseas assignments.

Here are some occupations for which a foreign language is an important asset:

book dealer	hotel manager	flight attendant
journalist	translator	interpreter
librarian	bilingual secretary	teacher
importer/exporter	museum worker	social worker
customs inspector	immigration officer	international sales worker
foreign service worker		

Even if you're not interested in one of these fields, any prospective employer will be impressed if you've spent time studying abroad. It shows independence, initiative, and resourcefulness.

It's important to choose the right program for you. Talk to your guidance counselor, your parents, and people who have been abroad themselves. Some programs designed specifically for recent high school graduates who want to study abroad are listed below; many have full or partial scholarships. Write to them for further information.

AFS International/Intercultural Programs
313 East 43rd Street
New York, N.Y. 10017

Offers summer program of ten weeks and academic program of one year for high school students or recent graduates of schools participating in the program. Emphasis on family and community involvement with exchanges between the United States and more than fifty-five countries as well as a domestic program providing exchanges for students within the United States.

American Institute for Foreign Study
102 Greenwich Avenue
Greenwich, Conn. 06830

Offers one-week programs during winter, spring, and summer in Europe, Mexico, and the United States; two- to five-week travel programs; two- to eight-week study programs for college credit; and year and semester programs. Students live with host families while going to school with other Americans in the program. An American teacher and program coordinator usually live in the community as well.

British American Educational Foundation
351 East 74th Street
New York, N.Y. 10021

Offers American high school graduates an opportunity to spend a year at a school in Great Britain. Its purpose is to develop participants' leadership qualities by challenging them with the unique educational and social environment of the British public schools (which are really private schools).

College Year in Scandinavia
Scandinavian Seminar
358 North Pleasant Street
Amherst, Mass. 01002

Offers a yearlong program combining intensive language study, a homestay, and attendance and boarding at a small Scandinavian college. Each student in the program is placed in a different college in order to strengthen language skills.

English-Speaking Union of the United States
16 East 69th Street
New York, N.Y. 10021

Scholarships are offered by British public schools to recent high school graduates for one year of study. Open only to students of participating schools. If you want to go to Britain and your school is not a participant in this program, you can apply to the next organization.

Experiment in International Living
Kipling Road
Brattleboro, Vt. 05301

Offers summer and academic semesters abroad in thirty countries for high school and college students. Students live with host families; language study is emphasized.

U.S. Student Travel Service
801 Second Avenue
New York, N.Y. 10017

Offers travel service for students traveling abroad, including summer jobs, homestays, language study, special-interest tours, and charter flights. Also arranges international music exchange programs.

Youth for Understanding International Student Exchange
3501 Newark Street, NW
Washington, D.C. 20016

Programs in Latin America, Asia, the Pacific, and Europe. Most are offered during summer, although there are some year-round academic programs. Students between the ages of 14 and 18 are accepted; they live with host families.

As with anything else, there are pitfalls to avoid in your search for an overseas study program. As you read the brochures, advertisements, and other literature, check for the following:

- A name of someone responsible for the program rather than just a title; a list of trustees, advisers, or board of directors provides further assurance
- An address you can verify rather than a post office box number
- The name of a specific university or institution at which you will be studying, rather than "famous university" or "internationally recognized institution"
- Accreditation—who awards it and to whom?
- Names of specific faculty members who will be teaching
- Detailed description of curriculum: hours spent in class, courses taught, extracurricular and travel opportunities
- Enumeration of exactly what your fee covers: transportation, course fees, books, room and board; paying for any of these as extras will add a considerable amount to the initial fee
- Description of living quarters provided: Are they adequate? Are they near the institution where you will be studying?

A pamphlet called "Work-Study-Travel-Abroad" will help you evaluate the program you are interested in. It's available free from the Council on International Educational Exchange (777 United Nations Plaza, New York, N.Y. 10017).

WORKING ABROAD

Working abroad is more complicated than studying abroad. There are strict labor and visa regulations that make it difficult for U.S. citizens to find jobs in foreign countries. For paid work, your best chances are in seasonal or service industries, in jobs that are short-term and require relatively few skills. This means hotel, farm, child-care, or domestic work. These jobs don't usually pay well. Better-paying jobs are teaching English as a foreign language, or leading tour groups from the United States, or working as a nurse. If your background qualifies you for work in these areas and you want to find out more, write to:

TESOL
School of Languages and Linguistics
Georgetown University
Washington, D.C. 20057

American Youth Hostels
National Headquarters
Delaplane, Va. 22025

Nursing Practice Department
American Nurses' Association
2420 Pershing Road
Kansas City, Mo. 64108

Volunteer work is easier to find and usually includes room and board. Work camps (that means lots of manual labor) often employ young students. There are also volunteer opportunities in community service—hospitals or recreation programs, for example—that you might want to consider.

Other organizations that can provide information on traveling, studying, and working abroad are the Institute of International Education (809 United Nations Plaza, New York, N.Y. 10017) and the Council on International Educational Exchange (address given above).

EXTERNAL DEGREES

Over 150 institutions currently offer external degree programs—also called open universities, adult education programs, lifelong learning, or universities without walls. These schools recognize that learning can take place outside the traditional classroom. Their emphasis is on what you know, not on how you learn it, and their programs are designed to fit your schedule and needs. Requirements for time spent on campus range from nothing to 25 percent of the total credit hours required for a degree. The rest of the degree is earned through classes at off-campus sites; independent study; courses through television or newspapers; credit for past experience; credit by examination; planned fieldwork; courses at libraries, art centers, or museums; internships; travel; seminars; or any combination of these.

While not all study options are offered by all programs, almost all award credit for prior learning and for successful completion of standardized tests such as CLEP, ACT, and Advanced Placement exams. Some schools also offer counseling and job placement assistance. Most programs require a high school diploma or equivalent for admission, and some do not accept out-of-state students. Because of the flexibility of the programs, you can enroll in most of them any time of the year. Costs are relatively low, though some charge more to students from out of state. Tuition is basically enough to cover administrating exams, evaluating experience for credit, record keeping, and advising. Again—be sure to check on the college's accreditation. This is just as important a consideration as it is for traditional colleges, maybe *more* important because the opportunity for fraud is greater.

The Guide to Undergraduate External Degree Programs in the United States (Eugene J. Sullivan, ed.; Washington: American Council on Education, 1980) lists numerous accredited programs throughout the country and is also a good source for more information on external degrees.

While many of the colleges offering external degrees don't require students to spend any time on campus, four programs are unique in that they don't even *have* a campus. They provide no instruction, and, since there is no campus, you don't even have to live in the same state. Degrees are usually awarded on the basis of your performance on a series of proficiency examinations, which you take at your own pace and which demonstrate your college-level knowledge. These four programs are:

Board of State Academic Awards
340 Capitol Avenue
Hartford, Conn. 06106

Board of Governors of State Colleges and Universities
Bachelor of Arts Degree Program
544 Iles Park Place
Springfield, Ill. 62718

Thomas A. Edison State College
101 West State Street, CN 545
Trenton, N.J. 08625

Regents External Degree Program
The University of the State of New York
Cultural Education Center
Albany, N.Y. 12230

We will discuss one of these in greater detail to give you an idea of how they operate: the Regents External Degree Program. Requirements for earning a Regents degree are determined by faculty members and administrators from New York colleges and universities. The degrees offered are Associate in Arts, Associate in Science, Associate in Science in nursing, and Associate in Applied Science in nursing (comparable to similar degrees from community colleges) and Bachelor of Arts, Bachelor of Science, Bachelor of Science in nursing, and Bachelor of Science in business (comparable to similar degrees offered by four-year institutions). There are no prerequisites—such as a high school diploma—for admission to the Regents program. Students may be of any age, have any level of education, and live halfway around the world. There is no time limit for completing the degree and advisers are available to students at any time. The Regents program is accredited by the New York State Board of Regents and the Middle States Association of Colleges and Schools, and its nursing programs are accredited by the National League for Nursing.

FINANCIAL AID

The cost of financing your education will depend on the college you go to. Whatever your choice, however, there are a number of sources for financial help. It will take a little investigation on your part to uncover them. Colleges' financial aid and admissions offices can help, as can the publications listed at the end of this section.

The federal government is a good place to start. Five programs for students offered by the U.S. Department of Education are

- *Pell Grant Program* (formerly the Basic Educational Opportunity Grant Program). This is the largest government aid program and is available to all eligible students at participating two- and four-year colleges and universities, vocational and technical schools, and nursing schools. The colleges receive enough money to cover all the eligible students they have enrolled, and they give it to those students as part of their financial aid package. A grant is an outright gift of money; you do not have to pay it back. To qualify, you must meet general requirements for eligibility as well as be considered a "needy" student, a determination based on a combination of factors such as your family's income and assets, family size, and the number of other people in your family also attending postsecondary school. These factors also determine the amount of money you receive.

- *Supplemental Educational Opportunity Grant Program.* This program is smaller than the Pell Grant Program. Colleges receive a set amount of money to award to accepted students of their choice as a supplement in their financial aid package. These grants also do not need to be repaid.

- *Guaranteed Student Loan Program.* This offers government-insured, low-interest loans available from banks, credit unions, and savings and loan associations. Eligibility for the loans is based on your or your family's financial situation. Applications are available directly from the lender or a college. The college you plan to attend must fill out part of it, then you submit it to the institution from which you are requesting the loan. If you obtain a loan, you do not have to start paying it back until six to twelve months after you leave school, and you have five to ten years to repay it.

- *National Direct Student Loan Program.* Under this program, needy students may obtain low-interest loans directly from their college or school. Repayment begins after you leave school, and you have up to ten years to repay.

- *College Work-Study Program.* This provides financial aid in the form of a job, either on campus or at a nonprofit organization, in which you earn money to help pay your education costs. The type of job and the work schedule are arranged by your school's financial aid administrator.

The amount and kind of aid available from these programs are subject to changes in the laws. For further, up-to-date information, write to the Office of Student Financial Assistance, Federal Financial Aid, P.O. Box 84, Washington, D.C. 20044.

Federal financial aid must be reapplied for every year and various circumstances affect your eligibility. In general, however, you must be enrolled in an eligible program at an eligible school (ask the school where you're applying if it is eligible), be a U.S. citizen or an eligible noncitizen, be at least a half-time student, and earn satisfactory grades. Whether or not you are independent of your parents is another factor affecting eligibility. If you live with your parents at least six weeks of the year, receive support from them, or continue to be claimed as an exemption on their tax return, you are considered to be dependent, and your parents' financial situation will be taken into consideration.

There are various other sources of aid. Many states have their own grant or scholarship programs. Write to your state's department of education to find out about these. In addition, schools may offer their own scholarship and loan programs, so it's worth talking to someone at the financial aid office of the institutions you are interested in. If you are currently employed and plan to continue working while you go to school, your employer may pay all or part of your tuition, particularly if the course work is related to your job. You may be eligible for veterans' benefits if you are a military veteran, so check with the local Veterans Administration. If you are handicapped, there may be special aid available; check with the local vocational rehabilitation office. If you are planning to study for medicine, nursing, dentistry, pharmacy, or an allied health profession, you can write for scholarship information to U.S. Public Health Service, Bureau of Health Manpower, Student Assistance Branch, Room G-23, Center Building, 3700 East-West Highway, Hyattsville, Md. 20782.

Privately sponsored loans and scholarship programs are available from community agencies, foundations, corporations, unions, religious groups, and civic and cultural groups. Depending upon their interest, such organizations award aid on the basis of academic ability, religious affiliation, ethnic or racial heritage, artistic talent, athletic ability, community service, etc. To find out about this kind of aid, check with the financial aid offices at local colleges and at the colleges you are applying to, as well as with the local library.

If you decided not to go to school because you thought you couldn't afford it, reconsider. There are almost as many ways of financing your education as there are institutions. Following is a list of additional publications that have been prepared especially for women. Be sure to take a look at them; although many of the listings are highly specialized, you may find some that apply to you without much competition. And, of course, check your library or guidance office for financial aid references that apply to both sexes, such as *The College Money Handbook,* published by Peterson's Guides.

Association for Women in Science. *Resources for Women in Science.* Washington: Association for Women in Science, 1980. (Available from Association for Women in Science, Room 1122, 1346 Connecticut Avenue, NW, Washington, D.C. 20036.)

Association of American Colleges, Project on the Status and Education of Women. *Financial Aid: A Partial List of Resources for Women.* Washington: Association of American Colleges, 1981. (Available from Association of American Colleges, 1818 R Street, NW, Washington, D.C. 20009.)

Business and Professional Women's Foundation. *Financial Aid, Where to Get It, How to Use It.* Washington: Business and Professional Women's Foundation, n.d. (Available from BPW Foundation, 2012 Massachusetts Avenue, NW, Washington, D.C. 20036.)

Clairol Loving Care Scholarship Program. *Educational Financial Aid Sources for Women.* New York: Clairol, 1981. (Available from Clairol Loving Care Scholarship, 345 Park Avenue, New York, N.Y. 10022.)

Directory of Federal Aid for Women and Minorities. Santa Monica, Calif.: Ready Reference Press, 1982.

Jawin, A. *A Woman's Guide to Career Preparation, Scholarships, Grants and Loans.* Garden City, N.Y.: Doubleday Publishing Co., 1979.

Schlacter, Gail Ann. *Directory of Financial Aids for Women.* 2nd ed. Santa Barbara, Calif.: Reference Service Press, 1982.

Society of Women Engineers. *Scholarship Programs.* New York: Society of Women Engineers, 1981. (Available from Society of Women Engineers, Room 305, 345 East 47th Street, New York, N.Y. 10017.)

Women's Sports Foundation. *The 1982 College Athletic Scholarship Guide.* San Francisco: Women's Sports Foundation, 1982. (Available from Women's Sports Foundation, 195 Moulton Street, San Francisco, Calif. 94123.)

The decision of what to do after high school is not one that is going to set irrevocably the course of your life for the next fifty years. It is only the first in a series of decisions that will shape your career. Whatever you do next, you'll have new experiences, acquire new interests, and meet new people, all of which can lead you in different directions. And, whatever direction you take, there will probably be a program somewhere to help you prepare for it.

This kind of flexibility may be shockingly innovative for people who are accustomed to the rigid convention of four years of college that begin when students are about 18 and end when they are about 21. You have to be flexible yourself if you want to capitalize on the new and creative types of schooling. And you must realize that throughout life you have to keep learning if you want to keep growing. Remember that whatever you do—school, job, or raising a family—will require motivation, discipline, and hard work.

One reassuring thing is that you don't have to make this decision all by yourself. Parents, relatives, friends, teachers, counselors, and books like this can provide information, advice, and direction. Sure, there are going to be things beyond your reach. Don't be discouraged. With so many possibilities open to you, you're going to find something that will satisfy your aspirations.

A Few Years Down the Road

Even if you've decided now to get an associate degree rather than a bachelor's degree—or plan to skip college altogether—there may come a time when you want that four-year degree. More and more women of all ages are returning to school for various reasons: the chance to meet new people and be in a stimulating environment, to get ahead in a current job, or to open new education and career options. Many schools welcome these students, finding that they bring a fresh perspective to the classroom because of their experience in the work world and a keener interest in their studies. After all, they've made a deliberate, conscious decision to return to school.

Returning to school after time away can be difficult. You'll probably have other obligations such as a family, a job, or social commitments that can't just be dropped because you're going to school. Somehow, your schedule will have to be worked out to accommodate them as well. Courses at night, weekend seminars, and summer semesters are designed for the person who has responsibilities in addition to school. Also consider other options, such as external degrees, credit by examination, and correspondence courses. Counselors, centers, and books are available to offer support, guidance, and advice.

Since you won't be able to devote all of your time to studying, it may take you longer than usual to get your degree. However long it takes, the effort you spend will be worth the rewards of expanded opportunities and a broader education.

WORKING WOMAN

Linda Cunningham McGee

Environmental Science Engineer

Television, that unblinking eye in the center of almost everyone's living room, has been decried as a bad influence on American youth. But influences come in different flavors, bad and good. Sometimes the set can turn *you* on, and that's what happened one day years ago when Linda Cunningham tuned in a Jacques Cousteau special. Thirteen-year-old Linda was entranced.

"I've always been interested in the outdoors and in sports," she recalls, "but when I first saw a Jacques Cousteau special on TV, I realized that the ocean held the greatest fascination for me. I decided then that I wanted to be one of Cousteau's divers or a member of his crew."

Even in Michigan, Linda could feel the "tidal pull." During high school, she still dreamed of working on—and in—the ocean. She saw, though, that she'd need more than a high school diploma to realize her ambition. Still, by the time she was 18, she had decided she didn't want to attend a conventional four-year college.

"I felt it wouldn't prepare me for an outdoors, get-your-hands-dirty type of job," she says. So she researched technical schools with programs in ocean studies and eventually chose the Cape Fear Technical Institute in North Carolina. The Institute's program, called Marine Laboratory Technology, prepares students to do fieldwork, lab work, and data analysis for scientists.

"We took classes in such things as small-boat handling, welding, and fishnet making and repair," Linda says. "There was also a class called 'Practical Experience' that covered whatever jobs needed to be done: chipping off rust from the boats, painting, repairing equipment, etc. Because I had taken a scuba-diving course in high school, I was able to participate in underwater projects as well.

"What I liked about technical school was that I only took classes in the things I was interested in; if I had taken a liberal arts program at a four-year institution, I would have had to spend too much time in classes that didn't have much to do with my interest in the ocean."

She found two drawbacks to the Cape Fear program: no dorms and no sports program. To Linda, however, these were minor problems, easily overcome.

"For the two years I attended CFTI, I lived in the home of an elderly woman who became like a grandmother to me. As for the sports—which I sorely missed—I introduced myself to the coaches at the local branch of the University of North Carolina and was eventually allowed to participate in team practices, although I couldn't actually compete with them."

Linda's program was small, about 100 students, half of whom were women. But the presence of women is a relatively recent phenomenon at many technical schools, and Linda ran into a few students and teachers who wished they could turn back the clock to the all-male days.

"In dealing with these people, I found that it was best to use a great deal of tact and to have a good sense of humor," she says. "I was thankful for the fighting spirit athletics has given me, which helped me to be firm in demanding challenging responsibilities and projects. But I also cooperated willingly if involved in anyone else's projects.

"Although I was teasingly called 'that Libber,' people treated me with respect and I had a great many friends. The skills I developed for dealing with people at CFTI have helped me through similar situations since."

While still enrolled at Cape Fear, Linda heard about a twelve-week ocean research program—Sea Semester, at Woods Hole, Massachusetts.

"I felt this was just what I needed to test myself, to see if I could take life at sea with Cousteau," she recalls. "I still had those romantic visions!" She convinced the Cape Fear admissions committee to substitute Sea Semester, plus two classes, for her last semester at CFTI.

The Woods Hole program began with six weeks of intensive classwork, including biology, navigation, and ecology. Then came the exciting part: six weeks at sea aboard the 100-foot schooner R/V *Westward*. On ship, the 22 students worked in the engine room, on deck, and in the galley and also performed scientific tasks.

"We had about an even mix of men and women," she recalls, "and were all treated equally. On a ship, everyone has to pull their own weight. We were all frequently pushed to our limits. As the cruise progressed, we were given increasing responsibility until finally we each served as watch officer, reporting directly to the captain. It was truly a terrific experience."

Then, armed with her Associate in Applied Science degree, it was time to see how well she could paddle her own canoe. She landed a job at a public aquarium in Mystic, Connecticut. It wasn't exactly a cruise with Jacques Cousteau, but for a year she busied herself with lab work, monitoring water quality and growing live algae, rotifer, and brine shrimp cultures to feed the fish.

"I liked that part of my job very much," Linda says. "After I'd worked there about a year, though, I began to sour on the idea of aquariums or zoos as a means of educating—or, more realistically, *entertaining*—the public. I didn't feel this justified the waste of aquatic life that I saw every day behind the scenes. For this reason, I decided to go back to school for further education in what was becoming a new interest of mine: aquaculture." (Sometimes known by the more descriptive term "fish farming," aquaculture involves using a natural or artificial body of water for the growing of fish, mollusks, and seaweed for food.)

The four-year degree that didn't seem to make sense when she was in high school had become sensible. At age 22, Linda enrolled at the University of Michigan because, besides being a very good school, it was less expensive (since it was her home state and she could pay the lower resident's tuition) and had a volleyball coach she liked. Believing that an engineering degree is more marketable than one in science, Linda eventually transferred from the University's School of Natural Resources to the environmental science engineering program.

"In this program," she explains, "the science part of your degree determines which engineering courses you take. I am specializing in water quality; other people in the program are studying things as varied as air pollution and urban planning."

She's found no prejudice against women engineering students.

"Here at the University of Michigan, women in engineering programs are not an uncommon sight. Although most are in programs like environmental science, computer science, civil engineering, and chemical engineering, there are growing numbers studying mechanical engineering, electrical engineering, and naval architecture. From my own experience with counselors, teachers, and other students, women in engineering are no big deal.

She's realistic about her job options after graduation. "In looking for a job, I have been stressing my background in water and wastewater treatments, hydrology, and environmental analysis more than in aquaculture, although that's my primary interest.

"There's not much research being done in this country in the area of aquaculture yet," she says, "but I think it is an up-and-coming field. I hope that when I have enough seniority and experience on my job, I will be able to propose projects in aquaculture to the company I work for."

Jacques Cousteau would be proud.

WHEN SHE WAS YOUNG

Golda Meir

Born in Russia in 1898, Golda Meir emigrated with her family to the United States in 1906 and later to Israel with her husband in 1921. There, she became involved in Israel's labor federation and the World Zionist Movement. Following the declaration of Israel's independence in 1948, Golda was the only woman member of the first provisional legislature. She went on to become the only woman member of the Cabinet, in 1956, and finally, in 1969, was sworn in as the first woman prime minister of Israel—at the age of 71, serving until 1974. This excerpt from her autobiography describes the conflict between Golda and her parents over her future. They wanted her to get married and settle down; she wanted to become a teacher.

When I was fourteen, I finished elementary school. My marks were good, and I was chosen to be class valedictorian. The future seemed very bright and clear to me. Obviously I would go on to high school and then, perhaps, even become a teacher, which is what I most wanted to be....

My parents, however—as I ought to have understood but did not—had other plans for me. I think my father would have liked me to be educated, and at my Fourth Street graduation ceremony his eyes were moist. He understood, I believe, what was involved; but in a way his own life had defeated him, and he was unable to be of much help to me. My mother, as usual and despite her disastrous relationship with Sheyna [Golda's older sister], knew exactly what I should do. Now that I had finished elementary school, spoke English well and without an accent and had developed into what the neighbors said was a *dervaksene shein meydl* (a fine, upstanding girl), I could work in the shop full time and sooner or later—but better sooner—start thinking seriously about getting married, which, she reminded me, was forbidden to women teachers by state law.

If I insisted on acquiring a profession, she said, I could go to secretarial school and learn to become a shorthand typist. At least, I wouldn't remain an old maid that way. My father nodded his head. "It doesn't pay to be too clever," he warned. "Men don't like smart girls." As Sheyna had done before me, I tried in every way I knew to change my parents' mind. In tears, I explained that nowadays an education was important, even for a married woman, and argued that in any case I had no intention whatsoever of getting married for a very long time. Besides, I sobbed, I would rather die than spend my life—or even part of it—hunched over a typewriter in some dingy office.

But neither my arguments nor my tears were of any avail. My parents were convinced that high school, for me at least, was an unwarranted luxury—not only unnecessary, but undesirable. From the distance of Denver, Sheyna (now convalescent and out of the sanatorium) encouraged me in my campaign, and so did Shamai [Sheyna's husband], who joined her there. . . .

In my secret letters to Denver I wrote in detail about the continuing fights over school that were making my life at home almost intolerable and were leading me to decide to become independent as soon as possible. That autumn, the autumn of 1912, I defiantly began my first term at Milwaukee's North Division High School and in the afternoons and on weekends worked at a variety of odd jobs, determined never again to ask my parents for money. But none of this helped; the disputes at home went on and on.

The last straw was my mother's attempt to find me a husband. She didn't want me to get married at once, of course, but she very much wanted to be sure not only that I would get married at what she considered a reasonable age, but that, unlike Sheyna, *I* at least, would marry somebody substantial. Not rich—that was out of the question— but at least solid. In actual fact, she was already discreetly negotiating with a Mr. Goodstein, a pleasant, friendly, relatively well-to-do man in his early thirties, whom I knew because he used to come into the store now and then to chat for a while. Mr. Goodstein! But he was an old man! Twice my age! I sent a furious letter to poor Sheyna. The reply came from Denver by return mail. "No, you shouldn't stop school. You are too young to work; you have good chances to become something," Shamai wrote. And with perfect generosity: "My advice is that you should get ready and come to us. We are not rich either, but you will have good chances here to study, and we will do all we can for you. . . ."

That letter, written from Denver in November, 1912, was a turning point in my life because it was in Denver that my real education began and that I started to grow up. I suppose that if Sheyna and Shamai had not come to my rescue, I would have gone on fighting with my parents, crying at night and still somehow going to high school. I can't imagine that I would have agreed under any circumstances to stop studying and marry the probably much-maligned Mr. Goodstein; but Sheyna and Shamai's offer was like a lifeline, and I grabbed at it.

In the years that have passed since that November, I have also often thought of Sheyna's last letter to me before I joined her in Denver. "The main thing," she wrote, "is never to be excited. Always be calm and act coolly. This way of action will always bring you good results. Be brave." That was advice about running away from home; but I never forgot it, and it stood me in good stead within a few years when I came to what was to be my real home, the land in which I was prepared to fight to the death in order to stay.

Drawing submitted by Suzanne M. Beebe, 16;
New Haven, Connecticut
Catalyst Cartoon Competition Winner

Hear What I'm Not Saying

"Mother—
 High school is over
 I'm leaving today
 To begin a new life
 On my own."

"Mother—
 Don't worry about me
 Yes, I will study
 Yes, I'll be good
 Yes, I can take care of myself."

"Mother—
 The time has come
 My bags are packed
 I'll call you next month
 Good-bye."

Mommy,
 I'll be far from you
 Alone and afraid
 To begin a new life—
 College.

Mommy,
 Please worry about me
 I need your support
 I'm terribly frightened
 Hold me.

Mommy,
 The time has come
 I don't want to go
 I'll miss you
 I love you.

Poem submitted by Frances K. Wang, 15;
Morgan Hill, California
Catalyst Poetry Competition Winner

12
A Job-Hunting Primer

"Cheshire-Puss,"... [said] Alice.... "Would you tell me, please, which way I ought to go from here?"

"That depends a good deal on where you want to get to," said the Cat.

—Lewis Carroll, *mathematician and writer*

When you learn to drive a car, you don't just jump behind the wheel, turn the key, floor the gas pedal, and merrily zip off. You'd be likely to zip right into the rear of that $40,000 Porsche in front of you. The next thing you'd see would be a flashing red light and a polite-but-firm face asking, "May I see your driver's license, ma'am?" No, unless you're Mr. Toad in *The Wind in the Willows*, you'll learn to drive by first mastering the rules of the road, then mastering the levers and dials, and finally edging cautiously away from the curb. At first, your awkwardness will be matched only by your anxiety, but practice will transform you into a skilled and confident driver, someone who knows how to get where she wants to go.

With the same kind of effort, you can develop job-hunting skills that you can use throughout your life. You'll learn how to find your first job and how to find another when circumstances—or your goals—

change. Frequently, changes in circumstances are beyond the control of individuals. In the 1960s, for instance, teachers had their pick of jobs. By the mid-1970s, the situation was different and some teachers were laid off. The teachers weren't to blame; the postwar baby boom had simply ended and there were fewer students to teach.

You'll change, too, as you get older. Maybe you find lab work really exciting right now and you can't imagine doing anything else. In ten years, however, management might begin to look attractive. You can't predict how you'll change in the coming years, but you *can* master the skills that will help you find a new job if your goals do change.

NINE TO GET READY

Go back in your mind to your childhood. Remember those last few weeks of summer each year, just before school started? Remember how excited you felt? You checked out last year's clothes to see which ones you'd outgrown. Maybe you got a new dress or a new pair of sneakers. You collected all the necessary equipment—lunch box, pencils, paper, a new loose-leaf notebook—and you were all set for the first day of school.

Preparing for your job search will give you that same feeling of excitement. What will you need? The basics include a Social Security number, a work permit (if you're under 16), a résumé, samples of your work, references, interview clothes, a datebook or calendar, and a job file. But first: Do you have a job target?

YOUR JOB TARGET

A job target isn't a bull's-eye labeled "lawyer." It's simply your idea of the job you want to have. It can be the job itself: "I want to be a paramedic." It can be an industry or place to work: "I want to work in the computer industry," or "I want to work in a library." Or it can be something else about a job, like advancement, opportunities to learn new skills, or a chance to work on a commission basis.

Michelle clarified her job target after talking with her guidance counselor. When she was a senior in high school, Michelle's father died. "I thought then that I would have to give up the idea of going to college and that I'd have to get a job," she said. "I was bitterly disappointed, partly because my father had always wanted me to go to college."

The guidance counselor at Michelle's high school told her there were companies that helped pay the college tuition of their employees.

That became Michelle's job target—to find a job with a company that would send her to college.

"Well, I found it. It took me a little longer to find this job, but I'm very happy here. Of course I'm working like crazy—day and night—but I'm going to have everything I wanted."

Without a job target, you'll waste time responding to every opening you find. You won't know how to answer when an interviewer asks you, "What kind of job are you looking for?" You won't even know when you've found what you wanted. You *must* have a job target.

Janet started out looking for "just any job." She didn't find one until she set a target.

"When I graduated from high school I had very little work experience to go on. I started answering ads and going to employment agencies. It was very discouraging. I didn't know what I wanted to do, and nobody seemed to want me.

"One evening I was talking to my older brother and his friends and one of them, remembering I was good in math, said, 'Why don't you look for a job in a bank?' I knew I wanted to be in business, so I thought I'd give banking a try. I talked to a friend of my mother's who worked in a bank, and that's when things started to click for me. All of a sudden I knew what I was looking for. I wanted to be a teller.

"I went into the city and applied for a teller's position at every large bank I could walk to in two days. The interviewers treated me differently because I knew what I wanted. And one summer job as a cashier counted for me. Banks like to have tellers who have had what they call 'cash experience.' That means they've worked with money before.

"But I didn't just take the first offer I got. I had worked one summer in a place with a terrible atmosphere. I decided I only wanted to work in a place where I would feel happy working. So I took my time and looked around some more. I think you can tell what kind of a place it is to work by how they treat you in the interview. I picked this bank because they really showed an interest in me. The people I met in their branches also seemed like really nice people who wanted to see me do the job well. I made the right choice. Four years later, I'm still at the bank and still enjoying my work. Only now I'm head teller at a major branch."

When you are thinking about a job target, dream a little. Look for something you really want, and aim for it. The earlier chapters in this book help you set a job target. They guide you through the process of career planning—from awareness of yourself to awareness of the work world.

Do You Have a Social Security Number?

Anyone who is employed, regardless of age, must have a Social Security number and a card. Employers use the number to report each employee's income to the Internal Revenue Service for income tax purposes. And Social Security contributions are deducted from your wages by your employer (who pays an equal amount) so that later, when you reach retirement age, you'll be eligible for Social Security benefits.

If you don't have a Social Security number, look up the nearest office of the Social Security Administration in the White Pages of your telephone book. Visit the office nearest you and fill out an application form. You'll have to take three pieces of identification with you: your birth certificate and two other "official" documents with your signature, such as a driver's license, a credit card, a school identification card, or any school record with your signature. Then, it usually takes about six weeks to get your number.

Do You Need a Work Permit or Age Certificate?

A work permit or age certificate is an official document that shows you are older than the minimum age for the job. Employers of minors keep age certificates on file to prove that they are not violating child labor laws.

All states and the federal government have child labor laws that restrict the kind of work people under 18 may do. The state laws vary, but they are fairly close to the federal requirements. Generally speaking, if you are not working for your parents or as an actor, newspaper delivery person, or farm worker, you are covered by these regulations:

- *Fourteen* is the minimum age for employment in most jobs, including office and clerical work, cashiering and selling, packing and shelving, delivery work, cleaning, and kitchen work. Certain more hazardous jobs—working with heavy machinery or dangerous chemicals, for instance—are not open to you at all if you are 14 or 15. Nor can you work more than 3 hours on a school day or 18 hours a week during school—unless it is in a school-run work or career program. On nonschool days, you can't work more than 8 hours a day, and during nonschool weeks you can't work more than 40 hours a week. Between June and Labor Day, you can work until 9 P.M., but the rest of the year you can work only between 7 A.M. and 7 P.M. You need a work permit or age certificate if you're 14 or 15.

- *Sixteen* is the basic minimum age for working. There are no special restrictions on the hours you may work, but you may not work in certain hazardous jobs until you are 18. These hazardous jobs (determined by the Secretary of Labor) include most coal mining jobs, most jobs involving explosives or ammunition, logging or sawmilling, power-driven metal forming, slaughtering, and jobs that involve exposure to radioactive substances. Some states require work permits or age certificates for 16- and 17-year-old workers, too.

- *Eighteen* is the minimum age for those hazardous jobs listed above. When you are 18, there are generally no special employment-related restrictions because of your age.

If you are under 18 and need a work permit or age certificate, ask your high school adviser or guidance counselor how to get one. Most employers who are accustomed to hiring 14- or 15-year-olds can also tell you how to apply, as can the state board of education.

YOUR RÉSUMÉ

A good résumé, like a good advertisement, provides information in a positive way. It's a summary on paper of your skills, accomplishments, and experiences. Résumés are sent in response to classified ads, handed in with application forms, or given to interviewers.

There are occasions when you don't need a résumé. If you're looking for your first job and have little or no experience, a completed application form may be all that's needed. The same goes if you're looking for a job through an employment agency. But even if you don't need one for your prospective employer, the process of preparing a résumé is useful. It helps you focus on your most important skills and achievements and relate them to your job target. It also prepares you to answer questions about your experience.

Sharon got her first job at her hometown drugstore. She wanted summer work and, knowing it was hard to find, started looking in April. She went from store to store, asking if they needed summer help. Whether there was a job opening or not, she left a very brief résumé at each store.

The results were good—three job offers. "If you leave something with them," Sharon reasoned, "you stand out as more mature and more organized than the other people looking for work."

Three sample résumés are shown on pages 255–257. The first is the short one Sharon used before she had much work experience. Résumés 2 and 3 are appropriate after a year's work experience. Like all three examples, *your* résumé should contain

- Your name, address, and telephone number
- Your education
- Your past jobs (where and when you worked, including volunteer work)
- Information about what you did on each job

Résumé 1 emphasizes Sharon's skills, and each skill listed is backed up with specific evidence. The fact that she had held only one paid job (in her school office) is deemphasized with this kind of presentation.

Résumé 2 is a straightforward summary of Sharon's work history, starting with her most recent job and going backwards from there. This "chronological" résumé is the kind most commonly used. If Sharon's job target is to get a job similar to the one she has now, this is a good format since it gives specific details about what she's accomplished.

Before preparing Résumé 3, a "functional" résumé, Sharon decided her job target was "sales trainee." She rearranged the data concerning her work experience to highlight sales and included high school accomplishments. Notice that Sharon placed a chronological summary of her experience at the end. Résumés 2 and 3 contain the same information but emphasize different things.

Select the résumé format that best suits *your* job target and circumstances. As you write, describe your skills and accomplishments as specifically as possible. Use action words (like "prepared" and "performed") and numbers (like "$2000 in sales") whenever possible.

Information about your health, weight, or marital status is unnecessary, and it only distracts readers from your job-related skills.

Whether you include a "Special Interests" section is up to you. If you have an interest that is a salable skill, such as photography, drawing, or carpentry, you should probably put information about that skill on your résumé. Interests like cooking, travel, or movies, unless directly related to the job, should be omitted.

Some final advice: All résumés, even brief ones, must

- Be neatly typed
- Contain no spelling or grammatical errors
- Be photocopied clearly, legibly, and straight on the page

Make sure you have a knowledgeable friend check your résumé for typographical and spelling errors. You can find help in writing your résumé from a high school guidance counselor, a state employment agency counselor, or sometimes from an employment agency recruiter. Workbooks, such as the Catalyst *Résumé Preparation Manual*, can be found at your library or bookstore and also provide detailed, step-by-step guidance in résumé preparation.

When you send a copy of your résumé to a potential employer, write and type a cover letter to go with it. This is your sales pitch for a particular job. In your cover letter, state your job target and reinforce or give more details about the skills and experience on your résumé. If you are sending your résumé in response to a classified ad, repeat the description of the job in the ad as closely as possible. Your cover letter should echo each requirement whenever possible. For example, if the ad states that the company is looking for someone with "one or two years' experience and exposure to quality control," you might say, "I have had almost a full year's experience in this field, and I was exposed to quality control through my department's activities in. . . ."

The cover letter that accompanied Sharon's functional résumé, which she sent in response to a classified ad for a sales trainee position, is on page 258. It mentions her job target, repeats words from the ad, and builds a strong case for hiring her.

Résumé 1: Minimal Work Experience

Sharon Corkum
32 April Road
Westford, Ohio 02134
227-6410

I am a Westford High junior looking for a summer job. I have skills you can use:

Typing: 55 words a minute (Typing I and II at Westford High School)

Clerical Work: Prepared bulk mailings (up to 1,000 pieces) and filed for high school office (after school)

Responsible with Money: Managed ticket sales worth $2400 for high school play

---

References: Ms. Helen Croft, Westford High School Office, 227-9100, Extension 235

Mr. Blake Radisson, Westford High School, 227-9100, Extension 210

Résumé 2: Chronological

Sharon Corkum
32 April Road
Westford, Ohio 02134
227-6410

Work Experience

June 1983 to present	Customer Service Representative, Haford Wales Inc., Dayton, Ohio

- Handle approximately 50 orders a day for manufacturer of boiler controls
- Perform inventory control procedures on Astra Business System (computerized)
- Manage customer complaints for Maintenance Division

1981–1982 1982–1983 (school years)	Administrative Support, Westford High School, Westford, Ohio

- Typed, mimeographed, prepared bulk mailings up to 1,000 pieces
- Typed general correspondence

1982 (summer)	Clerk, Ruabon Drugs, Westford, Ohio

- Handled sales
- Managed store in owner's absence
- Helped prepare and send out bills

Education

1983 Graduate, Westford High School, Business Major

Courses in: accounting, computer science, typing, shorthand

Special Interests

Photography and basketball

References available on request.

Résumé 3: Functional

Sharon Corkum
32 April Road
Westford, Ohio 02134
227-6410

Work Experience

Sales

- Handle 50 orders a day for boiler control manufacturer
- As sales clerk in drugstore, increased sales of cosmetics
- Sold $2000 worth of ads for high school yearbook
- Managed ticket sales worth $2400 for high school play
- Collected $1500 as junior high student for Oxfam America, Inc.

Administrative

- Perform inventory control procedures for boiler control manufacturer
- Helped prepare and send out bills for drugstore
- Managed store in owner's absence
- Typed, mimeographed, and prepared bulk mailings (up to 1,000 pieces) for high school office
- Typed general correspondence for high school office

June 1983 to present: Customer Service Representative, Haford Wales Inc., Dayton, Ohio

1981–1983 (school years): Administrative Support, Westford High School, Westford, Ohio

1982 (summer): Clerk, Ruabon Drugs, Westford, Ohio

Education

1983   Graduate, Westford High School, Business Major

Courses in: accounting, computer science, typing, shorthand

Special Interests

Photography and basketball

References available on request.

Sample Cover Letter

32 April Road
Westford, Ohio 02134
July 14, 1984

Mr. Arnold Roberts
Sales Manager
Jackson and Sons, Inc.
1127 Hillside Avenue
Westford, Ohio 02134

Dear Mr. Roberts:

I would like to be considered for the sales trainee position advertised in the Sunday <u>News Tribune.</u> I have been working in jobs where sales was only a part of what I was expected to do and have come to realize that, for me, sales is the most exciting part of the job. I am now aiming for a career in sales.

I am a responsible and highly motivated person. I am also familiar with some of your office equipment. I use your Business System in my current job (see enclosed résumé), so I know how your equipment fits into an office setting.

Please give me the chance to meet you and describe my qualifications in person.

Sincerely,

Sharon Corkum

Sharon Corkum

Enclosure

SAMPLES OF YOUR WORK

Showing samples of your work can often help you land a job, particularly if your experience in the field is very limited. One young woman got into a special training program after showing printouts of her computer programs. Another took clothes she'd made in school to dress stores and landed a job as a designer-in-training. A cabinetmaker was hired after showing photographs of furniture she'd built in shop class. A woman applying for a job as an auto body repairer told her interviewer, "If you'd like to see the kind of work I can do, come out to the parking lot and have a look at my car." A sample of your work that shows what you can do will help get the job you want.

If you're looking for a job as a photographer, cartoonist, graphic artist, writer, or drafter, a portfolio of work samples is essential. Display them neatly and attractively in a binder or notebook. The samples can be from school courses and from jobs you've had—anything that shows the kind of work you can do. Organize the samples in chronological order, starting with the most recent, and include only your *best* work. Start with a sample that grabs attention, something you're really proud of. When you show the portfolio, talk about what the interviewers are looking at, but let them look through it at their own pace. If possible, have a few extra samples or photocopies of your work to leave with an interested interviewer.

REFERENCES

Before making hiring decisions, employers often check to see that what you've said about yourself is true. They prefer references from people who have known you on the job over those from teachers or friends. At the beginning of your career, though, teachers or guidance counselors can also serve as references.

At the bottom of Résumé 1, Sharon listed one work-related reference and one teacher reference. Ms. Croft supervised her office work for the high school. Mr. Radisson is the high school drama coach. Because she asked them if they would be willing to write a recommendation for her, Sharon knew what each would say about her. Ms. Croft would say that Sharon was always on time and did her work well. Mr. Radisson would brag that Sharon sold more tickets to a school play than anyone else in the history of the high school.

Select your references carefully. Choose people who know your work and will be enthusiastic about you. *Always* ask before listing anyone as a reference. It's a good idea to tell each reference your job target and provide him or her with a copy of your résumé. (Once you land your job, remember to share your good news with your references and thank them for their help.)

Note that on Résumés 2 and 3, Sharon didn't list her references. She wanted to wait until she knew that she was being seriously considered for a job first. She could decide during the interview which references would be best for the job she wanted. And since her current employer didn't know yet that she was job hunting and she wanted to use him as a reference, she planned to wait as long as possible before telling him.

Sometimes employers use their own sources to check the qualifications of prospective employees. One boss may rely on his secretary's knowledge of "every family in town" before he hires someone. Another checks with a friend who teaches at the local high school for scuttlebutt about a job seeker. In these situations, you just have to keep your fingers crossed.

INTERVIEW CLOTHES

What you wear to a job interview is important for at least two reasons: looking good will boost your self-confidence, and it will create a favorable impression. But you don't have to go out and buy a new wardrobe—unless your closet contains only blue jeans and running shoes. Just pick clothes that fit well, are comfortable, and make you feel self-assured. Generally, a simple dress or skirt and blouse are good bets.

Many job counselors and company recruiters advise women *always* to wear skirts to job interviews, even at a place where women commonly wear pants. They say the only exceptions are jobs like telephone installer or auto mechanic, where pants are the "uniform." You can disregard this advice if you want to, but be aware that if you do wear trousers, you risk creating a less favorable impression with some interviewers.

Some final interview tips: Plan on getting to the interview a few minutes early so you'll have time to stop in the restroom, straighten your clothes, and comb your hair. This will lessen your anxiety about your appearance. (If pressure makes you breathless, take some relaxing deep breaths while in the restroom.) Lastly, if you're starting an extensive job search, try to have two sets of interview clothes so that one outfit will always be clean and ready at a moment's notice. This will also give you an alternate outfit if you have to go back to the same place twice.

YOUR DATEBOOK OR CALENDAR

Arriving late or on the wrong day for a job interview is one of the worst mistakes a job hunter can make. Avoid it by using a special datebook for your job search. You won't need anything elaborate, and it should be small enough to carry with you.

Enter every appointment you make in the datebook. Be sure you put down the time, the name of the person you're to see, the address, the phone number (in case you get lost), and clear directions (so you don't). It's a good idea also to note the dates you sent résumés to various employers and the dates when you expect to hear about each job. By writing this down and taking it with you, you'll never get stuck like this Boston job hunter:

"I had just made the appointment the day before so I was sure I remembered where to go. I went all the way out to Malden Center on the subway and got off and started looking for the street address. I couldn't find it. Then I started to get scared. Which town was it in? Was it in Malden or maybe was it in Medford Center? Or Medfield Center? Or Medway? When you get scared you can't remember anything.

"Well, it turned out to be Medford. I got there 2 hours late and even though I called to let them know, I wasn't really considered for the job. Now, I always write *everything* down."

YOUR JOB FILE

The last piece of "basic equipment" you'll need is a job file. A cardboard box will do; just make sure it's in a place where it won't be disturbed by little brothers looking for paper to draw on or cats looking for a cozy place to nap.

Keep all your job information and records—copies of your résumé and cover letters, notes on different employers you've researched—in the job file so you can find what you need right away. Also, use the file to help you organize your job search activities. That way, you'll follow up every option systematically. Put all your information about specific job openings and leads in a separate file folder or envelope. (Cut out classified ads and staple them to a regular-sized piece of paper so you won't lose them.) Then, as you investigate each one, draw a line through those that don't work out.

Remember, the more options you pursue, the more jobs you'll hear about, the more interviews you'll have, and the more positions you'll have to choose from.

HOW TO FIND THE RIGHT JOB

> "The trouble is," said Laura, "walking in Venice becomes compulsive once you start. Just over the next bridge, you say, and then the next one beckons."
>
> —Daphne du Maurier, *novelist*

Think about yourself for a minute. You are the center of your own personal world. In that world are all kinds of people you know and all kinds of places you're familiar with. You know some of these people and places intimately: your family and friends, the street you live on, the stores you usually shop in. Radiating from this inner circle are other circles of people and places you know fairly well; then, beyond them, circles you know casually; until you get to distant circles of people or places you've only heard about. Your personal world is your solar system, with you—like the sun—at the center.

The nature of your world is an important factor in your choice of a career. Because of it, you might be an expert on classrooms or cattle but know nothing about computers or carburetors. That's why you should stretch beyond the limits of your inner circle. Your personal world also shapes your job hunting because it determines the people you know—people who may hire you or guide you to a job. There's a lot of truth in the old saying, "It's not what you know but *who* you know that counts." When you're looking for a job, connections can make a big difference.

The simple truth is that most job openings are not advertised, and most people get jobs through people they already know. Maybe it's not fair, but it's a fact. A person who's qualified for the job and who has an "in" is more likely to be hired than someone who sends in a résumé (along with a hundred other people) in response to a classified ad.

If you put yourself in an employer's shoes, you'll understand that hiring new employees invariably involves some risk. Suppose you hire that friendly, energetic young woman you interviewed. Then she comes in late every morning and can't really operate a lathe as well as she claimed. You have a real problem. Do you fire her and go through the lengthy and expensive hiring process all over again? Do you arrange extra supervision or extra training for her? Employers try to reduce this risk by hiring an applicant they know or someone who is recommended by people they know; in fact, some companies even pay a bonus to an employee who recommends someone the company hires.

Jill got her job at a newspaper through the father of children she baby-sat for. "I knew he worked for a newspaper, and so I just asked him if he knew of an opening for someone like me. He even called the personnel office and recommended me. Of course I got the job."

Maria got a job through someone she met at a party. "The funny thing was, I almost didn't go to the party. I met someone who said he'd heard of a job opening and to call his friend on Monday. That conversation led to my job here. I think you've got to let everyone know you're looking for a job and what kind of job you want, and then follow up on every lead."

Maria's right. Once you've decided on your job target, tell *every-one* about it, particularly older people like friends of your parents (and parents of your friends), people you've worked for in the past, and teachers. When you're given a lead—the name of someone to call or see—write down that name and the name of the person who referred you. Then use the name of the person who referred you in the first sentence of your phone call or letter: "Hello, Ms. Marret, Bob Avery suggested I call you. . . ." Or "Dear Ms. Marret: I am writing at the suggestion of Bob Avery. . . ." Be sure, too, that you keep a record of all your job leads in a special part of your job file and follow up each one systematically. And thank the person who gave you the tip.

"I used to think it wasn't really fair somehow that I got my job because I knew somebody," says Jill. "But now that I've been working for a while, I know that's how the work world functions. I work hard at my job, and I'm sure I put out a little extra partly because I want to live up to my recommendation."

While you're following up on job leads, you might also want to use classified ads, employment agencies, and company personnel offices to help you find a job. These more formal ways of getting a job can be particularly helpful if you're new to the area. And in today's tight job market, many job hunters find it necessary to explore a variety of avenues to find job openings.

Classified Ads

Each day newspapers list job openings in the classified ads. Sunday papers generally contain the most. Each newspaper serves a limited geographical area, so if you're looking for a job in a particular town or city, be sure to check the local papers.

Most help-wanted ads are divided into categories such as Professional Help (for people with college degrees or advanced training), Business Help (which includes clerical, secretarial, and bookkeeping positions), Medical Help (which covers all kinds of jobs in hospitals, nursing homes, and doctors' offices), General Help (which lists jobs in manufacturing and skilled and unskilled jobs in the trades), Sales Help (all kinds of jobs involving selling), and Household Help (which contains ads for baby-sitters, housekeepers, etc.).

Read the ads in the sections that apply to your job target. Make sure you don't overlook the little ads with lots of abbreviations. (See the "Translator's Guide to Classified Ads" in this section.) When you find an ad that interests you, cut it out, staple it to a larger piece of paper, and note the newspaper name and the date.

Translator's Guide to Classified Ads

No, classified ads are not written in some obscure foreign language. But most *are* filled with abbreviations. Why? The shorter the ad, the cheaper it is to run. Here are some common abbreviations.

AA/EO employer	affirmative action/equal opportunity employer
acct	accounting
asst	assistant
bkkp	bookkeeping
EEO	equal employment opportunity
EOE	equal opportunity employer
exp	experience
f/pd	fee paid
ft or f/t	full time
hlpr	helper
hrs	hours
int'l	international
K	thousand a year ($13K means $13,000 a year
lic	license
m/f	male or female
mfg	manufacturing
m/f/h	minority/female/handicapped
mgr	manager
nat'l	national
oppt'y	opportunity
pt or p/t	part time
sec'y	secretary
sft	shift
trnee	trainee
w/	with
wpm	words per minute

Virtually every ad will tell you three important pieces of information:

1. What the job is
2. The qualifications needed to get the job
3. How to respond to the ad

After analyzing the ads you're interested in, be sure to respond exactly as the ad states. If you're instructed to call, try to get through to an interviewer. The person who answers the phone has been trained to screen out unqualified callers, so don't underestimate yourself or sell yourself short on the phone. When you get to the interview, the interviewer may give you a chance even if your qualifications aren't quite the ones mentioned in the ad. And, whether you respond by phone, by mail, or in person, use as many of the words from the ad as possible.

Don't be surprised if the ad proves to be somewhat exaggerated. Remember that it was written to attract attention. A perfect-sounding job in an ad might be perfectly terrible when you've taken a closer look. Learn to be a little skeptical; it's not likely that you'll earn $20,000 addressing envelopes in your spare time.

Too Good to Be True

Tired of just frills and no money? Make $500-a-week commission. No experience necessary.

$260 per week Comm. If you are ambitious and would like to get ahead, we will train you. . . .

I am 25 yrs. old and made $50,000 last year. I am looking for high school grads with no exper. . . .

The job advertisements quoted above involved selling products—vacuum cleaners, encyclopedias, pots and pans—door-to-door, and applicants actually had to buy the product or pay money in advance before getting a chance to work. In other words, the companies made money not by selling products to customers, but by selling products to would-be saleswomen and salesmen, people who ended up stuck with the merchandise. Do *you* need ten vacuum cleaners?

Another scam is used often with magazine sales. Applicants are promised an exciting sales job in another part of the country, special bonuses, paid room and board, scholarships, the works. What they *aren't* told is that they'll be herded around in an old converted school bus, dropped in an unfriendly neighborhood in a part of the country they aren't familiar with, and told to make their quota of sales or they won't be picked up again. After working for a month, they might be abandoned in a strange city with nothing to show for their work.

There *are* honest companies selling magazines, vacuum cleaners, encyclopedias, pots and pans, and other products door-to-door. But legitimate companies don't lure naïve job hunters with get-rich-quick promises, and they pay their sales force a reasonable commission. Here are some clues that will help you tell whether an ad is for a real job or a rip-off:

- Does the ad mention the product you'd be selling?
- Does the ad state the name of the company?
- Does the salary sound unreasonably high for the work involved?
- When you call, do you get an answering service?
- Does the interviewer refuse to discuss any negative aspects of the job, duck specific questions, and assure you that, no matter what your background, you'll be successful?

If you decide to follow up on a job selling products door-to-door, make sure you have someone you trust read any contract you're asked to sign. *Never* work for a company that asks you to pay money first in order to get the job or for one that no one has ever heard of. Remember: The job that sounds too good to be true probably is.

Employment Agencies

Sometimes companies with job openings use employment agencies. This saves the company the bother of advertising, answering phone calls, and interviewing unsuitable people. Usually, the specifications for agency jobs are precise: applicants must possess a certain skill, such as typing eighty words a minute, or be able to operate a certain machine. The employment agency representative tries to get a clear idea of the kind of person needed and then matches that as closely as possible with someone in the agency's files.

Employment agencies make money by connecting job hunters with jobs. Usually the agency doesn't earn a cent until the person is actually hired. Then, the agency's fee is based on a percentage of what the new employee will earn. That means that filling low-paying jobs is less lucrative than filling high-paying ones. The result? Naturally, agencies work longer and harder to fill the highest-paying jobs.

An employment agency can offer you some real advantages. For one thing, some job openings are listed only through an agency. Furthermore, many agencies will give you advice on interviewing and help you prepare your résumé. They usually know enough about a particular job to give you tips on what to wear and what to emphasize in the interview. Finally, they can save you time by screening out jobs that aren't right for you.

On the other hand, if you don't fit neatly into a job category, an agency might be unenthusiastic about getting you a job. Or, if you've been interviewed unsuccessfully several times, you might be passed over the next time. And if you do get a job offer, you will probably be pressured to take it. Remember: The more people they place in jobs, the more they earn. *Never* give in to this kind of pressure unless you believe the job is the right one for you.

Agencies tend to specialize, so make sure you go to one that fits your job target. You often can get some idea of an agency's specialization from its ad in the Yellow Pages or the newspaper. If you aren't sure what kinds of jobs a particular agency handles, it's easy to call and ask. Questions such as, "Do you place people in entry-level positions?" or "Do you place people in summer jobs?" or "Do you have management trainee listings?" can save you time.

Another thing to ask about (or look for in employment agency ads) is whether the agency handles "fee paid" jobs. That means that the employment agency is paid by the company with the job opening, not by the person looking for work. Most employment agencies work this way unless they're basically career counseling centers or government-run services, but it's best to find out in advance. Some agencies still accept "split fee" jobs (the company pays part and the job hunter pays part) and jobs that require the applicant to pay the entire fee.

In addition, before you go to any employment agency, check on its reputation. Have your parents, school counselors, or friends heard of the agency? Do you know someone who has used it? Some agencies are better run than others. Some take unfair advantage of people. Be cautious. Never sign any contract or agreement with an employment agency unless you have read it over very carefully. A good bet is to show it to a friend or relative who knows something about contracts. If they won't let you take it out of the office to do this, you have good reason to be suspicious of it.

When you go to an employment agency, expect to wait (even if you have an appointment). Bring a pen, since you'll fill out an application form (even if you've brought your résumé). Ask for two copies of the application form—just say that you want to keep a copy in your files. It's a good idea to keep a copy of every form you fill out in case you're asked questions about it later. If there's time before the interview, note your answers on your file copy. It's also handy to have two copies if you make an error. You won't have to go back and explain that you made a mistake.

After you've handed in your completed application and taken any tests, you'll be interviewed by an agency recruiter. Probably this interview will be more relaxed than an interview with a prospective employer. The interviewer may dress casually, call you by your first name, and try to draw you out and make you feel very good about your skills and abilities. Remember, however, that you are still being evaluated. Wear business clothes. Establish eye contact. Treat the interview seriously. The recruiter will be looking for things to use in "selling" you to a prospective employer. Boast about anything that makes you look good. The recruiter will tell you if being captain of your bowling team is a selling point or not.

As one employment agency recruiter put it, "All the time I'm interviewing a person, I'm thinking. Is this a front office person? Can this person present herself well in an interview? Does she act enthusiastic and responsible? Will she pass XYZ Company's dress code? I'm not just looking at someone with my own eyes, I'm looking at her through a company personnel officer's eyes, too."

If the agency has a job listing appropriate for you, you'll be sent for an interview. The agency recruiter will call you and prepare you for the interview and will call the potential employer to praise you and your qualifications.

State Employment Services

Each state offers employment services in major towns and cities. These offices operate a lot like private employment agencies; job hunters visit the office, fill out an application form, and are sent out on job interviews. There are some important differences, however. Employees of state services are paid salaries, not commissions, so there's less pressure on them to fill vacancies. State service offices can often tell you which kinds of jobs are short of applicants— important information if you're setting or adjusting your job target. In addition, some state employment services run training sessions in job-hunting skills, and most can refer you to special training or work programs offered by the state, major unions, and employers. To find your state's employment service, look under the state government listings in your telephone book.

Temporary Employment Services

If you don't have much work experience or you aren't sure of your job target, consider applying at a temporary employment service. They function much like employment agencies except that the jobs they're filling may last only a day and will probably last several months at most. Temporary workers perform special tasks or fill in for regular employees who are sick or on vacation or are themselves on special assignment.

The positions offered by temporary employment services are often fairly routine and don't always pay well. You aren't guaranteed any amount of work, either. But as a program director for one temporary employment service puts it, "When you come to us, if you're any good at all, you'll be working right away. No waiting around to see if you're hired or to get your first paycheck. Employers aren't as choosy about temporary help. They judge temporary help by a different set of standards. Were you there on time? Was your attitude good? That's 75 percent of what they will judge you by. They aren't as concerned about how efficiently you're doing the job. They expect you to still be learning. If you're there on time and if you're trying, they'll give you a good reference."

Collecting good references isn't the only reason to try a temporary agency. If you want to know what it's like to work somewhere—a hospital, a factory, or a large insurance company—working as a "temp" is one way to find out without making a long-term commitment. You'll be earning money, learning skills, and meeting "contacts"—and your relatively flexible work schedule will enable you to look for a permanent job when you aren't on a temporary assignment. Who knows? An employer may like you enough to offer a permanent position.

Usually it's not necessary to sign up with more than one temporary agency, provided you have skills that are in demand. And since you're hired and paid directly by the temporary agency, there's no second interview. Some services will give you a series of tests to evaluate your skills; some offer benefits like medical insurance to people who work with the service for six months or more; some even offer special training programs (like word processing or typing) for people who lack specific skills that are in demand. You'll probably be notified at least two or three days in advance of any job. Sometimes you may even get a choice of assignments. You have the right to refuse to take a temporary job assignment, but if you refuse too often the temporary service won't call you back.

Company Personnel Offices

Large employers—hospitals, universities, manufacturing companies, and state governments, for example—operate personnel departments or offices that work something like in-house employment agencies. If a research laboratory needs an apprentice pipe fitter, for example, the head of the maintenance division will send a job description or job order to the company personnel department. A staff member in that department will then be assigned to find appropriate applicants for the head of maintenance to interview.

A large employer doesn't list every opening in the classified ads. Notices of job openings are often posted on company bulletin boards so employees hear about them first. Often, too, applicants from within the company have a better chance of being hired. If you've decided on a particular industry or particular type of employer, however, it's probably a good idea to check with all the employers in that category in case they have unadvertised openings.

There are two schools of thought about whether you should call first and ask if there are any job openings. Calling is quicker and easier, of course. However, some personnel recruiters think it shows energy and initiative if you take the trouble to visit the office and fill out an application. And, as one personnel recruiter put it, "There is always the chance that if you call today, I'd say there was nothing available, but the next day I'd have just the right opening and no way of contacting you without that application form."

HOW TO FILL OUT AN APPLICATION FORM

Both company personnel departments and employment agencies use application forms as a shorthand way of getting to know you before you're interviewed and as a way of keeping track of applicants. From the application form, the interviewer can tell if you're qualified enough to be interviewed at all and, if you are, what should be discussed during the interview.

Again, ask for *two* copies of the application form so you'll have an extra one for your files or in case you make a mistake.

Application forms usually have four basic sections covering (1) personal information, (2) education, (3) work history, and (4) references. Here are examples of these four sections from real application forms.

Personal Information:

APPLICATION FOR EMPLOYMENT

IN ORDER THAT YOUR APPLICATION MAY BE
PROPERLY EVALUATED, IT IS ESSENTIAL THAT
ALL OF THE FOLLOWING QUESTIONS BE
ANSWERED CAREFULLY AND COMPLETELY.

6/15/84
TODAY'S DATE

Name (Last, First, Middle Initial) PLEASE PRINT	Area Code	Phone Number	Social Security Number
❶ McHenry, Rosemary G.	602	444-1243	**❷** 136-60-5472

Present Address (No., Street, City, State, and Zip Code)

170 Croghan St., Fremont, AZ 62435

Position Desired	Full-Time Part-Time Temp.	Pay Expected	Are you under 18 or over 70 years of age?
❸ Public relations	**❹** ☑ ☑ ☐	**❺** Negotiable	☐ Yes ☑ No

Do you have a physical or medical condition that should be considered in job assignment or that requires special accommodation? If so, describe.

❻ No

MILITARY	Have you ever served in U.S. Armed Forces? ☐ Yes ☑ No	From (Date) —	To (Date) —	Branch of Service —

Briefly describe the nature of your duties in the service.

—

Have you ever worked for this company? ☑ No ☐ Yes, when and where:	Do you have any relatives or a spouse employed by this company? ☐ No ☑ Yes, name and location employed: **❼** Gerald Bittersohn, Accounting Dept.

---

❶ This is the way they usually want your name.

❷ Bring this number with you.

❸ Write something as general as possible; there may be several possibilities for you.

❹ Check all kinds of employment you would accept.

❺ Try not to answer this question directly. One way out is to write "negotiable."

❻ Never give any medical history unless it's really relevant to your on-the-job performance. It may be used against you. Even if you are legally blind, if you're applying for a job for which your blindness is irrelevant, you should answer "no." In other words, if you *have* to answer "yes" to the question "Do you have a physical condition that limits your ability to perform the job?" you're probably applying for the wrong job.

7 Some companies refuse to hire relatives of employees in order to avoid charges of showing favoritism, but blanket antinepotism policies are no longer prevalent. In fact, a few companies pay bonuses to employees who bring in relatives to company jobs.

Don't leave any space blank. If there's a question you can't answer, write "N.A." ("Not Applicable") or a dash to indicate that you've seen the question but don't need to answer. Otherwise the interviewer might assume that you didn't read the application form carefully.

Education:

EDUCATION BACKGROUND				
Type of School	**8** Name & Address	**9** How Many Yrs. Attended	**10** Graduated	**11** Course
Grammar	St. Elizabeth's Elem. Sch. Tucson, AZ	8	Yes	N.A.
High School	Fremont Public H.S. Fremont, AZ	4	Yes	English and Art
College	Greene County Comm Clg. Fremont, AZ	2 months (freshman)	—	Journalism
Business or Trade	—	—	—	

8 You don't need the street address, just the city or town and state.

9 Put a number in the blank.

10 Just write "yes" or "no."

11 They mean "major" here.

When you have a form like this one that doesn't provide enough room for detailed answers, don't worry. Make the answers as simple and easy to understand as possible.

Work History:

12 FORMER EMPLOYERS List below last four employers, starting with last one first.				
13 Date Month and Year	Name and Address of Employer	Salary	Position	**14** Reason for Leaving
From June '83 To Sept. '83	Fremont Daily Journal 253 S. Post Rd. Fremont, AZ 62435	$40/wk. (part-time)	Classified Ad Dept.: clerk-typist	back to school
From July '82 To Aug. '82	Mrs. Inez Garcia 426 Oaklawn Dr. Fremont, AZ 62435	$25/wk. (part-time)	mother's helper	back to school
From To				
From To				

⑫ Make sure you list these in the right order.

⑬ What they're looking for here is consistency. Have you worked for one employer for a year or more, or do you move from job to job frequently? Have you had significant periods of unemployment? If so, why? The answer doesn't matter so much for someone just graduating from high school or technical school (no one expects them to have a consistent work history), but it *does* matter for people in their late 20s or 30s.

⑭ Write a brief, acceptable, and true reason (like "moved" or "laid off" or "advancement"), but never criticize a previous employer.

References:

This section is usually next to or related to the work history section.

⑮ PERSONAL REFERENCES	
Name & Occupation	**⑯** Phone Number
1. Maurice Thurston, mgr., Classified Ad Dept., Fremont Daily Journal	444-1968 Ext. 53
2. Inez Garcia, homemaker	444-3779
3. Linda Maynard, journalism prof., Greene County Comm. Clg.	444-5655 Ext. 14

⑮ Be sure you've asked people first before giving their names as references. If you don't want your current boss to know that you're job hunting yet, don't put her or his name down. Use another reference.

⑯ Bring these numbers with you or ask to use a phone book. Don't leave them blank.

Some application forms ask about your hobbies. Write down an activity or hobby that you'd like to be interviewed about. The purpose of this question is to help the interviewer get to know you.

Finally, some application forms end with contractual agreements requiring your signature. Read them. If you don't understand, ask. Such a contract typically contains provisions stating that you have completed the application form truthfully; that you agree to work according to the rules or personnel practices of the company; that anything you invent, create, or make on the job belongs to the company; or that you won't reveal the company's trade secrets.

HANDLING JOB INTERVIEWS

Did you ever have the measles, and if so, how many?

—Charles Farrar Browne (pseud. Artemus Ward), *humorist*

People are more worried about interviews than about any other part of job hunting. They see them as a combination of the Inquisition, a beauty contest, and a final exam. In reality, interviews are more like matching games. Do your experience and personality match the job opening? If you don't get the job after an interview, it's not your "fault." It's probably because you didn't match the job that was open or because another applicant was a better match. If you think about interviews this way, you'll realize that they are for you as much as for the employer. All you need to do is present yourself as you *are*. You don't have to fake anything.

There are three objectives in any job interview:

- To find out enough information about the job so that you can decide whether you want it
- To meet the person who can hire you
- To let that person know what your qualifications are and what you're like—and that you're interested in the job

Basically, there are two different kinds of job interviews: screening interviews and hiring interviews. *Screening interviews* are usually conducted in company personnel offices or employment agencies. The interviewer's objective is to find several qualified candidates to send to the hiring interview and to weed out unqualified candidates. During a screening interview, the questioner is thinking:

- Are you generally qualified for the job?
- What is your attitude toward work?
- Are you someone I can recommend for the job?

You usually aren't offered a job at the end of a screening interview. In fact, the interviewer probably doesn't have the power to hire you.

Hiring interviews, on the other hand, are conducted by people who do have that power. If you apply for a job at a small company and are interviewed by the owner or manager, you'll often skip the whole screening process. (However, if there are several really good applicants and the interviewer finds it difficult to make a decision, you might be asked to come back for a second meeting.) During a hiring interview, entirely different questions are running through the interviewer's mind:

- Can you handle the job?

- Will you need a lot of training, supervision, or prodding, or will you "hit the ground running"?
- Would I enjoy working with you?
- Will you make *my* job easier?

Interviewers in screening interviews are not likely to take risks or go on hunches, but hiring interviewers may be willing to take a chance. If a hiring interviewer wants to hire *you,* your qualifications might not matter quite so much. For example, one young woman applied for the job of administrative assistant to the head of the financial analysis office at a large nonprofit institution. "It wasn't strictly a secretarial job, but secretarial skills were needed. My secretarial skills are not spectacular, but when the manager met me, I could tell we hit it off immediately. She really wanted to hire me. The personnel office told her there were more-qualified candidates. Twice she actually rewrote the job description to make me the best candidate, and each time I had to go through the interview process again. I was beginning to get embarrassed. But she wanted me, and she got me. She was right, too. I'm the perfect person for the job."

Similarly, if the hiring interviewer wants to hire someone else, you probably won't get the job. Just keep in mind that if you have found out whether the job interests *you,* have met the person with the power to hire you, and have let that person know what you can do, what you're like, and that you're interested in the job, you've done all you can. The rest is up to the employer.

Here are more interviewing tips:

First of all, expect to have to wait at least a few minutes. Use the time to look over any material about the company that might be in the waiting room (such as an annual report or company newsletter), or jog your memory by reviewing the materials you've brought with you. (Bring two spare copies of your résumé, one for you and an extra one for the interviewer in case the first one you submitted has been misplaced or glued to a blotter or used to mop up spilled coffee. You'll look like the most organized person in the world.)

If you feel nervous and there are other candidates waiting or the secretary doesn't look busy, it can be helpful to exchange small talk. You could comment on how you like the office decor or the way the grounds are landscaped, if appropriate, or you might ask the secretary or receptionist how long he or she has worked there. Sometimes casual conversations like this can yield information that helps job hunters know whether they'd like working at a particular company.

You can also expect that the interviewer will be polite, interested in you, and—surprise!—somewhat nervous. Yes, interviewers are almost always a little nervous. They're facing a test too: "Will I miss a really good candidate?" "Will this person like me?" or "Will we establish good rapport, or will I have to drag all the answers out of her?" So, as soon as you're introduced, smile, shake hands, and look the interviewer in the eye. You'll both relax a little. After you're seated, the interviewer will probably make one of the usual remarks about the weather or traffic or something before getting down to business.

Many interviewers begin by briefly describing the job. (If you're handed a written job description, take a few minutes to read it carefully.) The first questions are usually easy ones about your education and job experience. Don't assume that the interviewer has remembered or even read anything you wrote on your application form or résumé. Repeat what you wrote down if necessary and don't worry about it. If you've brought along a portfolio or other work samples, this may be the time to show them to the interviewer.

Most interviewers have a standard list of additional questions that they use to get to know you. There are no right or wrong answers to these questions, but the interviewer *is* after specific information. Here are seven typical "getting-to-know-you" interview questions, an explanation of what the question usually means, and sample answers.

1. *What kind of job would you like to be doing five years from now?* (This question means, "Do you have any goals, or are you just drifting along?" This is your chance to tell the interviewer what your work-related goals are.)
   Good answers: "Five years from now I want to be an expert in personnel department policies and procedures." Or, "Five years from now I want to be a skilled machinist."
   Not-so-good answers: "I haven't thought about that; I'm just looking for a job." Or, "Whatever the company thinks I should be doing."

2. *Why do you want to be a _____?* (Translation: "Are you really enthusiastic about this job or committed to a career in this field?" Assure the interviewer that you are highly motivated.)
   Good answers: "I love to travel, and by working in a travel agency, I'll be helping to ensure that other people enjoy their trips." Or, "I understand that a major goal of your organization is providing information to consumers about their rights. I think that's very important."
   Not-so-good answers: "Because the pay is good." (A good answer if it's one of several reasons, but not as the only rea-

son. The interviewer may think you aren't motivated by anything *other* than the pay.) "Because it's such a fantastic, wonderful opportunity." (An opportunity for what? This sounds false and gushy, and it doesn't really answer the question.)

3. *Why do you want to work for this company?* (This question means, "Do you know anything about our company, what it manufactures or what its purpose is?" In your answer, demonstrate that you *do* know about the company by including specific facts.)
   Good answers: "I've shopped at this store frequently and have always been impressed by the atmosphere. The sales clerks are friendly and helpful." Or, "My brother bought a house recently and I found I was very interested in the real estate business."
   Not-so-good answers: "It seems like a nice place to work." (This is too vague.) Or, "It's close to my house." (This implies that's all you care about.)

4. *What is your greatest strength?* (Variations include, "How would you describe yourself?" or "Tell me a little about yourself." This is not the time for false modesty. Boast about yourself a little in job-related terms.)
   Good answers: "I like learning new things. The opportunity to develop my skills is important to me in a job." Or, "I really enjoy meeting new people. That's one reason this job is so appealing to me."
   Not-so-good answers: "I really couldn't say." Or, "I'm one of the most fantastic people you'll ever meet. . . ."

5. *What do you feel is your greatest weakness?* (This question is a real toughie. The interviewer wants to know if you can handle the pressure of a question like this one, so *how* you answer is as important as *what* you answer. Tip: Take any good quality and present it as a "fault," but make the answer *brief.*)
   Good answers: "I might be a little too conscientious. I'm never really satisfied until I've completed a task." Or, "Sometimes I'm so eager to get started on new projects that I feel impatient with people who don't seem to share my enthusiasm."
   Not-so-good answers: "I always oversleep in the morning." Or, "My biggest weakness is that I just can't get along with my parents. . . ."

6. *What did you like most about your last job?* (Translation: "Tell me about your responsibilities and accomplishments in your last job, especially the ones you really enjoyed and feel proudest of.")

Good answers: "I liked the opportunity I got to manage the shop when the owner was away." Or, "When I started working in the stockroom, I knew nothing about electrical equipment, but now I've learned a great deal, not just about stock but about. . . ."

Not-so-good answers: "I just loved the people. All my crowd from school worked there too." (The interviewer will probably wonder whether you were really working or just hanging out with friends.) "We got huge discounts on company merchandise." (This doesn't tell the interviewer what aspects of the job itself you really enjoyed.)

7. *What did you dislike about your last job?* (This seemingly simple question usually means, "Do you have a good attitude toward work and toward your supervisor?" Remember that *no* job is perfect, and that interviews are not the time to air complaints, no matter how valid. Even if your last boss was a tyrant, resist the impulse to sound off. It will backfire on you. An interviewer who doesn't know your previous boss will wonder whether you're hard to get along with, while an interviewer who *does* know your tyrant boss is actually asking you a trap question: "Do you tell all, or do you know when to keep quiet?" If an overly curious interviewer says something like, "I hear they're really terrible to work for; is that true?" try a shrug and a smile.)

Good answers: Any of the "why-are-you-leaving" reasons, such as the desire for advancement, personal growth, or learning new skills.

Not-so-good answer: "They wouldn't give me time off to be a quiz show contestant."

Interview Tips from Job Hunters

"Never be late to a job interview. They'll think you don't care about the job no matter how good your excuse is."

—lab assistant

"You're not supposed to look cool for a job interview; you're supposed to look interested."

—machinist

"I always say the interviewer's name when we're introduced, like, 'Hello, Mr. Blake.' That way I remember the name."

—junior account executive

"Never smoke in a job interview. You always end up with a long ash and no ashtray or lighting up the wrong end or being asked a question when you're trying to light up. Smoking always hangs you up."

—salesperson

"One of my friends says that chewing gum makes you look as if you are dumb. So I would never chew gum in an interview although I might on the job."

—assembler

"Practice interviewing with friends. One of you can be the interviewer, one can be the person looking for work, and another can watch and make suggestions." (Note: You might want to use real jobs from the want ads and the questions we've covered in this chapter—both the employers' and yours. Just don't memorize your answers. Unless you're Katharine Hepburn, memorized answers sound fake.)

—secretary

"I try and get them to look me in the eye at least once during the interview. If they look up and really look at me when I'm looking back at them, it gives me a clue as to whether they are interested in me."

—architect

"Interviews are always tough. So I always do something nice for myself right afterwards, like a movie or an evening with friends—something to look forward to."

—word processor

"My high school counselor told me that if you're scared going to a job interview, just imagine the interviewer sitting there in his or her underwear." (If you tend to giggle, better skip this one.)

—management trainee

"When I felt the interview wasn't going well for me, I asked the interviewer, 'Where could a person with my experience find a job in this industry?' And the interviewer gave me several names. That's how I found this job."

—technician

"Remember, in the interview, you're looking for a good boss. What kinds of questions is he asking you? How does he sound? You can usually tell if it will work out for you."

—chef

"If the interviewer is interrupted several times by phone calls or other people, don't let it bother you. Use the time to think about the questions *you* want answered."

—technical writer

"You have to sound excited about the job. That's how you get the job."

—cashier

Stereotypes: Theirs/Yours

You've probably heard older people make statements like these:

- Nobody in the younger generation knows how to spell or add or even speak correctly.
- People in their 20s are only interested in themselves.
- Kids today just want to goof off and get paid. They come in late. They call in sick. They loaf on the job.

Those may be mild compared to some comments you've heard. They're based on stereotyped images that some older people have of young people—mental pictures that are oversimplified and, obviously, inaccurate. Since older people do most of the hiring, you might have to deal with such views at job interviews.

How do you handle it? First recognize that if you do meet up with interviewers who express negative attitudes, you probably won't be able to change their minds. Resist the temptation to try, or you'll end up in an argument or staring at a closed door. The best strategy is to help them see you as an exception. "Well, maybe there *are* young people who only care about playing around, but *I'm* not like that. I want to work hard and do the job well." You don't have to say this directly, just convey the message by the way you act and present yourself. If you come across as an energetic and responsible person (you *must* be energetic and responsible; you're reading this book!), you'll increase your chances of getting the job.

Consider, too, whether *you* have any negative stereotypes. If you do, they're bound to affect your job search. Interviewers are at least as good at detecting them as you are, and they don't like them either. Worse, you'll be unable to see past your prejudices—and you might pass up a great place to work.

For instance, some young people believe that older people are completely incapable of relating to them. Some job hunters feel that most bosses are heartless slave drivers interested only in making a buck, and that most workplaces are little better than sweatshops. While some bosses *are* ogres and sweatshops *do* exist, most bosses and companies are neither. Some companies, with caring employers, are more like extended families. Some are like athletic teams with a sense of mission and excitement. Others are like small towns with all kinds of work opportunities.

By learning how to recognize and deal with stereotypes, you'll be better able to conduct a successful job search.

To Answer or Not to Answer: What Is the Question?

You're being interviewed for a job, and the interviewer, a friendly, fatherly sort, asks if you have a boyfriend. Or if you plan to get married, or how you spend your time on weekends, or what church you go to. Suddenly you think to yourself, "Gee, this doesn't have much to do with the job. Why does he want to know this? Do I have to answer? What are my rights?"

There are three federal laws that protect the rights of job hunters and thus affect the kinds of questions that may be asked in an interview and on job applications:

- Title VII of the 1964 Civil Rights Act, which prohibits discrimination due to sex, race, color, religion, or national origin in all employment practices—hiring, firing, promotions, salary, etc.
- The 1967 Age Discrimination in Employment Act, which is designed to promote the employment of older people on the basis of their ability rather than their age
- The 1973 Vocational Rehabilitation Act, which protects the right of the disabled to be hired for jobs that they are capable of doing

State and city laws often add further restrictions. When local laws are stronger than federal ones, they prevail; if they are weaker, federal laws prevail.

The only interview question specifically forbidden by federal law is, "Have you ever been arrested?" Other than this, however, no question is actually illegal by itself. It becomes illegal when the information in your response is used to discriminate against you in hiring. The information requested must be clearly relevant to and necessary for the job under discussion. Even the question about previous arrests, for instance, could be legal if the job involved national security.

Another criterion is that the same question be asked of all applicants. It's suspect to ask a woman how she plans to care for her young children while she's working without asking the same question of the men also interviewed. Other "questionable" questions sometimes asked of women concern their plans for having a family, what their husbands' occupations are, and how the husbands would feel about their wives traveling. While these may be only passing remarks or pleasantries, the underlying implication is that a woman with family responsibilities won't handle her job as well as a man would. As more women continue to enter the work force and show that they *can* handle both career and family successfully (and as men become more involved in running households), these questions will probably die the death they deserve.

But in the meantime, how should you respond to questions unrelated to your qualifications for the job? First, look behind the question to see what the interviewer is really asking. What is the interviewer concerned about? A question about your boyfriend, for instance, may mean the interviewer is worried that you will soon marry and quit your job. Reassurance from you that you *do* want the job, that you *are* seriously committed to a career, may be all that's needed to satisfy the interviewer. If the questions persist you have several options, all of them with some degree of risk:

- Answer the question frankly, knowing your answer may reduce your chances of getting the job.

- Run around the question. Don't actually give an answer. This may make you sound as if you are hiding something and cause you to lose the job anyway.

- Say that you don't understand how the question relates to the job. This may cause interviewers to become defensive, thinking you are accusing them of something.

- Say you believe that it is illegal to ask such a question and you are not going to answer it. This, of course, runs the risk of irritating interviewers so much that they end the interview right there. On the other hand, they may admire your honesty, guts, and awareness.

- End the interview yourself. If an interviewer poses a number of questions that seem blatantly discriminatory, ask yourself if you want to work at a company that seems to hold such attitudes.

How you answer questions you consider illegal—and the risk you take in either confronting the questioner or not answering—will depend on how badly you want the job and on what you feel comfortable saying. There is no simple way out. You'll have to judge each individual situation yourself and respond the way you think best.

Preemployment tests may also be illegal, if they are not validated (in this case, "validated" means tests that have been proven to predict success on the job) or if they disqualify substantially more minority group members or women than others taking the tests. While some tests—those measuring typing, stenography, and other manual skills, for instance—are fairly easy to validate, be wary of those purporting to measure intelligence, aptitude, or personality. As discussed on page 159, these are not very reliable indicators of job performance.

If you don't get a job and think it's due to discrimination, you *can* do something about it. The Equal Employment Opportunity Commission, which establishes guidelines on discrimination and has the major responsibility for enforcing relevant federal laws, is one place to go for help. There may be a local office in your area, or you could write to the national headquarters (2401 E Street, NW, Washington, D.C. 20507). You could also contact local women's centers, government labor and human rights agencies, or a lawyer who is familiar with the issues. Since local laws vary and all are subject to change, it's a good idea to contact one of these agencies before filing a complaint. They can help you determine whether you've been discriminated against and suggest what to do about it.

Advice for the Disabled

Following is Marlene Brill's article, "Disabled? Know Your Rights," which offers some helpful information.

"You just had your first job interview. During the interview, the personnel manager says, 'I'm sorry. We only hire brown-haired workers. They write better and work faster.'

You leave the office bewildered. What does hair color have to do with writing ability and work performance?

Nothing, of course. But to many disabled people, this exaggerated situation makes about as much sense as some of the excuses they hear when they are rejected from jobs.

Many people have misconceptions about the handicapped. These false ideas often are based on their own fears or lack of knowledge. They think because someone is unable to walk or see, they cannot hold a job.

Such reasoning, added to unnecessary physical barriers (turnstile doors, stairs), clearly limits careers open to the disabled. Not only are they blocks in job-getting, they also get in the way of school and recreation programs.

If you (or a friend) have ever been turned away from any program because of mental or physical problems, you may have been discriminated against. To prevent this from happening, there now are laws to protect your rights.

Section 504 of the Rehabilitation Act says that 'no otherwise qualified handicapped individual' can be kept away from a job, promotion, or service by any program receiving government money.

283

The law clearly spells out the meaning of 'handicap.' It includes the following:

- Speech, hearing, visual, and orthopedic impairments
- Cerebral palsy
- Epilepsy
- Cancer
- Diabetes
- Heart disease
- Mental retardation
- Emotional illness
- Learning disabilities

Alcoholism and drug addiction also are considered handicaps under this law.

Both Section 504 and Section 503 state that employers under federal contract must hire the handicapped.

With both laws, institutions are expected to make 'reasonable accommodations' for those who have disabilities. That is, the employer must try to do away with things that keep a disabled person from doing the job.

Accommodation means different things depending upon a person's handicap. The law says that special treatment of handicapped persons, *because of their handicap,* may be needed to give equal opportunity. To date, however, no guidelines have been set up to describe how much special treatment may be called for. Courts set standards case by case. Decisions have been based upon an agency's size and type, and on the cost of making changes.

Often employers do not know how to help the disabled to work for them. Many don't know what a disabled worker can do if given the chance. Those in charge of hiring workers worry about which questions they can ask.

Under Section 504, employers cannot ask about a person's handicapping condition in an interview. But they can ask if he or she can do the job-related tasks. An employer is discriminating by not hiring anyone who is qualified for a job or who can be helped by 'reasonable accommodation.' That same employer, however, may not reject an application simply *because* 'accommodation' would be needed. (To file a discrimination complaint, contact your local federal Office of Civil Rights.)

If you have a disability, you should know when you are within your rights. Sometimes minor changes will allow you to get that position you know is a perfect match, as in these cases:

Example 1: After being accepted by a university, Tom was able to have the school's animal restrictions relaxed. He then could move around campus on his own with his Seeing Eye dog.

Example 2: Miriam's cerebral palsy did not need to get in the way of her mailroom job. She was sometimes required to carry bulky packages. So she suggested to her boss that the bundles be rolled on a moving cart.

Example 3: Jerry was able to communicate with an employer who did not understand sign language. An interpreter for the deaf attended the interview.

Many groups will work with a disabled person who is unsure of how to go up against these kinds of barriers.

Depending upon where you live, you can find employment, housing, communication, medical, transportation, and legal help.

All of these services will help equalize your chances for the job or school you want. [Getting] the position, however, will depend on your experience and what you know. To be prepared,

- Know yourself—your skills, capabilities, and limitations.
- Know the law and how it is interpreted in your state.
- Know where you can go for help.

Do your homework so you can give yourself a fair chance to succeed. Be sure you're not rejected from your next interview because of 'hair color.' "

If you need more information, try these resources:

Center for Independent Living and Closer Look. *Taking Charge of Your Life: A Guide to Independence for Teens with Physical Disabilities.* Washington: Parents' Campaign for Handicapped Children and Youth, 1981.

Feingold, S. Norman, and Norma R. Miller. *Your Future: A Guide for the Handicapped Teenager.* New York: Richards Rosen Press, 1981.

Foster, June C., ed. *Guidance, Counseling, and Support Services for High School Students with Physical Disabilities.* Cambridge, Mass.: Technical Education Research Centers, 1977.

Mitchell, Joyce Slayton. *See Me More Clearly.* New York: Harcourt Brace Jovanovich, 1980.

YOUR QUESTIONS

One important objective of the interview is for you to find out if *you* want this job. So, before you leave the interview, be sure to ask some questions. The following are sample questions frequently asked by job hunters. All aren't appropriate for every job, so pick or adapt them carefully.

- What would I be doing during a typical day on the job?
- Whom could I go to with questions or problems?
- Would I be working alone most of the time or with a team?
- How is this job important to the company?
- What kinds of training are available to people in this job?
- May I talk to somone in your company with a similar job?
- What kind of advancement is there for people who are in this job?
- What kinds of jobs will this job prepare me for?
- Who would be supervising me? May I meet her (or him)?
- How would I get feedback on how I'm doing? Are there regular employee evaluations?

There's no need to feel hesitant about asking your questions. In fact, interviewers *prefer* that you ask questions. By doing so, you demonstrate that you take yourself and the job seriously. There is one commonsense rule you should keep in mind, however: ask questions that deal with more personal concerns (such as policies regarding vacation time, sick days, or insurance) *last.* That way, you'll avoid implying that you're mainly interested in the "extras."

Most job hunters aren't offered the job at the end of their interviews. If the interviewer doesn't bring it up, be sure to ask when the hiring decision will be made. Here are some ways to phrase it:

- When will you let me know about this position?
- Will you be contacting me, or shall I call your office next week?
- When will the decision be made about this opening?

The interviewer will give you a signal to indicate that the interview is over. Usually the interviewer will rise or say something like, "Well, thank you very much for coming in." That's your cue to stand up, shake hands again, thank the interviewer, and prepare to leave.

AFTER THE INTERVIEW

Once you're out the front door, find a place to sit—on a park bench, in a bus, in your car in the parking lot—and write down the name of the person who interviewed you; the job title, job description, and salary you discussed; and the date you'll be notified about the hiring decision.

Also jot down your first impressions. Now that you know more about the job and the company, were you impressed with what you learned? Disappointed? Did it look like a good place to work, a good company to work for? Was it a quiet atmosphere or a hectic one? These notes will come in handy because, after several interviews, it's easy to forget details. You'll also use them to compare various job possibilities.

Also analyze how you handled the interview. Was there a question you found difficult to answer? Were you so afraid of being thought immodest that you shied away from making positive statements about your abilities and accomplishments? Don't waste energy on regrets. Use what you've learned from evaluating this interview to help you handle the next one even better!

Finally, send a brief letter to the interviewer, expressing your appreciation for the opportunity to meet and discuss the job opening. Thank-you letters demonstrate your interest in the job as well as the fact that you're organized and conscientious. They also help interviewers remember you. Like your résumé, a thank-you letter should be carefully written and typed. (See the sample on the next page.) Be sure to send it promptly—within 24 hours of the interview is best.

WHAT HAPPENS WHEN YOU HAVEN'T HEARD?

In the job-hunting business, it's usually true that no news is bad news —but not always. If the company doesn't tell you their hiring decision by the date they specified, don't assume you didn't get the job. Call and ask. They might still be making up their minds. Tell them you're still interested and ask when the decision will be made. Call back on the next date and ask again. A little persistence just might work in your favor.

MAKING THE DECISION: HOW TO ASSESS JOB OFFERS

It's a long road, but I know I'm gonna find the end.

—Bessie Smith, *singer and songwriter*

Think back over your life for a few minutes. You've had many decisions to make—what courses to take in school, what friends to choose, what activities to become involved in. Some of these decisions were hard, some were easy. Some turned out well, some were disasters. Before you read any further, write down three decisions of which you're really proud. They don't have to be major life-changing decisions, just three decisions that worked out well for you.

Look at your list. Is there something those three decisions have in common? Many people discover that the decisions that pleased them most were those in which they had the biggest say—not that friends or relatives didn't have some influence but just that *they* made the final decisions for themselves.

Sample Thank-You Letter

223 South Washington Street
Rollinsville, N.C. 94176
February 19, 1984

Ms. Jessie Carlson
Director
Red River Camp
R.R. 6, Box 27
Morgantown, N.C. 94178

Dear Ms. Carlson:

Thank you for the opportunity to meet and discuss the position of junior counselor at Red River Camp for this coming summer. I am very impressed by the activities that you have planned, especially the new ecology-related projects.

As I told you in the interview, my long-term career goal is to become an elementary school guidance counselor. I believe that working at your camp would be an invaluable experience for me and hope that you'll give me the opportunity. I look forward to hearing your decision soon.

Sincerely,

Gwen Healy
Gwen Healy

When you're deciding whether to accept a job offer, you'll probably get a lot of advice and even some pressure from people. This will be particularly true if you were referred to the job by an employment agency, because agencies get paid for placing people in jobs. Remember, *you* are the person who would be working in the job. Only *you* can decide whether or not to accept it.

When a formal job offer is made, either the person who interviewed you or your future supervisor will call or write and ask you to take the job. Don't hesitate to ask for time to think it over. People often do, so an employer isn't likely to be surprised by your request. You'll probably just be told to let them know by a specific date, like "next Monday" or "tomorrow."

Some people grab the first job they're offered without stopping to consider whether they really want *that* job. Looking for a job is a difficult and stressful process, and accepting the first offer does get it over as quickly as possible. If you're broke and hungry, of course, you'll have to accept the first reasonable offer. But if things aren't that bad yet, stop to analyze the offer before you jump at it.

Make sure that you have the information you need to make the decision. The questions below will help you get the most important information. Writing down your answers, thoughts, and feelings will help you clarify them.

1. Does this job come close to my job target?
2. What is the salary? Is it appropriate for the job and for my background?
3. What are the fringe benefits?
4. What important skills will I develop that can be used in future jobs, when I'm ready for a change?
5. Will I have the opportunity to do things I like to do? If so, what?
6. What things will I be expected to do that I dislike?
7. Is this a good employer to work for?
8. Will I be able to advance in this company?
9. What hours and days of the week am I expected to work?
10. How will I get to work?
11. Have I met my future supervisor and coworkers, and do I like the thought of working with them?
12. Have I seen the place where I'd actually be working?
13. What personal goals will this job help me achieve?

If you discover that you're missing a piece of information that only the employer can provide—such as exactly what the fringe benefits are or what your work schedule will be—call and speak to the person who offered you the job. The company *wants* to hire you, so you won't be making a nuisance of yourself by asking a few more questions.

Next, on another sheet of paper, draw a line down the middle from top to bottom. On one side of the line, write down all the advantages of the job. On the other side, list the disadvantages. This step is especially helpful if you've had more than one job offer. Compare all the aspects of each job, not just the job title or salary. Which boss would be the better one to work for? Which could teach you more? Does one job provide a fringe benefit that's especially important to you? Was the atmosphere pleasantly busy at one place but frantically busy at the other?

It's during this stage of making up your mind that information and advice from other people might be useful. You could talk to friends, relatives, and anyone who's been particularly helpful in your job hunt. They might be able to point out an advantage that you've overlooked. Someone you know might be able to tell you that the company has a really good reputation for training their employees or that they seldom promote from within. If you know other women who work for the company, you might ask them how female employees are treated. Discuss the advantages and disadvantages of the job with a friend. Sometimes you'll find that as you explain them to another person, you clarify the decision for yourself.

Employee Benefits: How Can They Benefit You?

Once you have a firm job offer, you may have a tough time deciding whether or not to accept it. If you've considered such factors as the salary, working conditions, your boss-to-be, and opportunities for advancement and you believe there's nothing else to weigh, think again! The employee benefits a specific job provides just might help you make your final decision.

"Employee benefits" is a catchall phrase that includes everything from paid holidays to health insurance to inexpensive lunches in a company-subsidized cafeteria. Because you would otherwise have to pay these costs yourself (or do without), they really do add up to extra money. In fact, a recent U.S. Chamber of Commerce survey showed that the benefits employers pay now equal a national average of one third of an employee's salary.

It's not likely that your new employer will offer you stock options or the key to the executive washroom, and you probably aren't overly concerned about retirement plans at this point. Many benefits, however, can be very useful to you right now. For instance:

- *Compensatory benefits* are wages you are paid for days you don't work. In addition to a fixed number of paid holidays and vacation days, some companies also offer *personal days,* the number varying with each employer. Usually taken one at a time, these extra days off can be used, for example, to paint your bedroom, attend religious services, or cope with unexpected events such as a death in the family. *Floating holidays* are days off of your choice, which you exchange for holidays worked. For short-term illnesses and accidents, like colds and sprained ankles, most employers allow you a certain number of paid *sick days* each year. These are for illnesses and injuries not directly caused by your job, and the number of days you're allowed varies fom company to company.

- Employers are required to provide *worker's compensation* to employees who are either injured on the job or develop an occupation-related disease. Most employers have an insurance policy to cover this benefit. The amount of compensation you would receive varies according to the state administering the claim, but the federal government has recommended that you be paid no less than two thirds of your average weekly wage. Most often worker's compensation also covers all related medical costs, automatic cost-of-living adjustments, and, in the case of death resulting from such an injury or illness, weekly cash payments to dependents.

- If you become seriously ill or disabled by an off-the-job injury, you will probably receive *disability benefits.* These are payments that partially replace earnings lost because you are forced to remain off the job longer than the number of paid sick days you are allotted. Disability benefits laws vary from state to state. Usually you and your employer jointly cover the cost of this insurance; your share is deducted from your paycheck.

- Many companies pay for part or all of a *health insurance* plan, perhaps one of the most important benefits an employer can provide. A typical program such as Blue Cross/Blue Shield could pay for most of your hospital and surgical bills, follow-up care, and emergency treatment. Additional, more comprehensive insurance, called "major medical," is frequently tacked on to this basic insurance to supplement it by paying for visits to the doctor when you're sick, for medicine, and for therapy. Some plans also cover costs related to pregnancy and childbirth.

If you are currently covered by a parent's insurance policy, when you reach the age of 19 that coverage will probably expire unless you remain a full-time student. Bear in mind that you will not be covered by most employers' insurance plans until you've worked there at least a full month, that relatively few plans cover dental or mental health care, and that most don't pay for "preexisting conditions" (such as an illness already in existence when you were hired). In addition, before the insurance company begins to reimburse you for part or all of your bills, you are usually required to pay what's called a "deductible" (typically ranging from $50 to $200 a year).

- *Life insurance* policies vary with each employer and according to the employee's life-style, family size, and role in the family. If you die while employed by the company, a sum of money is paid to a person you have designated in advance, called your "beneficiary."

- Unless your employer has its own retirement program, under the Federal Insurance Contributions Act, *Social Security* payments will probably be deducted automatically from your paycheck by your employer, who pays a matching amount. After you retire, if you worked for and paid into the Social Security fund for a total of at least ten years, Social Security will provide you with an income and medical insurance called "Medicare."

- A company *pension plan* is similar to Social Security in that, together with your employer or union, you put aside some of your income each month into a special pension fund that will offer support later, when you retire. Companies' plans vary from one to the next, but all are optional.

- *Tuition reimbursement* plans can help you continue your education while you work. If the courses you take relate to your job—enable you to do the job better or prepare you to move up—employers refund you all or part of the cost of your tuition. Most companies offering this benefit require that you work a certain amount of time before you can take advantage of it.

- Under the Pregnancy Discrimination Act, employers are now required to treat pregnancy as any other disability. This means that any policy a company has that covers any short-term disability must also apply to pregnancies. (Only five states currently have short-term disability benefits laws, and the majority of women workers are not covered by private disability insurance.) Usually only large companies have formal, structured policies regarding *maternity benefits and parental leave.* Under such a policy, you might receive, for example, six to eight weeks of disability pay. If you take off more time, the company may give you paid leave or ask you to use accrued, paid vacation time; you may also be allowed a period of unpaid leave for up to six months, during which time your job will be held for you and you will still be covered by the company's benefits policy. Most companies do not have a standing policy providing for *paternity leave.* Men who request it often fear that their career commitment will be questioned, and it is most often an unpaid leave. But it's becoming an option that is increasingly available to parents.

- *Child-care assistance* is another benefit that is becoming more widespread. It may be available to you in one of four forms: a company may give financial assistance, such as subsidizing a day-care center or reimbursing parents for the cost of private day care; a company may offer flexibility in the time parents work or offer attractive part-time positions; a company may offer direct-care services on or near the work site; and, lastly, a company may offer an information and referral service to inform employees about available, affordable child care.

- If you're fired or laid off, you'll probably be covered by *unemployment insurance.* While there are some exceptions, most employers are required to contribute to the *unemployment compensation fund,* which provides willing, able, and unemployed workers with a small weekly income during the time they are out of work. Some companies also offer *severance pay.* The amount is usually one to three weeks' pay, depending on your salary and the length of time you were employed by the company.

- Large corporations typically offer lots of extras, or *"perks,"* that smaller companies don't provide. These might include car rental discounts, stock purchase plans, profit-sharing plans, and scholarships for employees' children. Some companies also offer discounts on their products or services to employees. For instance, if you work at a book publishing house, you might get free books at certain times of the year and a 50 percent discount the year round.

- A relatively new idea is the *flexible benefits* plan or "cafeteria plan." The employer provides a basic core of coverage—a minimum level of medical, disability, life insurance, and vacation time. Beyond that, employees are free to choose among the company's other benefits. For instance, under this plan you can decide whether you prefer tuition reimbursement or more life insurance, dental care or child care. Flexible benefits programs are tailored to the employee's needs, are more cost-effective for the employer, and show that some companies are recognizing that employees with diverse life-styles are happier and more productive with different benefits packages.

Now that you have some working definitions of benefits you might be offered, you can decide which will help you the most. When you receive a formal job offer, ask about employee benefits; if they don't match up to the ones on your list, you'll have to decide whether the particular benefits you had in mind are important enough to you to wait for another job offer. (This might be a hard decision, especially when you're just starting out in the job market.) But whatever your decision, take advantage of *any* benefits you are offered. And keep your eyes open—in the future, benefits packages are likely to become more flexible and more in tune with *your* needs.

WHAT IF YOU JUST CAN'T DECIDE?

If you've debated the pros and cons of a particular job until your brain throbs, your fingernails are nonexistent, and you're ready to start flipping coins, *stop thinking about it for a while.* Go roller-skating, see a movie, put on a stack of records and clean out your closet—do something that will help you calm down. Then, when you're more relaxed, try to pinpoint why you're having difficulty making the decision.

It's possible that you're in the clutches of the What-If-Something-Else-Turns-Up Problem, which usually goes like this: You've been offered a job that looks pretty good, but the job of your dreams is maybe, just maybe, going to be offered to you next week. Unfortunately you have to tell the "pretty good job" people your decision *this* week. What do you do?

This problem is not as impossible to solve as it seems. If the job of your dreams is a real job, one that you've already interviewed for, call up that interviewer. Explain that you've been offered another position, but the job at the interviewer's company is the one you want most. Then ask what the chances are that you'll be offered the job. The interviewer will probably level with you.

But if the job of your dreams is only a classified ad you've clipped or a job lead you've heard about, the situation is different.

You'll have to weigh the importance of meeting your job target versus the importance of a real job starting next week.

Other job hunters experience the It's-a-Great-Job-So-Why-Don't-I-Take-It Problem. The job seems fine; all your friends and family are proud of you for landing the offer—so what's the matter with you? Why don't you call them up and accept the offer? Here's how one job seeker describes this situation: "I knew I should have felt excited about the job offer and a little scared, the way all my friends did when they got job offers. I just felt dead—you know what I mean? I thought, 'Is that all there is to it? Am I going to end up *there*?' Nobody could figure out what was wrong with me."

If that's how a job offer makes *you* feel, don't take the job (unless an immediate paycheck is imperative), no matter how good it sounds or how many people advise you to accept it. Chances are you'd feel just as uncomfortable doing the job as you're feeling right now. Turn it down and look for another position. But first analyze *why* the job makes you feel that way. Is it the atmosphere at that company? Is it something about the boss or other people you'd be working with? Is it what you'd be doing? Adjust your job target to take into account what you've learned about yourself from this experience.

Another reason some people have difficulty making up their minds about a particular job offer is that they're having the What-If-I-Accept-This-Job-and-It-Turns-Out-to-Be-a-Big-Mistake Problem. The important point to keep in mind here is that you're not taking holy vows, just a job. If it turns out that you've made a mistake, you might feel unhappy, but you can always say those two little words: "I quit." It happens to almost everyone sooner or later.

One job hunter realized that she'd made a mistake not long after she began working as a cashier in a restaurant. As Martha describes it, "The manager treated everybody as if they couldn't do anything right. Some people weren't bothered by that and just joked around with him, but it made me miserable. So I thought to myself, if you're not happy at what you're doing, find something else. But find a good way to leave. So, first I found another job, but I made sure I was working just as hard at the restaurant. Then I went to my boss and told him I was leaving. I thought he would be mad. It was the hardest thing I had to do at that job, but I told him, and he wasn't as mad as I expected."

"Wrong" decisions like Martha's are never complete failures. Sometimes they're even more useful than "right" ones. Martha learned that to be happy in her work she needed a boss who respected her. She also realized that she wanted to work in a less pressured environment than a restaurant. Now she's a cashier at a large lumber company and hopes to be promoted in a year to a bookkeeping job.

If you find yourself in a job that is really wrong for you, do what Martha did and find a "good way" to leave. Don't just walk out or not show up for work, or you won't be able to list the job on your résumé or a job application. The work experience you had will count for nothing. If a prospective employer checks up and finds that you quit without notice, you'll have a tough time explaining it. By giving your present employer notice, you should still get a good recommendation. If possible, find the second job while you're still working at the first one. Job counselors agree that you're a much more interesting prospect to an employer if you already have a job.

Finally, some people have a difficult time making up their minds about job offers because they just hate to make decisions. If you have trouble deciding which flavor of ice cream to order or what to wear each morning, this might be your problem. If so, remember: Not to decide is to decide. If you don't respond to an offer, someone else will get the job.

SAYING YES

When you decide to accept a job offer, call the person who offered you the job and tell him or her your decision. Before hanging up the phone, be sure you know when and where to report for your first day.

Share your good news with your friends and family, and be sure to call or write and thank the people who've helped you in your job hunt. Then celebrate! You have a job, you've learned how to find a job, and you can do it again!

WORKING WOMAN

Sharyn Fink

Market Researcher

It was one of the earliest assignments in her new field, a kind of audition, and Sharyn Fink wanted to do a good job. But it wasn't going to be easy. She had to locate members of a political organization who were also cat owners *and* fed their cats a specific kind of cat food. Then she had to convince these political pet lovers to participate in a panel discussion on the relative merits of their brand of cat food.

Sharyn's field is market research, and it's a challenging one.

What do politics and pets have in common? Nothing much. But Sharyn knew that the roster of a political group would provide a variety of people.

"One way to find people for a survey is to go to an already existing organization," she explains. "A political organization will have a good mix of people—different educational levels, incomes, occupations, neighborhoods. That's a good cross section. You can't go to a PTA or a garden club and get that sort of variety."

In her current position as a field director for a market research data collection firm, Sharyn supervises consumer surveys at a regional shopping mall in Atlanta, Georgia. She manages a staff of 65 and consults with clients on the best way to collect the information they seek.

"We do consumer research for such clients as advertising agencies, major manufacturers, and marketing research suppliers—they're the ones who put together the actual surveys and analyze the information we gather. Our clients use what they learn from the surveys to develop strategies for marketing their products or services," Sharyn says. "My firm might be told, 'We're looking for males between 25 and 35 who own an American-made car and who have a major gasoline credit card.' Then I evaluate what the client is looking for and show the best way to survey this particular kind of consumer."

Before Sharyn got into market research, she managed the dress department for a department store.

"Then, after ten years in retail sales, I decided I wanted to make a career change," she recalls. "I quit my job and gave myself four months to find a new field. The first two months were spent in the library and talking to people; I used that time to research and evaluate different professions.

"Finally, a friend said to me, 'You like people, you aren't afraid to talk to strangers, you like to dig and find out what makes people click. Have you considered market research?'

"It seemed like a sensible question, so I decided to try it. I went to a firm and got an assignment on a free-lance basis—'Take this questionnaire and go talk to 50 people.' I was sent to a spot outside a store in Atlanta. It was wintertime, and it was *really* cold. But, despite everything, I finished the project and I enjoyed it."

This first job was followed by the cat-owner assignment. Sharyn was hooked.

"I decided to make a career of market research," she says. "I opened up the Yellow Pages and started calling firms. I said, 'I'm just starting out, but I really want to get into the business.' And I told them about my previous experience in management.

"I found a firm that took me on as an interviewer. In that job, you're just part of a group that's told to go out there and ask questions. I did this for about three months—sometimes six days a week, on weekends and evenings. I always was available and flexible. If they needed an interviewer, they knew they could count on me. At the same time, I helped my supervisor pull together her information to get the job done. She made me her assistant, and eventually I was made a supervisor myself.

"As a supervisor, I often worked directly under the president—it was a small firm. Again, I worked hard and was flexible, and after another three months I was promoted to overall mall supervisor, which involved training new supervisors, checking on current supervisors, and doing spot checks of the interviewers. I took on other duties, hired an assistant for myself, and began working with clients. In effect, I created a position for myself. I saw that the need was there and I filled it. I was working 12 hours a day; I guess I overburdened myself, but that's how you learn. I started with the firm in February and by January of the following year I was promoted to field director.

"When I look back over all the things I did and how hard I worked in the beginning, I don't know how I did it. I'm divorced with two children, and it seemed like I'd see my daughters for 10 minutes during a rushed breakfast and then not again until a few minutes at dinner. I had a boyfriend, too—when did I ever manage to see him?

"But in 1978, I started out managing 10 employees and now I am responsible for 65, so the hard work paid off."

Long hours are still one of the primary disadvantages of a supervisory job in market research data collection, Sharyn comments.

"A project may take 12 hours a day for weeks at a time," she explains. "And it has to be perfect—there are no shortcuts in this business. So, depending on the project, you might work a 60-hour week, or 40 hours, or 80 hours. And it involves a considerable amount of detail work."

She believes that there are three primary prerequisites for a successful career in market research—or any other field, for that matter. They are persistence, patience, and a positive attitude. She particularly stresses the last one.

"I know it sounds trite, but you have to wake up feeling positive about yourself and your work," she says. "If you're a manager, you have to evaluate your staff and find out what each person can do and do well. You have to be confident about yourself and your ability to accomplish whatever you set your mind to. Patience and persistence are also very important if you want to achieve the goals you set for yourself. You're not going to start out as an interviewer in market research and become a supervisor in a week. You have to build a career, step by step."

A good first step, Sharyn suggests, is to work part-time as an interviewer while you're still in high school or college.

"That kind of practical experience is invaluable," she believes. "It will give you some idea of what the research business is all about."

For young people looking for such work, Sharyn suggests checking with regional shopping malls to see if they house a market research operation. If that fails, she says to call the local Better Business Bureau for local research firms or do as she did and check the Yellow Pages.

"Even a person living in a very small city can find an interviewing job by contacting a market research firm in a nearby bigger city," she advises. "Then, when that firm needs to conduct a survey in the smaller town, they'll call you first."

Don't expect a big salary right away, Sharyn warns.

"The pay at the beginning is very low—it won't pay the bills," she says. "Usually, interviewers are paid minimum wage with a small increase, 5 or 10 percent, after the first ninety days. But it can be a good job for a student, and sometimes you can get college credit while you earn money."

Sharyn is already planning the next step in her own career; she wants to become a regional manager/personnel director for a data collection firm.

"Training new managers in expanding operations in other cities appeals to me. I can continue to have the people contact and institute the professionalism that the field requires."

WHEN SHE WAS YOUNG

Nelly Ptaschkina

Nelly Ptaschkina was born in 1903 in Russia. Her diary, begun when she was 10, covers the years of the Russian Revolution. Several of the notebooks were lost when Nelly and her family fled the Bolsheviks. A few were saved, however, and later published by her family in her memory. In this excerpt. written when she was 15, she talks about herself and the feeling that she is two people.

January 15, 1918. It has come into my mind that I have a kind of dual nature. It is pleasant, for I have a little of everything, but it is also annoying because I cannot define what I really am. I think it is because there is one part of me which soars high up among the clouds, and another which clings very much to the earth. To put it simply: there are in my nature materialism, idealism, and romanticism. This is what I call a dual nature.

When I go to the threatre or feel stirred up by any other cause, all my reasoning, my criticism, my hair-splitting suddenly become remote, barren and superfluous. Life seems full: and then I drift into another world, full of sweetness and beauty, that does not belong to our sphere. It holds enchantment—the clear beauty of the summer's day with its flowers in bloom and its azure sky.

In this respect, there is a different between Mummie and myself. She belongs much more than I do to the azure realm. Yes, I should hate to lose it. But when I live on this earthly planet, everything is reversed: here are the books, the cautious, reserved thoughts, the doubts. There is not a shadow of that other Nelly, pure, sensitive, lofty-minded. Down here she thinks and thinks, planning a reasonable, serious life, but the light that shines from that other world irradiates her thoughts and fancies.

I should like to remain many-sided and to go on belonging to both my worlds, so that the one may not thrust out the other. It would be dreadful if the whole of me were to be cast into the one mould, but I hope this will never happen. There are all kinds of things in me, and it is very difficult to know the whole of Nelly.

Drawing submitted by Philippa Alice Standley, 13; Mulvane, Kansas
Catalyst Cartoon Competition Winner

The Job Interview

Out to get a job today,
Went about it in the funniest way.
Got up too late,
Missed the bus.
It rained on my hair,
All that time and fuss!
Finally got there,
Took the elevator,
Got the space before some man,
Accidentally knocking his hat from his hand.
The door slid closed,
And crushed his hat,
Boy, mister, am I sorry for that!
Now it seems I remember seeing before,
That man—yes, down on the very first floor,
I bumped into him and his briefcase and books,
Gee, did he ever give me some looks!
So now as I sit down for my interview,
Oh, no, a crushed hat!
It's with—guess who!?!!!
Considering all of my many mistakes,
I wasn't surprised by his double take,
Better luck next time,
You're quick to say,
But no, I find
Sincerity pays
(Not to mention my new job)!

Poem submitted by Reagan Lee Brenneman, 14;
Lancaster, Pennsylvania
Catalyst Poetry Competition Winner

Appendix

Matching Yourself with the World of Work

by Gail M. Martin
and Melvin C. Fountain

In choosing an occupation, it is helpful to know as much as possible about what it demands. Whether you are trying to decide on an occupation now or you are preparing to enter it in the future, knowing what education or skills are required and something about the work environment of the job will help you make an informed choice. For example, knowing whether there are part-time opportunities in an occupation or knowing that a job does—or does not—require working with people or physical stamina can be important. And, the degree of employment growth or competition in a field may affect whether you get a job in it or how fast you advance.

The following guide was designed to help you compare these types of job characteristics with your interests and skills. Listed and defined are 16 occupational characteristics and requirements which are matched in the chart that follows with more than 250 occupations chosen from the 1982–83 *Occupational Outlook Handbook*.

One note of caution: The chart can be helpful in organizing occupational information, but it is intended only as a general exploratory

Gail M. Martin is an OOQ staffwriter.
Melvin C. Fountain is the editor of the OOQ.
Reprinted from *Occupational Outlook Quarterly*, Winter 1982.

tool. Before you eliminate an occupation from consideration because of a single characteristic, you should realize that the job characteristics presented in the table refer only to a typical job in the occupation. All jobs in an occupation are not alike. Most accountants, for example, work alone, but accountants who are auditors or investigators may work with others. Therefore, if you have an interest in an occupation, you should not disregard that career simply because one or two of its characteristics do not appeal to you. You should check further into the occupation—either through reading or by talking to your counselor to find out if some jobs in the occupation or occupational cluster better match up with your personality, interests, and abilities.

Following is a list—together with definitions—of the characteristics shown in the chart. Key words are sometimes listed to give an idea of the kinds of skills included.

Job Requirements

1. Leadership/persuasion—must be able to stimulate others to think or act in a certain way. Automobile sales workers who influence customers to buy and blue-collar worker supervisors are examples of occupations in which one must motivate others. Skills include organizing people and groups, supervising, directing, taking initiative, preaching, selling, promoting, counseling, speechmaking, negotiating, and mediating.

2. Helping/instructs others—helps others to learn how to do or understand something. Skills include treating, teaching, listening, and counseling.

3. Problem-solving/creativity—the development of new ideas, programs, designs, or products. Commercial artists who prepare the artwork in magazines and engineers who design machinery are examples of occupations that require creativity. Skills include designing, inventing, drawing, writing, and/or developing ideas programs.

4. Initiative—ability to determine what needs to be done and motivation to complete the job without close supervision. A department store buyer, for example, must use initiative in anticipating customers' preferences, buying merchandise at the right price, and seeing that goods are in store when needed.

5. Work as part of a team—essential interaction with fellow employees to get the work done. A school administrator, for example, works cooperatively with school principals, school committee members, and government officials.

6. Frequent public contact—ability to meet or deal with the public on a regular basis. Librarians must meet and deal easily with the public, for example.

7. Manual dexterity—adept with hands to make, build, fix, and do things. Skills include operating tools, growing plants, testing, drafting, carrying, instructing sports activities, and moving rhythmically.

8. Physical stamina—ability to endure stress and strain on the job, including heavy lifting, standing, or being uncomfortably confined for long periods.

Work Environment

9. Hazardous—conditions that could present danger because of use of dangerous or infectious materials or working in dangerous surroundings where accidents are common. Most of these jobs are not inherently dangerous, but they do require adherence to safety precautions. Medical laboratory workers, for example, must use precautions when handling infectious material.

10. Outdoors—work in which a major portion of time is spent outdoors, usually without regard to weather conditions.

11. Generally confined—work which requires staying in a specific place for most of the workday.

Occupational Characteristics

12. Jobs concentrated geographically—jobs located in or around one or a few geographic areas.

13. Part-time—many workers are employed for less than 35 hours a week.

14. Earnings—Estimated average earnings for 1980 were compiled for each occupation, and the earnings were ranked and divided into three levels:

    ○ lowest level

    ◐ middle level

    ● highest level

    Keep in mind that earnings within an occupation vary widely, and some workers earn more or less than the average level shown.

15. Employment growth—New job openings come about through employment growth and replacement needs. Job opportunities in a particular occupation usually are favorable if employment is expected to increase at least as rapidly as for the economy as a whole. But don't pick a job based solely on growth. Because of replacement needs, slow growing occupations may actually have more job opportunities than their growth rates indicate. Projected 1980–90 growth rates for each occupation were compiled, and the rates were ranked and divided into three levels:

   ○ lowest level

   ◉ middle level

   ● highest level

16. Entry requirements—Education and training requirements for each job were compiled and broken down into three levels:

   ○ entry-level—high school or less education is sufficient, and the basics of the job can usually be learned in a few months of on-the-job training;

   ◉ post high school training, such as apprenticeship or junior college, or many months of or years of experience are required to be fully qualified;

   ● 4 or more years of college usually required.

	1. Leadership/persuasion	2. Helping/instructing others	3. Problem-solving/creativity	4. Initiative	5. Work as part of a team	6. Frequent public contacts	7. Manual dexterity	8. Physical stamina	9. Hazardous	10. Outdoors	11. Confined	12. Jobs concentrated geographically	13. Part-time	14. Earnings	15. Employment growth	16. Entry requirements
Administrative and Managerial Occupations																
Accountants and auditors		●	●		●	●					●			◐	◐	●
Bank officers and managers	●	●	●	●	●	●					●			●	◐	●
Buyers	●		●	●	●									◐	◐	●
City managers	●	●	●	●	●	●								●	◐	●
College student personnel workers	●	●	●	●	●	●								1	1	●
Construction inspectors (government)		●	●	●	●		●		●					◐	●	◐
Credit managers	●	●	●		●	●					●			◐	○	●
Health services administrators	●		●	●	●	●								●	●	●
Health and regulatory inspectors (government)		●	●	●	●		●		●					1	○	◐
Hotel managers and assistants	●	●	●	●	●	●								1	●	◐
Medical record administrators	●		●	●										●	●	●
Occupational safety and health workers		●	●	●	●		●		●					●	1	●
Personnel and labor relations specialists	●	●	●	●	●	●								◐	○	●
Purchasing agents	●		●		●									1	○	●
School administrators	●	●	●	●	●	●								●	○	●
Underwriters			●											1	◐	●
Engineers, Surveyors, and Architects																
Architects		●	●	●	●	●								●	●	●
Landscape architects		●	●		●	●								1	●	●
Surveyors and surveying technicians				●		●	●		●					○	◐	◐
Engineers																
Aerospace engineers			●	●	●									●	●	●
Agricultural engineers			●	●	●									●	●	●
Biomedical engineers			●	●	●									●	●	●

Notes appear at end of table.

	Job requirements								Work environment			Occupational characteristics				
	1. Leadership/persuasion	2. Helping/instructing others	3. Problem-solving/creativity	4. Initiative	5. Work as part of a team	6. Frequent public contacts	7. Manual dexterity	8. Physical stamina	9. Hazardous	10. Outdoors	11. Confined	12. Jobs concentrated geographically	13. Part-time	14. Earnings	15. Employment growth	16. Entry requirements
Ceramic engineers			●	●	●									●	●	●
Chemical engineers			●	●	●									●	◐	●
Civil engineers			●	●	●									●	●	●
Electrical engineers			●	●	●									●	●	●
Industrial engineers			●	●	●									●	●	●
Mechanical engineers			●	●	●									●	●	●
Metallurgical engineers			●	●	●									●	●	●
Mining engineers			●	●	●									●	●	●
Petroleum engineers			●	●	●							●		●	●	●

Natural Scientists and Mathematicians

Mathematical scientists and systems analysts

	1	2	3	4	5	6	7	8	9	10	11	12	13	14	15	16
Actuaries			●	●							●			●	●	●
Mathematicians			●	●										●	○	●
Statisticians			●	●										◐	◐	●
Systems analysts	●		●	●	●						●			●	●	●

Physical scientists

	1	2	3	4	5	6	7	8	9	10	11	12	13	14	15	16
Astronomers			●	●										●	○	●
Chemists			●	●										●	◐	●
Geographers			●	●	●									●	◐	●
Geologists			●	●	●					●				●	●	●
Geophysicists			●	●	●					●				●	●	●
Meteorologists			●	●	●									●	○	●
Oceanographers			●	●	●					●		●		●	◐	●
Physicists			●	●										●	○	●

Life scientists

	1	2	3	4	5	6	7	8	9	10	11	12	13	14	15	16
Agricultural and biological scientists			●	●										1	◐	●
Biochemists			●	●										●	◐	●
Food technologists			●	●										●	○	●

	Job requirements								Work environment			Occupational characteristics				
	1. Leadership/persuasion	2. Helping/instructing others	3. Problem-solving/creativity	4. Initiative	5. Work as part of a team	6. Frequent public contacts	7. Manual dexterity	8. Physical stamina	9. Hazardous	10. Outdoors	11. Confined	12. Jobs concentrated geographically	13. Part-time	14. Earnings	15. Employment growth	16. Entry requirements
Foresters			●	●	●			●	●	●				⊖	○	●
Range managers			●	●	●			●	●	●				1	⊖	●
Soil conservationists		●	●	●						●				●	○	●

Social Scientists, Social Workers, Religious Workers, and Lawyers

Lawyers	●	●	●	●	●	●								●	⊖	●

Social scientists and urban planners

Anthropologists		●	●	●										●	⊖	●
Economists		●	●											●	●	●
Historians		●	●											●	○	●
Market research analysts	●		●	●	●									●	1	●
Project scientists		●	●	●	●									●	○	●
Psychologists		●	●	●		●								●	⊖	●
Sociologists		●	●			●								●	○	●
Urban and regional planners	●		●	●	●	●								●	●	●

Social and recreation workers

Recreation workers	●	●	●	●	●	●	●	●		●		●		○	⊖	⊖
Social workers	●	●	●	●	●	●								○	⊖	●

Religious workers

Protestant ministers	●	●	●	●	●	●								○	1	●
Rabbis	●	●	●	●	●	●								●	1	●
Roman Catholic priests	●	●	●	●	●	●								○	1	●

Teachers, Librarians, and Counselors

College career planning and placement counselors	●	●	●	●	●	●								⊖	1	●
College and university faculty	●	●	●	●	●	●							●	●		●
Cooperative extension service workers	●	●	●	●	●	●								⊖	1	●
Employment counselors	●	●	●	●	●	●						●		1	1	●
Kindergarten and elementary school teachers	●	●	●	●	●	●	●	●					●	⊖	⊖	●

	Job requirements								Work environment			Occupational characteristics				
	1. Leadership/persuasion	2. Helping/instructing others	3. Problem-solving/creativity	4. Initiative	5. Work as part of a team	6. Frequent public contacts	7. Manual dexterity	8. Physical stamina	9. Hazardous	10. Outdoors	11. Confined	12. Jobs concentrated geographically	13. Part-time	14. Earnings	15. Employment growth	16. Entry requirements
Librarians	●	●	●	●	●	●							●	◐	○	●
Rehabilitation counselors	●	●	●	●	●	●	●							1	1	●
School counselors	●	●	●	●	●	●								◐	○	●
Secondary school teachers	●	●	●	●	●	●								◐	○	●

Health Diagnosing and Treating Practitioners

	1	2	3	4	5	6	7	8	9	10	11	12	13	14	15	16
Chiropractors	●	●	●	●	●	●	●	●					●	●	◐	●
Dentists	●	●	●	●	●	●	●	●						●	◐	●
Optometrists	●	●	●	●	●	●	●	●					●	●	◐	●
Osteopathic physicians	●	●	●	●	●	●	●	●	●					●	●	●
Physicians	●	●	●	●	●	●	●	●	●					●	●	●
Podiatrists	●	●	●	●	●	●	●	●						●	●	●
Veterinarians	●	●	●	●	●	●	●	●	●					●	●	●

Registered Nurses, Pharmacists, Dietitians, Therapists, and Physician Assistants

	1	2	3	4	5	6	7	8	9	10	11	12	13	14	15	16
Dietitians	●	●	●	●	●	●							●	○	●	●
Occupational therapists	●	●	●	●	●	●	●	●						1	●	●
Pharmacists	●	●	●	●	●	●					●		●	●	○	●
Physical therapists	●	●	●	●	●	●	●	●						◐	●	●
Physician assistants	●	●	●	●	●	●	●	●						◐	1	●
Registered nurses	●	●	●	●	●	●	●	●					●	◐	●	◐
Respiratory therapy workers		●			●	●								◐	●	◐
Speech pathologists and audiologists	●	●	●	●	●	●	●							◐	●	●

Health Technologists and Technicians

	1	2	3	4	5	6	7	8	9	10	11	12	13	14	15	16
Dental hygienists		●			●	●	●	●			●		●	○	●	◐
Electrocardiograph technicians		●			●	●	●						●	1	●	◐
Electroencephalographic technologists and technicians		●			●	●	●							1	●	◐
Emergency medical technicians		●	●		●	●	●	●	●	●				○	◐	◐

	1. Leadership/persuasion	2. Helping/instructing others	3. Problem-solving/creativity	4. Initiative	5. Work as part of a team	6. Frequent public contacts	7. Manual dexterity	8. Physical stamina	9. Hazardous	10. Outdoors	11. Confined	12. Jobs concentrated geographically	13. Part-time	14. Earnings	15. Employment growth	16. Entry requirements
		Job requirements							Work environment			Occupational characteristics				
Licensed practical nurses		●			●	●	●	●					●	○	●	◐
Medical laboratory workers					●		●		●		●			○	●	2
Medical record technicians and clerks					●						●			○	●	2
Radiologic (X-ray) technicians		●			●	●			●				●	○	●	◐
Surgical technicians		●			●	●	●							○	●	◐

Writers, Artists, and Entertainers

Communications occupations

	1	2	3	4	5	6	7	8	9	10	11	12	13	14	15	16
Public relations	●		●	●	●	●								◐	◐	●
Radio and television announcers and newscasters	●	●		●	●	●						●		○	●	●
Reporters and correspondents	●		●	●	●	●								1	◐	●
Writers and editors	●		●	●	●							●	●	1	◐	●

Design occupations

	1	2	3	4	5	6	7	8	9	10	11	12	13	14	15	16
Commercial and graphic artists and designers		●	●	●		●							●	1	○	◐
Display workers	●		●	●		●			●					○	◐	○
Floral designers		●				●	●				●			1	○	○
Industrial designers		●	●	●		●								1	○	●
Interior designers		●	●	●	●	●								1	◐	◐
Photographers		●	●			●	●						●	○	○	◐

Performing artists

	1	2	3	4	5	6	7	8	9	10	11	12	13	14	15	16
Actors and actresses		●	●	●	●	●		●				●	●	○	◐	◐
Dancers		●	●	●	●	●	●	●				●	●	○	◐	◐
Musicians		●	●	●	●	●	●	●				●	●	○	○	◐
Singers		●	●	●	●	●	●	●				●	●	1	○	◐

Technologists and Technicians, Except Health

	1	2	3	4	5	6	7	8	9	10	11	12	13	14	15	16
Air-traffic controllers		●	●	●	●		●				●			●	○	●
Broadcast technicians			●		●		●				●			○	○	◐
Drafters					●		●				●			◐	●	◐

	Job requirements								Work environment			Occupational characteristics				
	1. Leadership/persuasion	2. Helping/instructing others	3. Problem-solving/creativity	4. Initiative	5. Work as part of a team	6. Frequent public contacts	7. Manual dexterity	8. Physical stamina	9. Hazardous	10. Outdoors	11. Confined	12. Jobs concentrated geographically	13. Part-time	14. Earnings	15. Employment growth	16. Entry requirements
Engineering and science technicians		●		●		●			2	2	2			◐	◐	◐
Legal assistants			2	●	2									◐	●	○
Library technicians and assistants		●		●	●	●							●	○	○	○
Programmers		●		●							●			◐	●	●
Technical writers		●	●	●							●			1	●	◐
Marketing and Sales Occupations																
Advertising workers	●		●	●	●									1	1	●
Automobile parts counter workers		●				●		●						○	◐	◐
Automobile salesworkers	●		●		●									◐	●	○
Cashiers					●	●					●		●	○	●	○
Insurance agents and brokers	●	●	●	●		●							●	◐	◐	◐
Manufacturers' salesworkers	●	●	●	●									●	●	○	●
Models					●	●		●				●	●	1	1	○
Real estate agents and brokers	●	●	●	●		●				●			●	◐	●	◐
Retail trade salesworkers	●					●	●						●	○	◐	○
Securities salesworkers	●	●	●	●		●							●	●	●	●
Travel agents	●	●	●	●		●								1	●	◐
Wholesale trade salesworkers	●	●	●	●		●								◐	◐	◐
Administrative Support Occupations, Including Clerical																
Airline reservation and ticket agents		●	●		●	●					●			◐	○	○
Bank clerks					●						●		●	○	●	○
Bank tellers					●	●					●		●	○	◐	○
Bookkeepers and accounting clerks					●						●		●	○	○	○
Claim representatives		●	●	●	●	●								○	●	◐
Collection workers	●			●	●	●					●			○	◐	○
Computer operating personnel		●		●			●				●			○	◐	◐
Hotel front office clerks		●	●		●	●					●			○	○	○

	1. Leadership/persuasion	2. Helping/instructing others	3. Problem-solving/creativity	4. Initiative	5. Work as part of a team	6. Frequent public contacts	7. Manual dexterity	8. Physical stamina	9. Hazardous	10. Outdoors	11. Confined	12. Jobs concentrated geographically	13. Part-time	14. Earnings	15. Employment growth	16. Entry requirements
Mail carriers						●	●	●		●				◐	○	○
Postal clerks					●	●	●	●			●		●	◐	○	○
Receptionists		●				●	●				●		●	○	◐	○
Secretaries and stenographers				●	●	●	●							○	●	○
Teacher aides	●	●			●	●	●	●						●	○	◐
Telephone operators		●				●					●			○	○	○
Typists							●				●		●	○	◐	○

Service Occupations

Protective service occupations

	1	2	3	4	5	6	7	8	9	10	11	12	13	14	15	16
Correction officers	●	●			●		●	●		●				1	●	○
FBI special agents	●	●	●	●	●	●	●	●	●	●				●	1	●
Firefighters		●	●		●	●	●	●	●	●		●		◐	◐	○
Guards						●	●	●	●		●		●	○	◐	○
Police officers	●	●	●	●	●	●	●	●	●	●				◐	◐	○
State police officers	●	●	●	●	●	●	●	●	●	●				◐	○	○

Food and beverage preparation and service occupations

	1	2	3	4	5	6	7	8	9	10	11	12	13	14	15	16
Bartenders				●		●	●	●			●		●	○	◐	◐
Cooks and chefs				●			●	●			●		●	○	◐	◐
Food and counterworkers				●		●	●	●			●		●	○	●	○
Meatcutters						●	●	●	●		●			○	○	◐
Waiters and waitresses					●		●	●	●				●	○	◐	○
Waiters' assistants and kitchen helpers					●		●	●	●				●	○	●	○

Health service occupations

	1	2	3	4	5	6	7	8	9	10	11	12	13	14	15	16
Dental assistants						●	●	●	●					○	●	○
Medical assistants						●	●	●						○	●	○
Occupational therapy assistants		●			●	●	●	●					●	1	●	◐
Optometric assistants						●	●	●						1	●	◐
Physical therapy assistants		●				●	●	●	●					1	●	◐

		Job requirements								Work environment			Occupational characteristics				
	1. Leadership/persuasion	2. Helping/instructing others	3. Problem-solving/creativity	4. Initiative	5. Work as part of a team	6. Frequent public contacts	7. Manual dexterity	8. Physical stamina	9. Hazardous	10. Outdoors	11. Confined	12. Jobs concentrated geographically	13. Part-time	14. Earnings	15. Employment growth	16. Entry requirements
Cleaning and building service occupations																
Hotel housekeepers and assistants						●	●	●						○	◐	○
Personal service occupations																
Barbers						●	●	●			●		●	○	○	◐
Bellhops and bell captains				●	●	●	●						●	○	○	○
Cosmetologists				●	●	●	●				●		●	○	○	◐
Flight attendants	●			●	●	●	●							◐	○	○
Agricultural and Forestry Occupations																
Forestry technicians							●			●				1	●	◐
Mechanics and Repairers																
Vehicle and mobile equipment mechanics and repairers																
Aircraft mechanics		●		●		●	●	●	●					●	○	◐
Automobile body repairers		●				●	●	●		●				◐	◐	◐
Automobile mechanics		●			●	●	●	●		●				○	◐	◐
Farm equipment mechanics		●												○	◐	◐
Truck mechanics and bus mechanics		●				●	●	●		●				◐	◐	◐
Electrical and electronic equipment repairers																
Appliance repairers		●	●		●	●								○	◐	◐
Central office craft occupations		●		●		●	●	●						1	○	○
Central office equipment installers		●		●		●	●	●						1	○	○
Computer service technicians		●	●		●	●								◐	●	◐
Electric sign repairers		●				●	●	●	●	●				1	1	◐
Line installers and cable splicers		●		●		●	●	●	●					◐	○	○
Maintenance electricians		●	●		●	●	●	●						◐	◐	◐
Telephone and PBX installers and repairers		●		●	●	●	●	●						◐	○	○

	Job requirements								Work environment			Occupational characteristics			
	1. Leadership/persuasion	2. Helping/instructing others	3. Problem-solving/creativity	4. Initiative	5. Work as part of a team	6. Frequent public contacts	7. Manual dexterity	8. Physical stamina	9. Hazardous	10. Outdoors	11. Confined	12. Jobs concentrated geographically	13. Part-time	14. Earnings	15. Employment growth	16. Entry requirements
Television and radio service technicians		●	●		●	●			●				●	◑	●	◑
Other mechanics and repairers																
Air-conditioning, refrigeration, and heating mechanics		●					●		●					◑	◑	◑
Business machine repairers		●	●	●			●							◑	●	◑
Elevator constructors		●					●	●						●	◑	◑
Industrial machinery repairers		●					●	●	●					◑	◑	◑
Millwrights		●					●		●					●	◑	◑
Piano and organ tuners and repairers							●							○	○	◑
Pinsetter mechanics							●							1	○	◑
Vending machine repairers		●	●				●							1	○	◑
Watch repairers		●	●	●			●				●		●	○	○	◑
Construction and Extractive Occupations																
Construction occupations																
Bricklayers and stonemasons		●					●	●	●	●				◑	●	◑
Carpenters		●					●	●	●	●				◑	◑	◑
Cement masons and terrazzo workers		●		●			●	●	●	●				◑	●	◑
Drywall installers and finishers							●	●	●					◑	●	◑
Electricians (construction)		●					●	●	●	●				●	◑	◑
Floorcovering installers					●	●	●							○	◑	◑
Glaziers		●		●			●	●	●	●				○	◑	◑
Insulation workers							●	●	●					◑	●	◑
Ironworkers					●		●	●	●	●				●	◑	◑
Painters and paperhangers					●		●	●	●	●				○	○	◑
Plasterers							●	●						◑	○	◑
Plumbers and pipefitters		●				●	●	●	●	●				●	◑	◑
Roofers					●		●	●	●	●				○	○	◑
Sheet-metal workers		●					●	●	●					◑	◑	◑

		Job requirements								Work environment			Occupational characteristics			
	1. Leadership/persuasion	2. Helping/instructing others	3. Problem-solving/creativity	4. Initiative	5. Work as part of a team	6. Frequent public contacts	7. Manual dexterity	8. Physical stamina	9. Hazardous	10. Outdoors	11. Confined	12. Jobs concentrated geographically	13. Part-time	14. Earnings	15. Employment growth	16. Entry requirements
Tilesetters							●	●						⊖	●	⊖
Extractive occupations																
Coal mining operatives							●		●	●	●	●		⊖	●	○
Production Occupations																
Blue-collar worker supervisors		●	●	●	●		●		●					⊖	○	⊖
Precision production occupations																
All-round machinists			●				●	●	●		●			⊖	⊖	⊖
Automobile repair service estimators	●	●	●		●	●	●							⊖	⊖	⊖
Boilermaking occupations			●				●		●					⊖	○	⊖
Bookbinders and bindery workers			2				●	●	●		●	2		○	○	⊖
Compositors							●	●	●		●			○	○	⊖
Coremakers (foundry)							●	●			●			○	○	⊖
Dental and laboratory technicians							●							○	●	⊖
Dispensing opticians							●							1	●	⊖
Furniture upholsterers							●	●			●	●		○	○	⊖
Instrument makers (mechanical)		●	●	●			●				●	●		⊖	⊖	⊖
Jewelers		●	●	●			●				●		●	○	⊖	⊖
Lithographers							●				●			●	●	⊖
Molders (foundry)							●	●	●		●			⊖	○	⊖
Ophthalmic laboratory technicians							●				●			○	○	⊖
Patternmakers (foundry)							●	●			●			●	○	⊖
Photoengravers							●				●			1	○	⊖
Photographic process workers							●				●			○	○	○
Shoe repairers							●							○	○	⊖
Tool-and-die makers			●				●	●	●		●			●	○	⊖
Plant and system operators																
Stationary engineers		●					●	●	●					⊖	○	⊖
Waste-water treatment-plant operators		●	●				●		●	●				○	○	⊖

	1. Leadership/persuasion	2. Helping/instructing others	3. Problem-solving/creativity	4. Initiative	5. Work as part of a team	6. Frequent public contacts	7. Manual dexterity	8. Physical stamina	9. Hazardous	10. Outdoors	11. Confined	12. Jobs concentrated geographically	13. Part-time	14. Earnings	15. Employment growth	16. Entry requirements
			Job requirements						Work environment			Occupational characteristics				
Machine operators, tenders, and setup workers																
Boiler tenders							●	●	●					◐	○	◐
Electrotypers and stereotypers							●	●			●			◐	○	◐
Forge shop occupations							●	●	●			●		◐	○	◐
Machine tool operators			●				●	●	●		●			◐	◐	◐
Machine tool setup workers			●				●		●		●			◐	◐	◐
Printing press operators and assistants							●	●	●		●			◐	○	◐
Production painters							●	●	●		●			○	◐	○
Fabricators, assemblers, and hand working occupations																
Assemblers			●		●						●			○	◐	○
Automotive painters							●	●	●		●			●	●	◐
Welders and flamecutters							●	●	●	●				◐	◐	◐
Transportation and Material Moving Occupations																
Motor vehicle operators																
Intercity busdrivers			●		●	●	●				●		●	●	○	◐
Local transit busdrivers			●		●	●	●				●		●	◐	●	◐
Local truckdrivers			●				●	●			●			◐	◐	○
Long-distance truckdrivers			●				●	●			●			●	◐	◐
Other transportation and material moving occupations																
Airplane pilots		●	●	●			●				●			●	○	◐
Merchant marine officers	●	●	●	●			●		●	●	●	●		●	○	●
Merchant marine sailors			●				●	●	●	●	●	●		◐	○	◐
Operating engineers (construction machinery operators)							●	●						◐	○	◐
Helpers, Handlers, Equipment Cleaners and Laborers																
Construction laborers				●			●	●	●	●				○	◐	○

1 Estimates not available.
2 Vary, depending on job.

Notes

1 Who Are You?
[1] *Personal Awareness: A Psychology of Adjustment* (New York: Houghton Mifflin Co., 1979).
[2] *Choosing Success: Transactional Analysis on the Job* (New York: John Wiley & Sons, 1978).

2 Threads in the Tapestry
[1] *The Uses of Enchantment* (New York: Random House, 1977).

3 What Are Your Needs?
[1] *Motivation and Personality* (New York: Harper & Row, Publishers, 1954).

4 What Are Your Values?
[1] Theodore Caplow with Howard Bahr, Bruce A. Chadwick, Reuben Hill, and Margaret Holmes Williamson, *Middletown Families: Fifty Years of Change and Continuity* (Minneapolis: University of Minnesota Press, 1982).
[2] Jody Gaylin, "What do you want out of life?" *Seventeen*, March 1980.
[3] Daniel Yankelovich, "What's next for women," *Family Circle*, August 1981.
[4] Gaylin, *op. cit.*
[5] Martha Hewson, "Right now," *McCall's*, May 1981.
[6] Julia Kagan, "Survey: Work in the 1980's and 1990's," *Working Woman*, June 1983.
[7] Hewson, *op. cit.*
[8] Gaylin, *op. cit.*
[9] Caplow, *op. cit.*
[10] Yankelovich, *op. cit.*

6 What Are Your Interests?

[1] *Making Vocational Choices: A Theory of Careers* (Englewood Cliffs, N.J.: Prentice-Hall, 1973).

[2] *Encouraging Girls in Mathematics: The Problem and the Solution* (Cambridge, Mass.: Abt Books, 1980).

[3] Mathematical Association of America, "You Will Need Math" (Washington, 1982).

8 The Great Beyond: Of Myths, and Women

[1] Allyson Sherman Grossman, "Special labor force reports—summaries," *Monthly Labor Review*, May 1981; Howard Hayghe, "Marital and family patterns of workers; an update," *Monthly Labor Review*, May 1982.

[2] Mary-Ellen Verheyden-Hillary, "Girls will be workers," *Occupational Outlook Quarterly*, Fall 1981.

[3] "The facts and resources," *Spokeswoman*, November 1981.

[4] Robert Cassidy, "How we're viewed by the men we boss," *Savvy*, July 1982.

[5] *We Were There: The Story of Working Women in America* (New York: Pantheon Books, 1977).

11 Getting Skills and Credentials

[1] *Profile II: A Second Profile of Women's Colleges/Analysis of the Data* (Washington: Women's College Coalition, 1981).

[2] Association of American Colleges, Project on the Status and Education of Women, "The Classroom Climate: A Chilly One for Women?" (Washington, 1982).

[3] *Ibid.*

[4] Del Marth, "Campus/job: Shuttles to careers," *Nation's Business*, December 1981.

Source Notes

In Chapter 1, Katherine Mansfield is quoted from *The Journal of Katherine Mansfield*, edited by J. Middleton Murry (Philadelphia: Richard West, 1979); Katharine Hepburn from *Kate: The Life of Katharine Hepburn*, by Charles Higham (New York: W. W. Norton & Co., 1975); Eleonora Duse from *Vita de Arrigo Boito*, by Piero Nardi (Milan: Mondadori, 1942); Mary Cassatt from *Sixteen to Sixty, Memoirs of a Collector*, by Louisine W. Havemeyer (New York: Private print for the family of Mrs. H. D. Havemeyer and the Metropolitan Museum of Art, 1961); Lina Wertmuller and Leonor Fini from *Interview with the Muse*, by Nina Winter (Berkeley: Moon Books, 1978); and Rosalyn Yalow, Muriel Siebert, Shirley Hufstedler, Addie Wyatt, and Billie Jean King from *Particular Passions: Talks with Women Who Have Shaped Our Times*, by Lynn Gilbert and Gaylen Moore (New York: Clarkson N. Potter, 1981).

In Chapter 2, Samuel Johnson is quoted from *The Idler* (1758–1760); Edith Ronald Mirrielees from her book *Story Writing* (Boston: Writer, 1972); Marjorie Rosen from her *Popcorn Venus* (New York: Avon Books, 1974); Anne Frank from her *Diary of a Young Girl* (Garden City, N.Y.: Doubleday Publishing Co., 1952); Doris Tarrant, Sophenia Maxwell, Judith Grant McKelvey, and Inez Ruth Hill from *Conversations: Working Women Talk About Doing a "Man's Job,"* edited by Terry Wetherby (Millbrae, Calif.: Les Femmes, Celestial Arts, 1977); Anica Vessel Mander from *Interview with the Muse*, by Nina Winter (Berkeley: Moon Books, 1978); Althea Gibson from *Out of the Bleachers*, by Stephanie L. Twin (Old Westbury, N.Y.: Feminist Press, 1979); Anne Lasoff, Connie Young Yu, May Stevens, and Alice Walker from *Working It Out*, edited by Sara Ruddick and Pamela Daniels (New York: Pantheon Books, 1977); Irene Joliot Curie from *A Long Way from Missouri*, by Mary Margaret McBride (New York: G. P. Putnam's Sons, 1959); Sarah Ellis from her *Pictures of a Private Life* (1834); and Edith Hamilton from the *Bryn Mawr School Bulletin* (1959).

In Chapter 3, the Agnes Repplier quotation is from her introduction to *Philadelphia: The Place and the People* (1898).

In Chapter 4, Marilyn Horne is quoted from *Divas*, by Winthrop Sargeant (New York: Coward, McCann & Geoghegan, 1973).

In Chapter 5, the Kathe Kollwitz quotation is from her *Diaries and Letters* (Chicago: H. Regnery, 1955).

In Chapter 6, Gertrude Kasebier is quoted from *The Woman's Eye*, by Anne Tucker (New York: Alfred A. Knopf, 1973).

In Chapter 7, Lewis Carroll is quoted from *Alice's Adventures in Wonderland* (New York: Dover Publications, 1965) and Tristine Rainer from her book *The New Diary: How to Use a Journal for Self-Guidance and Expanded Creativity* (Los Angeles: J. P. Tarcher, 1978).

In Chapter 8, the Simone Weil quotation is from the essay "Classical Science and After," in *On Science, Necessity, and the Love of God*, edited and translated by Richard Rees (London: Oxford University Press, 1968).

In Chapter 9, the Gerda Lerner quotation is from her book *The Female Experience* (Indianapolis: Bobbs-Merrill Co., 1977), and the Dorothea Dix quotation is from *Letters from New York*, Vol. 2, edited by Lydia M. Child (1845).

In Chapter 10, Colette is quoted from "The Photographer's Missus," in *The Tender Shoot and Other Stories*, translated by Antonia White (New York: Farrar, Straus & Cudahy, 1958).

In Chapter 11, the Mark Twain quotation is from *Puddinhead Wilson* (New York: Braun, Wilbur, 1958).

In Chapter 12, Lewis Carroll is quoted from *Alice's Adventures in Wonderland* (New York: Dover Publications, 1965), Daphne du Maurier from her *Don't Look Now* (New York: Avon Books, 1977), and Charles Farrar Browne from his *Artemus Ward, His Travels: The Census* (1865).

Have You Seen These Other Publications from Peterson's Guides?

SAT Success:
Peterson's Study Guide to English and Math Skills for College Entrance Examinations: SAT, ACT, and PSAT
Joan Davenport Carris and Michael R. Crystal

This brand-new step-by-step text is designed as an effective self-instruction aid to build both the skills and the confidence of students preparing for college entrance examinations. Quiz-filled verbal and math sections plus mock SATs and actual questions from recent tests are included for practice.

8½" x 11", 380 pages   Stock no. 2081
ISBN 0-87866-208-1   **$8.95** paperback

Peterson's Annual Guides/Undergraduate Study
Guide to Four-Year Colleges 1985
FIFTEENTH EDITION
Managing Editor: Kim R. Kaye
Book Editor: Joan H. Hunter

The largest, most up-to-date guide to all 1,900 accredited four-year colleges in the United States and Canada. Contains concise college profiles, a reader guidance section, and two-page "Messages from the Colleges" that are found in no other guide. September 1984.

8½" x 11", 2,100 pages (approx.) Stock no. 2316
ISBN 0-87866-231-6   **$12.95** paperback

Peterson's Annual Guides/Undergraduate Study
Guide to Two-Year Colleges 1985
FIFTEENTH EDITION
Managing Editor: Kim R. Kaye
Book Editor: Joan H. Hunter

This Guide covers over 1,450 accredited U.S. institutions that grant associate degrees. It contains basic college profiles, 1,800-word college essays written by admissions directors who chose to provide in-depth information, and directories of colleges by geographical area and by major. It serves as a companion volume to the *Guide to Four-Year Colleges 1985*. October 1984.

8½" x 11", 400 pages (approx.)   Stock no. 2324
ISBN 0-87866-232-4   **$9.95** paperback

Peterson's Guide to College Admissions:
Getting into the College of Your Choice
THIRD EDITION
R. Fred Zuker and Karen C. Hegener

This updated edition takes students behind the scenes at college admissions offices and gives current advice from admissions directors all

across the country. Contains dozens of campus photos and capsule profiles of 1,700 four-year colleges.

8½" x 11", 366 pages   Stock no. 2243
ISBN 0-87866-224-3   **$9.95** paperback

College 101
Dr. Ronald T. Farrar

The first book to answer the questions college-bound students most often ask—about money, health, social life, sex, and academic concerns. Written with empathy, common sense, and knowledge, this book can serve as a springboard to frank discussions of all college-related topics.

6" x 9", 187 pages   Stock no. 2693
ISBN 0-87866-269-3   **$6.95** paperback

Peterson's Competitive Colleges
THIRD EDITION
Editor: Karen C. Hegener

The only book that determines college selectivity from objective data—and gives you the facts to work with. *Peterson's Competitive Colleges* presents a full page of comparative data for each of 302 colleges that consistently have more undergraduate applicants—with above-average abilities—than they can accept.

7" x 10", 344 pages   Stock no. 2677
ISBN 0-87866-267-7   **$7.95** paperback

The College Money Handbook 1985:
The Complete Guide to Expenses, Scholarships, Loans, Jobs, and Special Aid Programs at Four-Year Colleges
SECOND EDITION
Editor: Karen C. Hegener

The only book that describes the complete picture of costs and financial aid at accredited four-year colleges in the United States. The book is divided into three sections: an overview of the financial aid process and ways to make it work for you; cost and aid profiles of each college, showing need-based and merit scholarship programs available; and directories listing colleges by the type of financial aid programs they offer. October 1984.

8½" x 11", 500 pages (approx.)   Stock no. 2820
ISBN 0-87866-282-0   **$12.95** paperback

Winning Money for College:
The High School Student's Guide to Scholarship Contests
Alan Deutschman

The first complete guide to scholarship competitions that students can enter and win on their own. It is the only compilation of facts, figures, dates, and advice pertaining to America's most prestigious—and most financially rewarding—privately offered scholarships. Includes over 50 national contests that cover public speaking, science, citizenship, and more.

6" x 9", 220 pages   Stock no. 2618
ISBN 0-87866-261-8   **$7.95** paperback

How to Order

These publications are available from all good booksellers, or you may order direct from **Peterson's Guides, Dept. 4615, P.O. Box 2123, Princeton, New Jersey 08540.** Please note that prices are necessarily subject to change without notice.

- Enclose full payment for each book, plus postage and handling charges as follows:

Amount of Order	4th-Class Postage and Handling Charges
$1-$10	$1.25
$10.01-$20	$2.00
$20.01-$40	$3.00
$40.01 +	Add $1.00 shipping and handling for every additional $20 worth of books ordered.

Place your order TOLL-FREE by calling 800-225-0261 between 8:30 A.M. and 4:30 P.M. Eastern time, Monday through Friday. Telephone orders over $15 may be charged to your charge card; institutional and trade orders over $20 may be billed. From New Jersey, Alaska, Hawaii, and outside the United States, call 609-924-5338.

- For faster shipment via United Parcel Service (UPS), add $2.00 over and above the appropriate fourth-class book-rate charges listed.
- Bookstores and tax-exempt organizations should contact us for appropriate discounts.
- You may charge your order to VISA, MasterCard, or American Express. Minimum charge order: $15. Please include the name, account number, and validation and expiration dates for charge orders.
- New Jersey residents should add 6% sales tax to the cost of the books, excluding the postage and handling charge.
- Write for a free catalog describing all of our latest publications.